D0457987

WE WERE PIRATES

A Torpedoman's Pacific War

Between 1942 and 1945, the USS *Tambor* made 13 war patrols in the Pacific Theater. She played a key role in U.S. Naval operations throughout the Pacific. Illustrative of the vast territory the *Tambor* patrolled during the war, this map highlights her encounters with Japanese merchant and naval vessels, encounters that included torpedo attack, battle surface, and enemy attack by depth charge and aerial bomb. Working out of Pearl Harbor and Western Australia, she saw significant action at the decisive Battle of Midway in 1942 but experienced her heaviest action in the sea lanes around the Philippines and off the China coast.

WE WERE PIRATES

A Torpedoman's Pacific War

Robert Schultz and James Shell

NAVAL INSTITUTE PRESS

Annapolis, Maryland

Naval Institute Press
291 Wood Road
Annapolis, MD 21402

Library of Congress Cataloging-in-Publication Data

Schultz, Robert, 1951 Sept. 20–

We were pirates : a torpedoman's Pacific war / Robert Schultz and James Shell.

p. cm.

Includes bibliographical references and index.

ISBN 978-1-59114-778-7 (alk. paper)

1. Tambor (Submarine) 2. World War, 1939–1945—Naval operations—Submarine. 3. World War, 1939–1945—Naval operations, American. 4. World War, 1939–1945—Campaigns—Pacific Ocean. 5. Hunt, Robert, 1919– 6. United States. Navy—Biography. 7. Submariners—United States—Biography. I. Shell, James, 1957– II. Title.

D783.5.T34S34 2009

940.54'51092—dc22

[B]

2009024610

Printed in the United States of America on acid-free paper

14 13 12 11 10 09   9 8 7 6 5 4 3 2

First printing

To Robert Hunt, who wishes, for himself,
to dedicate this story to his wife, Barbara.
—*Robert Schultz*

To the memory of my father, who served in the Coast Artillery
in San Francisco during World War II, and, like Bob Hunt,
always considered it one of the formative experiences of his life.
—*James Shell*

CONTENTS

ILLUSTRATIONS

PHOTOGRAPHS

MAPS AND FIGURES

PREFACE

THIS BOOK HAS BEEN ASSEMBLED from many sources and contains many voices. The chief source is Robert Hunt, torpedoman on the USS *Tambor* for twelve of its thirteen war patrols; but even he has contributed in different ways. The young man's voice, in one of its modes, survives in the laconic notes he jotted in his diary, the one that he kept in his footlocker in the *Tambor's* forward torpedo room and that he repaired with duct tape when a rat got on board and nibbled the binding. The older man's voice is the vigorous, emphatic one I heard in conversations and interviews when he began to tell me stories and we decided to make this book. And yet other tones and perspectives come from the 207-page, single-spaced draft he banged out at my instigation as a way of spilling onto the page in rough form the remarkable memories he had carried for over sixty years. The text here draws upon Bob's several voices, young and old, written and spoken.

It also draws upon the official, written voices of the four officers who captained the *Tambor* during Bob's service on the boat from December 12, 1940, to September 1, 1944. The submarine command required detailed reports on every mission, and the performance of each sub and captain received a written critique, called an "endorsement," with both report and critique distributed to every other sub captain in the Pacific Fleet. It was a mode of ongoing training as the role and tactics of subs evolved dynamically during the war, often the result of bold innovations at sea by young, aggressive captains who gradually replaced older, peacetime-trained officers. Distributing the reports was also, no doubt, an inspiration to captains who knew their colleagues would be reading about their decisions when they returned to port. These reports and endorsements were declassified in 1972, and, combined with Bob's perspective as an enlisted man, they provide a bifocal view of twelve patrols that mirror the course of the Pacific war.

An additional perspective is offered, of course, by the many histories that now provide us with an overview of the war that Bob experienced so close at hand in the *Tambor's* forward torpedo room, on surface watch, manning a gun for battle surface, or handling the bow planes in the control room with the captain at the periscope behind him. The result is a layered telling comprising a torpedoman's view of the war, both at the time and in recollection, along with the broader overview of captains and historians.

Another, less apparent voice helps to make up this account as well. My co-writer, James Shell, revised Bob's early draft and contributed additional research, writing, and revision. Our many discussions of the material and its treatment proved invaluable in shaping this book, and James drafted several of the book's chapters. The narrator's voice here, purportedly mine, is in many places a composite, growing out of an agreeable collaboration with a talented writer.

It has required the combination of many voices and sources to tell this story, but in the end the story is that of Robert Hunt, whose twelve consecutive war patrols are perhaps unsurpassed in number among those who served in the all-volunteer force that made up the silent service.

Many hands contributed to produce this account, and the authors would like to acknowledge the skilled and generous assistance of Julie Anderson, Mary Jorgensen, and Judy Syverson, who helped Robert Hunt handle innumerable requests for information and materials over our months of long-distance work together. Much more than clerical assistants, these women are Bob's longtime friends who have become, in the end, partners in the making of this book. Others in Bob's hometown of Decorah, Iowa, got involved along the way. Kyrl Henrickson of Real Good Creative produced a video recording of Bob recounting some of his wartime experiences, and David Cavagnaro took excellent photos of Bob, his war diary, his combat pin, and the *Tambor* battle flag.

Thanks to Paul Cora, director of the Baltimore Maritime Museum, who gave James Shell an informative tour of the USS *Torsk*. And when Bob, James, and I visited the Wisconsin Maritime Museum in Manitowoc, Michelle Hill, who was curator at the time, kindly accompanied us on a leisurely tour through every compartment of the USS *Cobia*, with Bob providing explanations and reminiscences. It was an invaluable experience to stand with Bob between the forward tubes and get a lesson on the process of firing and reloading torpedoes; to see the position of the bunk in the forward room that was his wartime home; and to sit across from him in the mess where so many sailors lost so many dollars to Bob in their long games of poker.

I would like to thank Channing Johnson for the secretarial assistance she cheerfully provided. And Tom Carter, a former naval officer and current colleague, helped to reconstruct the complex movements of the *Tambor* and Japanese cruisers during the Battle of Midway. Special thanks are due to my friend David Wyatt, whose lively interest in this book helped to sustain the long process of making it. As ever, his conversation and his discerning comments on drafts were invaluable. And, finally, to my wife, Sally, I again acknowledge, with gratitude, help less easily summarized.

ROBERT SCHULTZ
Salem, Virginia

Note: The numbering of the *Tambor's* war patrols used here differs from the Navy's, which conflates the boat's service in the Battle of Midway (May 21–June 16, 1942) with the separate patrol that followed (commencing July 24, 1942). Correcting the misleading count that appears in the official logs and records, this book numbers the Midway battle as the *Tambor's* third, increasing the number labeling each subsequent mission by one.

CHAPTER ONE

"You never know who your neighbors are"

Robert Hunt, torpedoman on the USS *Tambor*, saw the fires on Wake Island when the Japanese hit the American base there a few hours after the attack on Pearl Harbor. Sixteen days later he held the bowline on the deck of his leaking submarine as it entered Pearl, sliding through oil slicks and bumping through debris. "What a mess," he wrote in his diary. During the Battle of Midway he was on night watch at the port lookout as the *Tambor* stalked an unidentified convoy. When their quarry—four Japanese cruisers—spotted the sub and took evasive action, two collided and were badly damaged. On the *Tambor*'s eighth patrol Bob was in the forward torpedo room when they sank a freighter off the coast of China, then had to apply right full rudder to dodge one of their own torpedoes that had run in a circle and come back at them. About the incident he wrote in his diary: "It wasn't half an hour ago so am still a little shaky—first time really scared." On the boat's tenth mission the *Tambor* made a night surface attack on a Japanese convoy, was silhouetted by a burning tanker it had torpedoed, and was almost rammed by a Japanese patrol boat. A crew member manning a deck gun probably saved the sub with extremely accurate 20-mm fire along the length of the patrol boat's deck. The boat missed the *Tambor* by a mere twenty yards, close enough for the captain to read the numbers on the Japanese hull by the light of the machine gun's tracers. The same night, after the *Tambor* sank another freighter and tanker, Bob and the crew sat on the bottom at 270 feet and listened to the screws of a destroyer passing over time and again, emptying its racks of depth charges. After seventeen hours submerged, severe damage to the sub included the destruction of its radio antennae, so all communications were cut off until temporary repairs could be made. Only when they returned to port did the crew learn that Tokyo Rose had reported the *Tambor* destroyed with all hands.

Bob was on the *Tambor* from December 1940 to September 1944 and sailed on twelve consecutive war patrols under four captains. The usual pattern was to serve on four patrols, rotate to a land-based relief crew, then return to sea when a different sub required a sailor with your specialty. Bob's experience, therefore, provides a uniquely continuous perspective among the subs' all-volunteer sailors. Bob's patrols included special missions to lay mines in the Hainan Strait, land guerrillas in the Philippines, search for the disabled USS *Houston*, and conduct coordinated patrols with other subs. According to records kept by the crew, the boat sank 26 ships totaling over 100,000 tons, but after the war the Joint Army-Navy Assessment Committee (JANAC) was able to confirm only 11 ships totaling 33,479 tons. For "exceptional skill and proficiency at his battle station" and for his "calm manner and devotion to duty" Bob was awarded a special commendation by Commander in Chief of the Pacific Fleet Admiral Chester W. Nimitz. After he left the *Tambor* he ran a torpedo tube school near San Francisco, and when the Japanese surrendered he was roughed up in the V-J day "peace riots" that killed eleven people.

The young man from Decorah, Iowa, was twenty years old when he enlisted in the Navy, and he marked his twenty-third birthday at sea on the *Tambor*'s third patrol. He was one of the older enlisted men on the boat and its best poker player. He sent his winnings home to his father whenever he reached port, and by the war's end they were sufficient to help the family buy a farm. Patrols regularly lasted more than a month and many extended to as many as sixty days, most of the time spent in tight quarters below decks. When these men—in their teens and early twenties—returned to base, they popped ashore like corks out of champagne bottles. Pale and haggard, often plagued by prickly rash because of the *Tambor*'s faulty air conditioners, the crew headed for the beaches, the bars, and the brothels. They had survived, and they knew they'd go back to sea as soon as the sub was ready, so they made the most of their few days of R and R at the Royal Hawaiian in Honolulu or, later in the war, at the Ocean Beach or the King Edward in Perth, Australia. They probably didn't know that nearly one in four submariners would die—the highest mortality rate in any branch of service—but they knew their duty was hazardous. Everybody had known someone on another sub that had been lost with all hands, like the *Trout*, the *Shark*, and the *Grayling*.

Bob and his crewmates were young, and they'd been flung across the globe to live and die. They lived hard when they could, and Bob lived as hard as any, brawling and drinking and womanizing. After one fight on Pearl he was taken in by the women in a house he frequented, who bathed him, put him to bed, washed the blood out of his clothes, and hid him from the MPs until morning. Bob was also responsible for setting up the onboard still that transformed the oil-laced "pink lady" torpedo fuel into drinkable alcohol while at sea.

Photo 1. *Tambor* signalmen made this battle flag on board using linens and deck paint. It was given to Bob at a crew reunion after the war. (Courtesy Robert Hunt)

I heard some of these stories standing with Bob in my driveway under the big walnut on Pine Street in Decorah, where Bob was my neighbor two doors up. We'd spoken briefly many times, but after I published my first novel he sauntered down and said, "You never know who your neighbors are." It was as true for me as it was for him. He told me about the whore with the cash register tattooed below her navel and the sailor with the fly tattooed on the head of his penis. He told me about the girl in Australia who thought he was an American cowboy and whose neighbor, a sheep rancher, asked him to ride an unbroken horse. The girl was a beauty so he jumped on the horse, despite misgivings, and crashed it into the house. He gave me boxes of documents, maps, photos, and letters. He showed me his war diary and the nude picture of his Australian friend and the Japanese propaganda leaflet dropped on British troops, featuring a drawing of a Yank soldier with a naked British woman back in "Merry Old England." He showed me the *Tambor* battle flag made at sea out of sheets and deck paint, with an eagle holding a torpedo in one set of talons and a Japanese ship in the other. I asked him if the boat had flown both the American flag and the battle flag, and he said, "On patrol we didn't fly a flag. We were pirates."

He asked me to help him write a book and I told him how to set down a rough draft. That winter, when I walked past his house, I saw the bare lightbulb burning in the tiny window of his unfinished basement "study" where he kept his archive, typewriter, and computer. There he was, the submariner in Iowa, below ground among exposed pipes and wires, tapping out his memories of the silent service. His wife, Barb, had been an editor with the *Decorah Newspapers*, and she still wrote a weekly historical feature, "Echoes of the Past," but this was Bob's project. When he asked for my help, he said, "I've got to get this out. It's my life." A year later he presented me with a 207-page, single-spaced typescript.

Throughout the typescript that he handed to me Bob referred to himself in the third person. About his opportunity as a Navy clerk typist to volunteer for sub duty, he wrote:

> One morning Bob was looking out the window at the boats and a young ensign walked over to Bob and said that he was always looking out the window at the boats and would he like to serve on one of the subs—Bob's answer was that he would give anything to do just that and the ensign explained that the new construction of subs was far ahead of the trained personnel and the sub school could not furnish the people to man all the new boats—now the big brass of the base decided that if they could train new sub sailors right on the boats, it would help the problem and would Bob like to go aboard without sub school as a test case—would he like to volunteer—Bob almost lost it with excitement and said you got your man— the ensign then said for Bob to get his gear together and report aboard the USS *R10* the next morning for duty.

It seemed as though the Robert Hunt that I knew—Decorah's retired director of Parks and Recreation—looked back and saw another man, a self so distant now he couldn't claim him with the pronoun "I." It was another life, strange to remember, and when he spoke of it a look of wonder came into his face, a grin of disbelief that it had all really happened—hunting ships and men across the Pacific, being hunted, escaping into booze and women and fights on shore, his hands shaking from too much drinking, too little sleep, or something else. He stood before me, the longtime husband of Barb; the fit retiree who rode his bike around town with a tennis racket strapped to the back; the man who, a few years earlier at the age of seventy-five, had shown my daughter how to downhill ski at the rope-tow hill over by the college. Here he stood, in the shade of a big walnut, telling me stories from another life sixty years in the past.

Robert Hunt's story provides a valuable perspective on the war in the Pacific. As a submariner and a torpedoman, he was in the belly of the beast. He was at Wake Island, Pearl Harbor, the Battle of Midway, the Australian sub bases, the Philippines, the South China Sea, the Hainan Strait, and off the coast of Japan—nearly everywhere that Japanese and American forces clashed. And he describes the experiences from the point of view of an enlisted man peering through binoculars for bumps on the horizon. Or playing poker at a table in the mess compartment until the humidity made the cards too damp to shuffle and cigarettes went out for lack of air. Or jumping out of his bunk when a big aerial bomb killed the lights and running barefooted over a deck that seemed to burn his feet. When he'd closed and dogged the watertight door and secured the room, he checked his soles by flashlight and saw the glass on the deck from the shattered lightbulbs. Equally candid about the war patrols and liberties, Bob recounts the alternation of confinement and release, of deprivations and desperate compensations. The women, too, seemed desperate, thrown by world war into a time apart in which they took their chances as they came along.

Official history, with its statistics and maps, with its grand narrative seen from above, tells one story. Bob Hunt's follows a young man from the hills of northeast Iowa to the bottom of the Pacific listening to the screws of a Japanese destroyer passing overhead. It follows him through the war patrols and the wild liberties. It is not an officer's account or a historian's. Both are valuable, of course, but compared with the experience of a common seaman, an officer knows both too much and too little, and the historian's account can feel detached and skeletal. A story like Bob Hunt's puts flesh on the bones and gives them a beating heart.

And so the narrative recorded here is, in addition to a war story, a story of two starkly contrasting lives, the one at war and the one after, as the old man remembers the young man's adventures and trials. In this sense the story of Robert Hunt echoes his generation's defining experience and the oldest of war stories. Like Homer's *Odyssey*, it speaks of war and return—and the haunted life of survival.

CHAPTER TWO

Real War

On the USS *Tambor*'s second patrol, Robert Hunt, torpedoman 2nd class from Decorah, Iowa, stood watch on the lookout platform, eyeing the wide Pacific sky for planes and scanning the horizon with binoculars. It was December 7, 1941, and the *Tambor* operated on station four miles north of Wake Island. With a second sub, the *Triton*, to the island's south, the boats' mission was to protect the U.S. base on Wake from invasion. Though America was not at war, the crew sensed that it soon might be. They had shipped out from Pearl with a full complement of torpedoes, ammunition, and provisions for a long patrol.

Their first patrol had seemed equally ominous. Fully armed, they'd cruised to Midway Island and found it bustling with construction. There, they had tested the newly dredged channel, maneuvering at night into the bay where a sub base was going up at a frantic pace. Bob felt a certain amount of tension as he scanned his quadrant, watching for bumps on the horizon or telltale smoke plumes. Nevertheless, the hardest part of standing watch that day was maintaining the belief that you might actually see something. The ocean was calm and the sky was blue and wide.

Bob's crewmates seemed never to tire of Iowa jokes, especially on topside watch. Most had to do with the flat reaches of ocean resembling the Great Plains. "If you could only grow corn on saltwater, right Bob?" "Perfect spot for a farm—if pigs could swim." But Decorah wasn't like that. The northeast part of the state, near the Minnesota border and the Mississippi River, featured rolling hills with spring-fed streams winding between them. In Decorah itself the Upper Iowa River ran beneath high limestone bluffs. There were Indian burial mounds on the ridges overlooking the Mississippi, and every spring the plows in the fields turned over a new crop of arrowheads and scrapers. The chamber of commerce called the area "the Little Switzerland of Iowa," which was quite a stretch, but hills and valleys were plentiful. Back home Bob had hunted and fished the meandering valleys like any other kid, sitting for hours with a rifle in his lap or a fishing rod in his hands, but he'd never dreamed he'd be way out here, in the Pacific, hunting men.

From his lookout post, Bob heard shouting coming up from below. Then word reached the topside watch: Gordon "Red" Mayo, the radio operator, was running through the boat yelling, "The Japs have bombed Pearl Harbor!" He'd shouted into the after battery and engine rooms, then run to the control room and yelled the news again: "We're at war! The Japs have hit Pearl!" Then, remembering that he hadn't told the captain, he'd hustled to the officers' quarters to correct his mistake.

So now it was real. Within hours of the attack on Pearl there were Japanese planes over Wake. That night, when the *Tambor* ran on the surface to recharge its batteries, Bob and the other lookouts saw fires and gun flashes on the island. The *Tambor*'s orders had been to avoid contacts and to maintain the secrecy of its position, and as far as the crew understood, not even the Americans on Wake knew they were here. But once hostilities commenced, the boat's captain, Lt. Cdr. John W. Murphy Jr., ordered Bob's forward torpedo room to keep one tube loaded and ready to fire at all times.

Over the next four days they patrolled their assigned position, watching for an invasion fleet. At night on watch Bob saw more fires on the island and the sparks of welders' torches. On December 11 the *Tambor* saw the gun flashes of Japanese ships across the island, approached them, but turned back to avoid penetrating the *Triton*'s patrol area. That day the *Triton* fired a torpedo at a ship bombarding the island and missed. The action occurred as the Marines on Wake repelled a first invasion attempt, sinking two enemy ships and damaging several others with the 3- and 5-inch guns dug in behind the beaches. They were the first Japanese ships sunk during the war, but to the north of the island the only indication of serious battle was the aerial bomb that shook the *Tambor*. In his diary Bob wrote, "Bomb hit quite close today—think it was meant for us."

A storm blew in and churned the sea, and the submarine pitched and rolled with it. When it was Bob's turn to check the live tube, he had to grab onto whatever he could to keep from falling. Once, when a big wave slammed the boat, it threw him into the hand-firing key—and *Whoosh*—there went a ten-thousand-dollar torpedo out into empty ocean. "My Navy career is over," Bob thought. But with everything that was going on nobody said much, and Bob found it prudent to deny that he had touched the firing key. "The boat was pitching and it just went off." That was his story and he stuck with it. Later he saw the captain's report: "Shortly after surfacing at dark, while our torpedomen were shifting the ready torpedo tubes, the ship lurched and caused a torpedoman inadvertently to strike the hand-firing key of number 3 tube, which was ready for firing. The

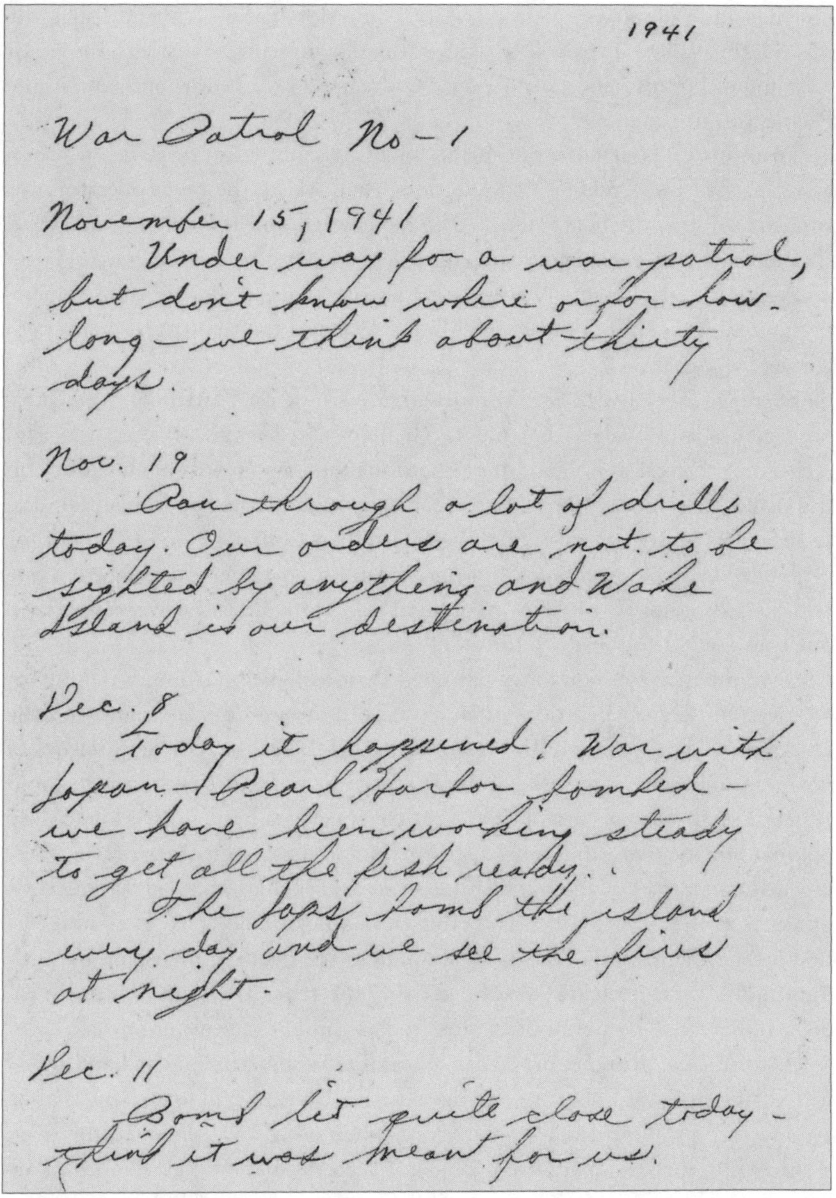

1941

War Patrol No - 1

November 15, 1941
      Under way for a war patrol,
but don't know where or for how
long — we think about thirty
days.

Nov. 19
      Ran through a lot of drills
today. Our orders are not to be
sighted by anything and Wake
Island is our destination.

Dec. 8
      Today it happened! War with
Japan — Pearl Harbor bombed —
we have been working steady
to get all the fish ready.
      The Japs bomb the island
every day and we see the fires
at night.

Dec. 11
      Bomb let quite close today —
think it was meant for us.

Photo 2. The first page of the diary Robert Hunt kept throughout the war, which records the beginning of the war, an eyewitness view of the attacks on Wake Island, and a bomb blast that damaged the *Tambor*.

torpedo ran hot, straight, and normal." So everybody knew what had happened, but Bob had not been named and there were no repercussions.

At dusk on December 15, still patrolling the northern approach to the island, Captain Murphy scanned the sea by periscope. He was watching for a Japanese sub to surface. The *Tambor* had picked up underwater sounds, but couldn't be sure it wasn't its own propeller noises echoing off the atoll's coral. Still submerged, he ordered all silent and placed his best sound man on the listening devices. With noise-making machinery shut down, including the trim pump, the boat would not hold its depth, and as the crew listened the sub drifted down. At a depth of two hundred feet the captain ordered all ahead to regain control, but the maneuvering room reported a scraping sound along the side and recommended that the propellers be stopped. Without power, the *Tambor* settled to 270 feet and Murphy ordered the main ballast tanks blown. "We caught at 310 feet and surfaced," he wrote laconically in his report, but the dip exceeded the *Tambor*'s maximum test depth of 250 feet.

The next day there was a disturbing development in the forward room: at a depth of 140 feet, a serious leak appeared near one of the torpedo wells and gradually worsened. The dip to 310 feet the night before apparently had been too much for a large gasket under a plate giving internal access to a pair of sound heads, and the jolt by the aerial bomb may have been a factor. At first the leak bubbled like a spring, but eventually it sprayed up hard. Mechanics determined that it couldn't be repaired at sea, so the *Tambor*, which had already suffered the failure of one of its diesel engines, was ordered to head back to Pearl. That day Bob wrote in his diary: "Have a leak in the forward room that we can't fix—heading for home with our fingers crossed. Wake has been burning every day—have seen welders working on the radio tower. We communicated with the island by blinker the other night."

The *Tambor* had asked the Marines defending Wake if they needed the sub to relay a message, and the men on the island replied in the negative. Apparently their repair work on the radio tower had been successful. Soon after, one of the messages they sent back to Hawaii became famous. Asked by headquarters if they needed anything, the commanding officer was said to have replied, "Send more Japs." Reported widely stateside, the remark cheered a public hungry for reassurance in the anxious days following the devastation of Pearl Harbor. Here were Americans fighting back, courageous and irrepressible. Newspapers covered the defense of Wake Island as the lone bright glimmer in a dark time.

The little atoll between Hawaii and Guam—less than four square miles of land—was deemed of strategic importance by war planners in both the United States and Japan. A U.S. possession since 1898, Wake had been included by the American military as part of a defensive screen west of Pearl Harbor. The Japanese, for their part, would not tolerate a base that could allow heavy bombers to reach their important outposts in the Marshall Islands, at Taongi, and in the Kwajalein Atoll. Despite all this, in 1941 the island was lightly defended. The military presence included the 13 officers and 365 enlisted men of the Marines' 1st Defense Corps, a Marine fighter squadron dispatched to the island in the days before the Japanese attack, and a 6-member Army communication detachment. Helping to build the base were about one thousand civilian construction workers. When Bob was topside there was little to see. The island's highest point was twenty-one feet above sea level and there were no palms—only shrubs and salt-stunted trees. The wildlife consisted of birds, hermit crabs, and rats. It was a place of importance only because of its location. So, as Bob was being tossed by heavy seas in the *Tambor*'s forward torpedo room, the Japanese continued to send bombers against the island's defensive positions. And as the *Tambor* limped home with a serious leak, the small American garrison, armed only with cannons scavenged from old battleships, four working fighter planes, machine guns, and rifles, continued to hold off a vastly superior force, hoping for reinforcements.

None arrived. A belated rescue attempt sent ships and troops from Pearl to within a day's cruising of the island, but the convoy was called back when the Wake commander reported "Enemy on Island—Issue in Doubt." In an anguished choice, Vice Adm. William Pye, acting commander of the Pacific fleet after Adm. Husband E. Kimmel was relieved, deemed it less important to save the Wake defenders than to preserve what was left of the Pacific Fleet. As Wake's two senior officers considered their options, Maj. James Devereux asked Cdr. Winfield Scott Cunningham, USN, if the American subs were still offshore. They weren't. The damaged *Tambor* had been ordered home days earlier and the *Triton* had been called back to make sure it didn't mistakenly fire upon the rescue convoy that was never to arrive. On December 23—the day the *Tambor* reached Pearl Harbor—the Americans, assailed on several fronts by Japanese landing forces, had no choice but to surrender. They had lost fifty-two men, and seventy civilian contractors had been killed by bombs or gunfire in the siege. The estimated Japanese losses were 820 dead and 1,153 wounded.

Heroic as they were, the Wake defenders never said, "Send more Japs." After the Marines had fended off a first invasion attempt, Commander Cunningham sent a message reporting enemy losses. The message was encoded, and, following standard procedure to protect the code, the actual message was preceded and followed by strings of nonsense. Prefacing Cunningham's message, therefore, his decoder had added the words: "SEND US STOP NOW IS THE TIME FOR ALL GOOD MEN TO COME TO THE AID OF THEIR PARTY STOP CUNNINGHAM MORE JAPS. . . ." Someone in the Navy's Honolulu offices, either thinking they'd detected a defiant hidden message or seizing upon a public relations opportunity, combined the opening and closing words of gibberish and passed the phrase along.

Though invented, the brave reply made a story Americans wanted to believe about themselves, and the news media flashed it around the world. Within days even the Wake defenders heard it on the radio: "Wake Marines, asked if they need anything, answer: 'Yes, send more Japs!'" The men on Wake were not amused. Fighting with insufficient forces, firepower, planes, and spare parts, the last thing they needed was more of the enemy. Yet, when the island had fallen and Cunningham became a prisoner of war, a cultured Japanese officer who spoke good English asked him, "Did you send the message saying, 'Send more Japs'?" When Cunningham denied it, the officer smiled and said, "Anyhow, it was damned good propaganda."[1]

By maintaining their chain of command and military discipline, most of the Americans taken at Wake survived four grueling years of imprisonment, forced labor, and malnutrition. Of those who didn't, five were beheaded in a ritual overseen by Lieutenant Toshio Saito aboard the cargo ship transporting the captives to a prison in Shanghai. The bodies were then mutilated and thrown overboard to avenge the heavy toll taken upon Wake's Japanese invaders. Another atrocity came to light only after the war, during one of the war crimes trials held in the Pacific. About a hundred American construction workers had been kept at Wake by the Japanese to help build fortifications. On the night of October 7, 1943, fearing an invasion, the Japanese defenders marched their captives to the beach on the north side of the island, machine-gunned them, and buried them in a mass grave.[2]

~~~~~~

It took the *Tambor* eight days to return to Pearl, and for Bob and the rest of the crew in the forward torpedo room, the leak in their compartment was a constant presence and concern. Even when they slept in their bunks hung from the room's bulkheads, tucked below and above the reload torpedoes, the water seeped and bubbled in the corner. But what could they do besides tend to their work and keep quiet about their worries?

At last, when they neared Pearl Harbor, Bob was taking a shift in the control room, manning the bow planes, and Captain Murphy stood directly behind him at the periscope, watching for the destroyer that would lead them safely into the harbor. There were minefields to negotiate, planes on alert, and a sub screen to be drawn back upon the approach of a friendly boat, all of which required an escort. The base was on high alert. So it was a shock when Captain Murphy, normally not a demonstrative man, let out a loud *Whoop!* "There she is—there's the *Litchfield*," he said, "and it's quite a sight! You've all got to see this." Bob was closest and went first. There, magnified in the scope's shimmering optics, was the old four-stack destroyer flying the biggest American flag Bob had ever seen.

Here, in the first days of war, that big Stars and Stripes fluttering in the wind gave him a shiver.

The *Tambor* surfaced, the *Litchfield* signaled "Welcome home," and the sub tucked in close behind so the American air patrols wouldn't mistake it for an enemy craft stalking the destroyer. The *Litchfield* negotiated the minefields, and when they approached the mouth of the harbor the anti-sub net was retracted. Then Bob's number-one line crew was ordered topside, and he took his position at the very front of the deck, just above the prow. Tying the boat to the dock took skill and coordination by the line crew and the men waiting on the dock, but it was also a lot of fun. Bob had become proud of his accuracy with the heaving line, a rope with a rounded lead weight called a "monkey fist," woven into one end. The line crew often had informal competitions on the way in or out of port, throwing the heaving lines at pilings, buoys, or seagulls, and Bob bragged that he could land the monkey fist in front of the guy on the dock from several hundred feet.

On deck Bob's little crew stood, happy and excited, congratulating each other for bringing the leaking boat safely home. Only now did they admit that back at Wake they hadn't thought their chances were very good of ever seeing Pearl again. But the mood of relief changed abruptly when the sub made its first turn into the harbor.

Now the *Tambor*'s hull slid through a heavy oil slick, and debris in the water bumped off the bow. First the grounded battleship *Nevada* came into view, sunk in shallow water, its stern to the beach. The *Tambor* crew had been told that the surprise attack had inflicted damage, but no one was prepared for what they were seeing now, and the line crew stood in silence. As the boat continued into the harbor, the battleship *Oklahoma* slid into view, but only the bottom of its hull showed above water. Workers were cutting holes all over it, still looking for trapped sailors or simply recovering bodies. Farther along on the left, the superstructure of the sunken *Arizona* jutted from the water at a severe angle. As they passed the naval air station at Ford Island they saw the wing of a crashed Zero sticking up from a pile of debris, its bright red "meatball" insignia showing clearly. Everywhere they looked they saw ships of all kinds damaged or destroyed, and as they pulled into the submarine base Bob spotted a miniature Japanese sub that had been dragged ashore.

The naval assault by midget submarines had been one of the few failures of the attack sixteen days before. Five small subs, each eighty feet long and manned by a two-sailor crew, had been launched from a parent sub operating near the mouth of Pearl Harbor. Their mission was to penetrate the harbor and launch their two torpedoes at the ships moored there. With a sixteen-hour endurance, they hoped to return to their mother subs for rendezvous or rescue. None returned and there were no confirmed hits on U.S. ships by the small craft, though it was for a time believed that one of the minis might have struck the *West Virginia* and *Oklahoma*. That craft, launched from the Japanese I-16 attack sub, has never been found, though the fates of the other four minis are known. One suffered mechanical failure outside the harbor, where a second was sunk by a cannon shot through the conning tower by the destroyer USS *Ward*. A third was rammed and destroyed with two depth charges from the USS *Monaghan* inside the harbor, and the beached sub Bob spotted had been captured when it ran aground.

More successful by far were the two waves of aircraft launched from the carriers *Akagi*, *Hiryu*, *Kaga*, *Shokaku*, *Soryu*, and *Zuikaku*. After the fleet's undetected thirteen-day transit from the Kuril Islands, the first wave of aircraft achieved complete surprise, with 184 planes sweeping in low from the west at 8:00 AM, December 7. In the last minutes of their approach they were detected by radar, but the operators on Oahu found it inconceivable that a formation so big could be anything but American planes arriving from the mainland. The combination of Japanese high-altitude bombers, torpedo bombers, dive-bombers, and fighters inflicted heavy damage. Forty-nine Kate high-altitude bombers were particularly effective along "Battleship Row," and the dive-bombers and Zeros struck Hickam Field, destroying many planes on the ground and neutralizing Pearl's air power. The attack of the first wave sent curtains of black smoke into the air that obscured visibility for the second wave of 171 aircraft arriving an hour later, perhaps sparing the harbor's important oil storage tanks from destruction. The final death toll from the attack included 2,403 American servicemen killed and 1,178 injured, with 103 civilian casualties. All 8 U.S. battleships were hit, with 4 sinkings and a grounding; 3 destroyers were lost; 2 cruisers were badly damaged; and 198 aircraft were destroyed, with another 174 damaged. The Japanese lost just 29 of 355 attacking planes, though another 111 were damaged.

The Japanese had calculated that destroying four battleships would delay American countermoves in the Pacific long enough for them to secure a source of raw materials from Southeast Asia, the Philippines, and other island groups, and to establish a defensive shell. They hoped to buy a six-month window during which they could achieve a long-sought Asian sphere of influence, defensible enough that the next clash with American naval power would result in stalemate and an advantageous negotiated settlement.

The attack did remove from operations all seven ships moored along Battleship Row, at least temporarily. Two battleships, the *Arizona* and the *Oklahoma*, remained permanently out of commission. Most dramatically hit was the *Arizona*. A bomb struck its forward magazine, causing a huge explosion and fireball that killed nearly one thousand sailors, badly burned many others, and sent the ship down within minutes. The final death toll on the *Arizona* was 1,177 men. A third battleship, the *Nevada*, was run aground after receiving extensive damage, though massive reconstruction eventually restored it to service. The *West Virginia* and *California* would also return to service, but required over two years of repair work. More lightly damaged were the battleships *Maryland, Tennessee,* and *Pennsylvania,* all of which were repaired in a matter of weeks.

The daring attack made plain that aircraft carriers would play a major new role in the war, and fortunately for the Americans two of its Pacific carriers had been at sea, and a third, the *Saratoga,* had been in port at San Diego. In fact, the damage inflicted upon battleships at Pearl Harbor would force the U.S. Navy to rebuild its tactical units around carriers rather than the big gunboats. More immediately, however, the only recourse open to American strategists was to launch an all-out submarine offensive against Japanese shipping of all kinds. And, remarkably, the two waves of Japanese air attacks had left the Pearl sub base completely unharmed. From the beginning, then, the *Tambor* would be in the thick of it, and Bob would serve on twelve of its thirteen missions—patrols that would mirror the turns and progress of the Pacific war.

Now, two days before Christmas, 1941, Bob saw from the *Tambor's* deck details of U.S. sailors swarming the base, cleaning up from the attack, and young soldiers patrolling with rifles. Once the boat was secured at dock, its officers sent their mess attendant ashore to check them into officers' quarters, and the nervousness on the base became fully apparent. When the mess aide didn't return as expected, the officers made their way to quarters on their own, and it was hours before their attendant showed up in the hands of MPs who wanted to verify his identity. A Filipino, he'd been taken for a Japanese agent and arrested.

When night fell the island was blacked out entirely, adding to the general air of unease. It was eerie—and hard to walk around—but Bob and a few others picked their way from the docks toward the base until they were challenged by men with rifles demanding a password. They hadn't been given one and it took a while to convince the guards that they were *Tambor* sailors out for a stroll. When they were finally allowed to return to their boat they felt lucky that they hadn't been shot. Everyone on the island was tense. That night Bob mustered only a few words for the diary: "Pearl Harbor—what a mess."

The next day the sight across the channel of the *Arizona's* upper structure sticking out of the water at a 45-degree angle was a sobering reminder of the devastating attack. Only 337 of its crew of 1,514 had survived, and many of the survivors were badly injured, most with terrible burns. Bob's brother, Dick, who was two years younger than he, could have been one of the dead or injured. After Dick and Bob enlisted and trained together, Dick's first assignment was to the doomed battleship, but he had been accepted into officers' training and so had transferred stateside before the attack.

Bob and Dick enlisted in the Navy late in 1939, leaving behind their father Russell (whom everyone called R. C.), their older sister, Marge, and the town of Decorah. Dick had just graduated from Decorah High School, and Bob, on a football and track scholarship, had completed a year at Coe College in Cedar Rapids, Iowa, but had run out of money. The war in Europe had barely begun and the United States was in the grips of a depression. There were no jobs and no prospects, so enlistment was a practical decision as much as a patriotic one. Both had led sturdy outdoor lives all over the upper Midwest. Born in Mason City, Iowa, Bob moved to Fredericksburg when R. C. bought a hardware store there.

After a few years it was on to Colby, Wisconsin, where R. C. bought the Elmbrook Guernsey Farm. The farm was so big that the whole family had to pitch in, bottling and selling the milk, which was delivered in wagons bearing the slogan "You can whip our cream, but you can't beat our milk." They also raised and sold ponies and dogs, and Bob had a pony of his own. Then, however, R. C. became a manager for Montgomery Ward and the family was on the move again—from La Crosse, Wisconsin, to Fargo, North Dakota, to Hibbing, Minnesota, to Duluth, Minnesota. All that moving, hard is it was, had served as good preparation for living on a boat that was constantly in motion.

A boyhood spent moving from town to town had prepared Bob for navy life in other ways, too. In each new town he'd had to establish his place in the "pack" of local boys, dealing with bullies and earning respect. A naturally gifted athlete with strength, coordination, and speed, he learned to fight. In La Crosse when Bob played marbles according to the rules he'd learned in Colby, the kids at recess told him he was wrong. They argued, and a big kid shoved Bob to the ground and kicked him in the stomach. A year later in Fargo, playing by La Crosse rules, Bob again was told he was wrong. This time when the leader of the pack stepped forward Bob wasted no time. He lowered his head, rammed the kid, knocked him down, and didn't stop punching until the other kids pulled him off. After that the Fargo kids played marbles Bob's way.

School proved more difficult to manage in the classroom than on the playground. Moving from one curriculum to another, Bob did well in courses that repeated what he'd studied earlier but struggled with classes that assumed prior knowledge he hadn't learned. Summers were better. In Fargo the hunting and fishing were the best he'd ever seen. The entire family, Bob's mother and sister included, spent weekends on lakes in Minnesota, just to the east. On the way Bob, Dick, and R. C. shot at gophers and jackrabbits out the car windows. When fall arrived Bob turned to sandlot football and discovered he was good at it. But when the Arctic wind blew down from Canada, the ball froze, making it hard to kick and easy to fumble.

Bob liked Hibbing even better. His dad bought a cabin on a lake about twenty miles from their house, with a smaller cabin out back for Bob and Dick. They

Photo 3. First extant photo of Robert Hunt, in Mason City, Iowa, in sailor's suit and with boat. (Courtesy Robert Hunt)

Photo 4. Hunt family milk truck with (left to right) R. C., Dick, and Bob, ca. 1925.
(Courtesy Robert Hunt)

spent most of their free time on the lake, and joined the Boy Scouts. It was good to have a place to go for peace and quiet, because Hibbing was a tough town. Bob and his family lived on the south side, but the iron miners' kids would come into their neighborhood from their homes on the north side to fight and loot. Bob's new Montgomery Ward bicycle disappeared from in front of his house one afternoon, and he never saw it again. Bob also learned to play hockey in Hibbing, first on roller skates and then on the city rinks and the backyards that were flooded as soon as the temperature dropped below freezing.

Mostly, though, when Bob thought of Hibbing he pictured the lake and cabin. Out there, sitting in a duck blind or standing hip-deep in the lake waiting for a strike had taught Bob the virtue of patience, just as his fights had taught him the value of aggressiveness. It was, perhaps, an unusual pair of traits to find in a young man, but invaluable for a future submariner. On the lake in winter, Bob, Dick, and R. C. went ice fishing. R. C. drilled a hole in the thick, opaque ice with an auger, and the three of them huddled around it, sitting on their creel buckets and holding their short ice-fishing rigs with gloved hands. Sometimes Bob imagined a fish gliding beneath the frozen surface and tried to will it onto his hook. He never thought that one day he would be the one gliding below silently, and that someone above would be fishing for him.

When Bob was a high-school sophomore, his father, tired of the frequent moves with Montgomery Ward, rented a building in downtown Decorah and opened a Ben Franklin five-and-dime store. The family moved into a house on Oak Street, and the town welcomed them warmly. Bob's father, as a new professional in town, soon rose to positions of leadership in the local businessmen's clubs, and Bob quickly established himself as a star on the football, basketball, and track teams.

If Bob's midwestern upbringing had, until then, taught him fighting skills and patience, in Decorah he acquired yet another ability that would prove beneficial in the Navy. Bob had played poker from early boyhood, and now there was always a game going at one of the city parks. One of his friends, and one of the most avid players, was the son of a car dealer; when it rained they would commandeer an old hearse on his father's used-car lot, drive it to Phelps Park, and play poker in the back. Bob also caddied at the local country club, and there were always games going in the caddy shack to pass the time between loops. That was all kid's stuff, however, compared with what he learned from a man he got to know at the country club. The old gentleman, a retired insurance man from North Dakota, had suffered a crippling accident and couldn't drive. One summer he hired Bob as his chauffeur, a job that most nights involved taking the man to the clubhouse for dinner and the serious poker games that were played afterward. Bob stayed with him until he was ready to go home, which was often after midnight, and he witnessed a lot of money changing hands. It was always straight poker, nothing wild or fancy, and the stakes were high. But his boss always came out ahead. Standing behind him, watching how he played and bet the hands, Bob received his graduate education in poker. It was knowledge that would prove more useful, and more profitable, than anything he had learned in school.

One shadow hung over those Decorah years. Bob' mother, Bessie, was sick. Ill before the move, her condition worsened, and finally she was diagnosed with cancer. Within a year she was gone. She died on a Friday night, October 12, 1936, only forty years old. Bob was playing tailback for the Decorah football team and had an important game that night. R. C., Dick, and Marge told him to go, that his mother, if she could, would tell him to play. But when he rushed back from the contest and found that she had died, it was hard to take, and it was hard not to feel guilty.

Though the family was new to Decorah, the town turned out for the funeral. The high school closed for the day and most of Bob's classmates came to be with him. That was the kind of town Decorah was. Still, Bessie's death was a heavy blow, and R. C. took it especially hard. Marge had enrolled at Luther College as part of the first group of women to matriculate there, and Dick, two years behind Bob, was a high-school freshman. The kids pulled together and watched out for one another as their dad attended to his duties at the store the best he could.

When Bob graduated (Best Athlete in the Class of '37), he worked at the town's new outdoor swimming pool over the summer, then did a year as a Coca-Cola salesman and truck driver, moonlighting on weekends at the concession stand at Niagara Cave in Minnesota. He would haul soda, ice cream, and candy to the cave's stand in his Coca-Cola truck, with a cooler full of beer for himself and the friends he occasionally took along to help. With his earnings he bought a car. "It was my first car, a Model A convertible," Bob remembered. "I paid $100 and drove the bejesus out of it." One of the girls in his group of friends was Barb Bishop, daughter of the town's newspaper publisher, and the two of them took the car to nearby New Hampton for a swim at the public pool there. It was, Bob remembered, his first date with the woman he would marry after the war. "I met her when I got to Decorah. She was a year ahead of me in school. Six or seven of us would go swimming together. Somebody's dad owned a gravel pit where we could go. And sometimes we'd hitchhike to the public pool in New Hampton. When I got the car we could drive over, and one day I asked Barb. I guess it was our first date." At the time, however, marriage was the furthest thing from his mind. "I only got serious after the war," he said. "I didn't want to leave anybody behind when I went into the service. When we went to sea—when we threw off the lines—I didn't want to have anybody waiting for me."

Bob enjoyed his year of work after high school—"I was partying pretty good then"—but he could see there was no future in it. With the help of one of his high-school coaches he was able to land a football and track scholarship to Coe College in Cedar Rapids, 125 miles south of Decorah. In addition to being his high-school team's starting tailback, he'd finished second in the conference meet in the 440, and had won the pole vault. The flagpole in front of his dad's store was removable, so he'd used it for practice in a backyard pit. The school had the latest bamboo pole, however, and he used it to clear the bar at 10' 6", a school record.

Bob's athletic scholarship covered tuition and books, but he still had living expenses. Sister Marge was teaching now, and she helped with a little something each month out of her paycheck. Coe gave Bob a work-study job, and he also worked at a downtown hotel for meals. Still, it was tight. Nevertheless, Bob made friends quickly and easily, hung out at a bar and restaurant near the college, pledged a fraternity, and went to the many Greek-sponsored parties. Money for dates was scarce, an acute problem when a dance was billed as formal, requiring clothes Bob didn't have, but the young women were understanding and everyone tried to help each other out. The summer after his first year at Coe, Bob worked a summer job at the college, as did his brother Dick, who had just graduated from Decorah High.

That fall—it was 1939—Bob and Dick sat down with R. C. "Dad was in a bad way," Bob recalled. "Mom was gone, he had two boys out of school, there was no more money for college, and there were no jobs." The depression was affecting the family store, as it was small businesses around the country. The family had to give up the house on Oak Street and move into an apartment behind the store. "Dad was the one who first mentioned the Navy, and Dick and I said, 'Why not? We can give that a try.'" On November 21 the two brothers enlisted as apprentice seamen and the next day were sent to the Great Lakes Naval Training Station in North Chicago. Germany had invaded Poland in September, but the European war seemed a distant thing compared with the economic straits the Hunts faced at home.

~~~~~~~~~~~~~~~~~~~~~~~~~~~~~~~~

The Hunt brothers were assigned to a training company with about 120 other recruits, but Bob and Dick were the only ones with prior military training of any kind. Bob had enrolled in the Reserve Officers' Training Corps at Coe and Dick had undertaken a similar training program in high school. Even their leader, a chief torpedoman named Paugh, didn't know how to march in close- or open-order drills, and he was always taking a manual out of his pocket and flipping through it with a puzzled frown. After a couple of days during which very little got accomplished, Paugh divided the company into two groups, put Bob in charge of one and Dick the other, and picked another kid named Sullivan, from Waterloo, Iowa, as the head of the company. Sullivan's older brother was in the Navy, so he knew his way around. Somehow, gradually, the company began to bear a resemblance to a military unit. The five Sullivan brothers would become world-famous in November 1942, when they all perished in the sinking of the USS *Juneau* by a Japanese submarine. A destroyer was named for them, the USS *The Sullivans*, and a movie about them, *The Fighting Sullivans*, was released in 1944.

Bob enjoyed both the camaraderie within his own unit and the competition with other units. Late in the training period, when the recruits finally received a night off, they hit the Chicago bars. At one, good-natured ribbing between members of two units escalated into a drunken brawl. Bob tried to stay out of it but had to intervene to pull a rival off his brother, Dick. In response, the guy threw a wild left hand that caught Bob squarely in the eye. It didn't hurt much, and Bob gave the guy a good pasting after that, but the next morning he awakened with a ring around his eye three different shades of purple. As it happened, that was also the morning the new recruits were to receive their first inspection from the admiral in charge of the station.

Nearly everyone in Bob's unit was groaning from a hangover or aching from the fight, but they managed to assemble on the parade ground for inspection on time and in fair order. Bob stood at attention at the head of his group, hoping the frigid wind blowing in off the lake would help to revive them. After what seemed an interminable wait, the admiral finally appeared, gold braid gleaming, trailed by a pack of aides. As soon as he came within sight of Bob, he broke away from his aides and walked directly to him, drawing so near that the shiny black bill of his cap almost grazed the bridge of Bob's nose.

Then he said, in a deep rumble, "What does the other guy look like?"

"Worse than me," Bob managed to say.

"Way to go, sailor," the admiral replied, and the men behind Bob erupted into a cheer.

Soon after they finished their training, Bob developed an infection in his foot, a result of athlete's foot and the black socks that were part of the sailor's standard uniform at the time. He went to the hospital for treatment, while Dick and the rest of the company were shipped to an outgoing unit to await their final assignments. The infection cleared up after a few days, but it proved difficult to obtain his release. He hoped that if he got out in time he could be assigned to the same ship as Dick, but he learned from some of the corpsmen who worked in the hospital that the officers in charge liked to keep all the beds full to protect the facility from cuts in staffing. By the time Bob was finally released, Dick had shipped off to the *Arizona*, and Bob was sent to another outgoing unit. The next day one of the officers came into their barracks and asked if any of them knew how to type. Bob remembered Sullivan telling him that his brother had advised him never to volunteer for anything. "A good way to wind up cleaning latrines," he explained. But Bob had taken a typing class in school, and acute boredom prompted him to raise his hand. After passing a typing test, he and two others were assigned desks and typewriters at a small office on the other side of the base. Their main duty was to type stencils of orders assigning recruits to their ships. The chief in charge of them, a veteran Navy man and an old sub sailor, told them how many men were needed on each ship, and they plucked the names off the roster. It didn't matter who went where, as long as everyone went somewhere.

When the workload was light, the chief would pull up a chair in the middle of their office, sit on it backward, and tell submarine stories. According to the chief, sub duty was the best in the Navy. You got the best food, extra pay, and as long as you did your job nobody bothered you. No spit and polish and no saluting. You could even grow a beard if you wanted. The moral of each tale was the same, and invariably the chief ended his story with this line: "You boys should try to get yourselves on a sub." Bob and another typist named Harvey were sold—the third man didn't like tight spaces—but how could it happen? "Just stick with me," the chief said. "One of these days we'll get a call for volunteers at the New London sub base, and we'll just send you guys there."

Before the month was out an order came in requesting three volunteers for sub training. Bob pulled a stencil out of his desk, typed his name in one space, Harvey's in the second, and a name picked off the roster at random in the third. The chief signed the orders, and Bob was promoted to seaman second class and sent to New London.

They arrived on March 23, 1940, and quickly discovered that Connecticut wasn't much warmer than Iowa or North Chicago. Bob and Harvey were immediately assigned to duty, not on a submarine but in an office high on a hill that overlooked the row of piers where the training subs were moored. It was a tantalizing and frustrating view. All day Bob sat and pounded on a typewriter just like the one he had left behind at Great Lakes, chafing in the dress whites they were required to wear in the office, pausing every few minutes to look out the window at the sailors working on the training subs. A class went out to sea each morning and afternoon, dressed in dungarees and wearing their white hats any way they wanted—forward, backward, inside out, or not at all. Nobody seemed to care, just as the chief had said. On his mess break and any other time he could sneak out, he walked down to the docks to talk to the trainees. They called him a "yeoman striker," which he thought at first was a sarcastic reference to what he did to the keys of his typewriter all day, until one of them explained that a "striker" is the navy term for a sailor who has chosen his specialization. When Bob made it clear to them that he hadn't chosen to sit behind a desk all day, they assured him that it was he and not they who had the best job in the Navy. This he could not understand. They lived in barracks, inspections were few, they seldom had to wear their dress whites, and they were allowed to keep beer in their lockers.

One month to the day after he arrived in New London, he was standing at the window watching the trainees man the subs for their morning run when a young ensign who worked in the same office building came and stood beside him.

"You like watching the boats?" he asked.

"Yes, sir." Bob had been afraid for a moment that he would get in trouble for gazing out the window, but this ensign never threw his weight around, and all the men liked him.

"How would you like to get on one?"

"I'd give anything to get on a sub, sir. That's why I volunteered to come here, not to sit behind a typewriter."

"I might be able to help you with that," the ensign told him. And he explained that new sub production was outstripping the sub schools' ability to train crew. To speed things up the brass was thinking about training sailors right on the boats. "They're looking for someone untrained to go aboard as a test case, so if you'd like to volunteer . . . "

"You've got your man!" Bob said, unable to contain his excitement. And, on the spot, the ensign told him to get his gear together and report the next day to a training sub, the *R-10*.

When Bob walked up the gangplank and onto the deck of the *R-10*, the first man he saw was a stubby fellow wearing a CPO (chief petty officer) insignia and a sour expression. Bob dropped his sea bag to the deck, snapped off a sharp salute, and barked out, "Seaman Hunt reporting for duty, sir!"

"In the first place," the CPO replied, "don't salute me and don't call me sir!" His face, which resembled a crumpled paper bag, reddened slightly as his voice gradually rose. "I am not an officer, I'm chief of the boat. Name's Pig Kelley. You call me *chief!* Also—I don't know what your rate is, but you can leave it on the gangplank! You are now a member of the *crew* and we all work together no matter what we are." It was Bob's first lesson in life aboard a submarine.

Kelley assigned Bob a locker and bunk in the housing barracks and explained his duty: He was to learn as many different jobs as he could during the morning and afternoon training sessions so that he could then teach them to the new sailors coming in from sub school. His curriculum included lookout, steering, bow and stern planes, forward torpedo room, hydraulic manifold, trim pump air manifold, main ballast flood valves, and topside line handling and heaving. His main tutors were Youtsey, Barton, and Slaybecker, all old-timers with four years or more in the service. Barton and Slaybecker were both torpedomen, just back from four years in the China station. There were also two men who had been on board the USS *Squalus* on May 23, 1939, when it sank during a test run off the Isles of Shoals, near the navy yard at Portsmouth, New Hampshire. A massive valve failure flooded the boat, and half the crew drowned. The old chief back in Chicago had neglected to mention the incident when he'd painted his glowing picture of submarine duty.

But Bob remained undaunted, even when the *R-10* ran aground on the beach of Fisherman's Island one afternoon in a heavy fog. They were able to break loose without damaging the boat and dropped anchor to wait for the fog to lift. That evening the captain, a skinny, likable fellow named Weiss who didn't look much older than Bob, called a meeting and told the crew that, since it would make neither them nor him look good to report the incident, they wouldn't.

Bob learned quickly and was soon promoted to seaman 1st class, and one day—in a surprise to everyone—he got to dive and surface the boat. A young officer who Captain Weiss was training to be the diving officer froze up so badly he could hardly talk, and Weiss told him to switch positions with Bob, who was on the bow planes. Bob stood up and gave the order to take her down to sixty feet and level her off. Whenever he forgot an order, the captain whispered it in his ear and Bob relayed it to the crew, who, delighted to have one of their own in charge, responded with a snappy "Aye, sir!" Captain Weiss then ordered Bob to surface the boat, and gave him a "well done." The tongue-tied young officer, sitting at the bow planes the whole time, suffered acute humiliation, as intended.

Craps games and "periscope liberty" were the main amusements between training sessions. Bob prized the model sub he won at craps, a three-foot aluminum model of the *Porpoise* (SS-172) a sailor had fashioned in one of the shops on base. It was too big to keep, so Bob sent it to R. C. in Decorah. Every Memorial Day and Veterans' Day during the war, R. C. put it on display in the window of Hunt's Variety Store with the sign "My son Bob's submarine, at war in the Pacific." "Periscope liberty" consisted of spying on couples who wandered away from the picnic area on an island across the Thames River from the sub docks. When the weather was nice at least one of the boats would have its periscope up, and if anyone saw anything interesting, he would pass the word to the lookouts, who had very powerful field glasses. The word would go down the line to the other boats, and the docks would ring with cheers of encouragement when the guy on the island was making out well and groans of disappointment when he wasn't. That was how the island acquired the nickname "Shag Island."

Before the war started sailors had a bad reputation in New London, so most would buy civilian clothes, rent a locker at the bus station, and change out of uniform before a night out. One evening, Bob and three of his shipmates had just received their first round at their favorite bar when another sailor ran in and told him that a local girl was looking for him, and that she was going around town telling everybody he had gotten her pregnant. He didn't want to leave the party, so he grabbed his drink and crawled under the table, which was draped in a long checkered cloth. The woman never arrived, but Bob stayed under the table for the rest of the evening, just in case. Another night Bob went to a local bar with a shipmate, and as soon as the guy finished his first drink he took a bite out of the cocktail glass, chewed on it, and spit it out. He'd been a fire- and glass-eater at a carnival, he told Bob, and lit a cigarette. Then he flipped the lit end into his mouth, chewed up the whole thing, and spit it out. Bob was duly impressed, and after a few more drinks he allowed the man to teach him to chew glass. He managed to do it without cutting his mouth, but decided to pass on the cigarette trick.

On a five-day leave Bob went to New York to see the World's Fair, with its signature Perisphere and Trylon, the big white spherical building and its companion seven-hundred-foot spire. Wandering amid the modernist architecture, he saw "Democracity"; the Radio Corporation of America building shaped like a radio tube; and the Works Projects Administration building, with the great tableau of workers above its entrance. The "Electrified Farm" featured livestock, greenhouse, orchard, pasture, and "over 100 applications of electricity." Bob walked by the Lagoon of Nations and the Court of Peace. He read that the pentagonal base of the League of Nations Building symbolized "the five continents and the five races of mankind" and its circular turret signified unity. But the Polish and Czechoslovakian pavilions, open in 1939, were now closed.

Bob also visited Coney Island and Times Square, but his two most lasting memories were of seeing Gypsy Rose Lee in a burlesque house and having a city cop bang on the soles of his feet with a nightstick when he tried to grab a nap on a bench in Grand Central Station. He had run out of money and was stranded in the city. When he begged a cup of coffee from the counterman at an all-night diner and explained his situation, the man gave him a handful of subway tokens and told him how to get out to the Boston Post Road. And from there Bob hitched a ride back to New London.

Bob also went to Boston occasionally with Pig Kelley, who had a girlfriend there. Bob was assigned the tasks of watching out for the highway patrol on the drive (Kelley drove fast) and keeping the girlfriend's teenage daughter occupied. The girl was a little young and silly for Bob, who was twenty-one by then, but Kelley gave him money to take her out to dinner and got them Red Sox and Bruins tickets.

The only other time he left New London was when the *R-10* was ordered to join a parade of fighting ships in Norfolk. The brass left it to them to worry about how to get a training sub in shape to make the trip. The crew lived, ate, and slept in barracks, and the fellow who was supposed to be the ship's cook only knew how to bake ham, so he ordered so many that there wasn't enough refrigerator space to hold them all. So they stored the excess hams in an empty torpedo tube, thinking it would be cool enough to preserve them. When the cook opened the tube in the forward torpedo room to get one, however, the boat was flooded with the stench of rotten meat. The tube was leaking salt water through its outer door, the hams were spoiled, and the ventilation system carried the smell throughout the boat. The odor persisted until they fired the number-one tube and sent the hams rocketing out to sea.

They made it into Norfolk in rough seas and a driving rain. Some of the sailors were seasick by the time they tied up in the harbor, but Bob was fine, and of course so were the old-timers on board. They had been to Norfolk many times before and were eager to take him out for a night on the town. Since there was no shower on the *Tambor,* two of Bob's shipmates suggested that they board the big ship tied up alongside them for a shower and shave. It was still raining hard, so they found three raincoats in the after-battery storage compartment and put them on before disembarking. Bob had never been on a Navy ship before, and he was surprised at how courteous the crew was to them. The deck watch welcomed them aboard, they were given a personal escort to the showers by one of the sailors, and another sailor came running up with towels and robes for them all. *They really do treat you right when you serve on a submarine,* Bob thought. It wasn't until after they went back to the *R-10* that they saw the stenciled lettering on the backs of the raincoats: "CAPTAIN," "EXEC. OFFICER," and "1st LIEUT., GUNNERY OFFICER." It gave them a start, and they hustled the raincoats back to the after-battery compartment so they wouldn't get court-martialed for impersonating officers.

On September 21, Bob finally passed the last of the seemingly endless battery of written and hands-on tests required to qualify on the *R-10*. On November 12, he was promoted to torpedoman 3rd class and began torpedo school, and four weeks later he received orders to transfer to Portsmouth, New Hampshire, to join a new boat that had just been commissioned, the USS *Tambor*. He was now officially a submariner and had the insignia of the twin dolphins sewn onto his left sleeve.

Photo 5. Bob Hunt in his early days as a submariner. (Courtesy Robert Hunt)

CHAPTER THREE

Tambor Class

A s the spring of 1940 turned to summer, then to fall, unprecedented events had occurred in the country and in the life of Bob Hunt. In early May, a week after Bob had reported aboard the *R-10*, President Roosevelt held the Pacific Fleet at Pearl Harbor as a warning to and defense against an increasingly imperialist Japan. In September, the Japanese signed the Tripartite Pact, formally aligning themselves with the Nazis. Just six days before Bob qualified on the *R-10*, the Royal Air Force (RAF) turned the tide of the Battle of Britain and averted a German invasion. And his promotion to torpedoman 3rd class and assignment to torpedo school came just a week after the 1940 presidential election.

It had been one of the most unusual elections in American history, matching the Republican challenger Wendell Willkie, who had never held elective office and had been a Democrat until two years before, against Franklin D. Roosevelt, the first president ever to gain his party's nomination for a third term. The experts predicted a close contest, but FDR prevailed easily, 449 electoral votes to 82. With the exception of Maine and Vermont, Willkie's electoral strength ran straight down the middle of the country and right through Bob's home region, including Iowa. Some analysts attributed Willkie's success in the Midwest to dissatisfaction with Roosevelt's farm policies, some to anti-third-term sentiment, others to resentment which the large population of German descendants in the region had toward Roosevelt's strongly pro-British, anti-Nazi foreign policy.[1]

Although Willkie was himself an internationalist, his party was still dominated by isolationists, so FDR's victory and the retention of strong Democratic majorities in both houses of Congress seemed to make an eventual American entry into the war more likely. The presence in the White House of a former assistant secretary of the Navy who had long been an advocate of the submarine also made it more likely that, when war came, submariners like Bob Hunt and his comrades would find themselves very much in the thick of it. And only four weeks after he had entered torpedo school, Bob got an early Christmas present—his transfer orders to the *Tambor*.

Bob's new boat was the fastest and finest in the American submarine arsenal, the first in a new class of fleet boat. The USS *Tambor* (SS-198) looked much longer, sleeker, and fiercer than anything Bob had seen before, with its sharklike snout, its deck gun, and the streamlined conning tower bristling with antennae. This, clearly, was a war-making machine, and along with contemporary events, the imposing sight of his new sub suggested to Bob that America's entry into the war was only a matter of time. For the next three years and nine months, the *Tambor* would be his home, his workplace, his restaurant and recreation hall, and sometimes his makeshift chapel. The submarine would be his very exoskeleton, and on more than one occasion it would nearly become his coffin.

The U.S. Navy bought its first submarine, the USS *Holland*, in 1900, and established its fleet with the acquisition of seven more subs in 1903. In 1905 FDR's cousin, Theodore, had squeezed his presidential bulk down the hatch of the submarine USS *Plunger* and taken a test dive. But efforts to perfect the design of a fleet submarine, a vessel that could cruise fast and far enough to serve as a weapon to rival the German U-boats of World War I, had largely failed. By the time the *Tambor* was designed and built, so many different but equally unsatisfactory models had been designed—among them the World War I–vintage R series on which Bob trained in New London—that the Navy departed from its alphabetized naming system. From this point on, each new series would be named for the first of its kind, and the *Tambor* class would remain the ultimate in American sub design until December 31, 1941, when the namesake of the *Gato* class was commissioned. Based on the *Tambor*-class subs, the *Gato* featured modified diesel engines and batteries for increased patrol duration, and reconfigured internal spaces for crew comfort. After the introduction of the *Gato*, only minor changes in sub design were allowed, expediting the massive shipbuilding effort required to produce new subs; the chief modification to the *Balao*-class submarines, whose namesake was commissioned in February of 1943, was a thicker steel pressure hull that increased the subs' official test depth from three hundred to four hundred feet. The *Tambor* had gone down to 268 feet on its first deep submergence, on December 19, 1940, and Bob received the traditional certificate to commemorate the occasion, signed by the boat's captain, the diving officer, and by "Davy Jones" and "Neptunus Rex."

At a little over three hundred feet, the *Tambor* was nearly 40 percent longer than the *R-10*. But at only twenty-seven feet across the beam and with a crew of about sixty-five enlisted men and five officers aboard, along with yard workmen completing their last tasks, Bob found the interior just as close and cramped as his former boat. After his experience with Pig Kelley when he first boarded

Photo 6. The *Tambor* (SS-198) shortly after its 1940 commissioning. (U.S. Navy)

the *R-10*, he kept a low profile this time, but no one paid attention to him anyway. He finally found the chief of the boat, Bill Blakenbaker, and got his bunk and locker assignment in the forward torpedo room. Then he began to learn his way around and start the long process of qualifying all over again on a fleet submarine.

Half of Bob's shipmates were electrician's mates, machinist's mates, and torpedomen like himself; the other half were assorted specialists such as quartermasters, cooks, gunner's mates, radiomen, the pharmacist's mate (the closest thing the boat had to a doctor), and unrated firemen and seamen. The chief of the boat was in charge of all the enlisted men's affairs. Each of the officers had a specific set of duties, overseen by the sub's captain, Lt. Cdr. John Murphy. The officers kept to themselves when not at battle stations, had their own mess, and stayed mostly in their quarters, so the crew had limited contact with them.

Many of the enlisted men were younger than Bob, but quite a few old-timers were also aboard—guys like Rex Harvey, whose name sounded like a movie star's, or Jake Schultz, whose wife ran a whorehouse in Honolulu and had bought him a ring set with an impressive diamond, or Charles "Chesty" DeBay, the balding, barrel-chested deep-sea diver who had participated in the salvage of the *Squalus*. The experience had apparently left him with a complement of nervous tics, since he constantly picked at his face and head and pulled a comb out of his pocket to run through his sparse fringe of hair. There was also Harry Behrens, the tall, rugged quartermaster who was nicknamed "Tarzan" by a female admirer for his impressive physique, and who would go on to serve twelve war patrols on three different submarines. And the "Gold Dust Twins," the crew's nickname for Warren Link and Ray Bouffard, who seemed always to be together. After the war, they married sisters. Also on the crew was a fellow with a fly tattooed on the head of his penis, and another with a screw propeller on each ass cheek. It was a rough bunch, almost as rough as some of the yard workmen, many of whom were from the Portsmouth Navy Prison. Most had been jailed for slugging an officer. It was an important lesson. "You can beat up on your shipmates as much as you want," Bob learned, "but no matter how much you hate an officer, never poke one in the snout."

Bob's conversations with his shipmates took place mostly in the forward torpedo room. He was one of six sailors assigned to it, but others often came in to visit when they weren't on duty, since it was the *Tambor*'s largest compartment, fitted into the tapered shark's snout at the boat's forward tip. Not that it contained any more open space than anywhere else on the boat; it too was crowded with pipes, valves, and tubes. At first it all looked to Bob like so much plumbing, but soon he would learn the function of every valve and control. Bob's living and sleeping space was confined to one of the eighteen bunks scattered among the reload torpedoes running all the way along both sides of the room. His diary and all his other possessions were stashed in one of the lockers, which were no larger than wall safes and were stacked along the bulkhead behind the bunks and torpedoes. When the crew worked on the torpedoes or made reloads, the bunks were folded up and slid out of the way. A small padlocked emergency food locker was mounted low on one bulkhead, but it was no bigger than a first-aid kit and usually contained more liquid than solid nourishment. There was also an aluminum bin for disposing of the oily rags the crew used to wipe their hands after working on the torpedoes, and contraband often surfaced here as well; a signalman once pulled a bra and panties out of the bin as the boat came into port and tied them to the periscope, next to the battle flag.

The main entrance to the forward torpedo room was through a watertight door in the center of the after bulkhead, which was closed and dogged shut when the collision alarm sounded, when the boat was under depth-charge attack, or any other time flooding was a danger. Each compartment had a similar door, so that each could be sealed off from the rest of the boat if necessary. A hatch and escape trunk were fitted into the overhead in the forward part of the room, and Momsen lungs for emergency escape were stored in bins behind the torpedoes and bunks. The crew had little confidence in the Momsen lungs, which were named for the naval officer who invented them, but five men on the *Tang* were to use them to escape to the surface when their boat was blown up by a circular run of one of its own torpedoes in October 1944. Among them was Henry Flanagan, who put the *Tambor* in commission and served in its after torpedo room before being transferred.

At the rear of the room was the head, affording the crew rare glimpses of the officers as they walked silently to it from their quarters and just as mutely returned. Sound heads that sat under steel plates in the forward room were wired to the control room and conning tower, allowing the captain and soundmen to listen for noises made by enemy ships. Two flapper valves handled air circulation, and a monitor was positioned to detect any poisonous gas emissions from 126 storage battery cells in the forward battery compartment, just aft and below the room. A series of ballast tanks at the forward end of the room helped regulate the boat's trim and buoyancy, air tanks supplied the high-pressure air that fired the torpedoes, and several large motors bolted to the overhead ran the bow planes and other electrical mechanisms. Of special interest to the crew were the fifty-five-gallon tanks, one on each side of the hull, that held torpedo fuel—pure alcohol laced with a pinkish oil that accounted for the fuel's nickname, "pink lady."

Most of the room's space was taken by its full complement of sixteen torpedoes—one in each of the six tubes and ten reloads waiting behind them on skids—and by the machinery that fired them. The tubes, which only the torpedomen were allowed to touch, were stacked in rows of three on each side of the room, with a narrow, green linoleum–lined alley between them that filled up quickly when the crew was at battle stations. Bob's own station was in this alley, as one of two men assigned to check the angle of the gyroscope on each torpedo and to man the hand-firing key in case the fish didn't fire electrically. Two other crewmen waited at the ranks of tubes to open their inner and outer doors and to operate the blow and vent manifold which kept the boat's weight balanced as the fish were fired. This manifold also sucked the air bubbles produced with each firing back into the boat, preventing them from floating to the surface and giving away the sub's position. Behind the men who operated the tubes, the reload crew raised and lowered chain falls on the overhead, moving the skids that swung the reload fish into position. The torpedoman 1st class choreographed the operation, standing behind the rows of tubes, wearing headphones connected to every other compartment on the boat, passing orders and information to the crew.

Just aft of the forward torpedo room, perched atop the forward battery room, was officers' country, housing their bunks, dining area, ward room, and the captain's tiny "stateroom"—actually little more than a desk, a bunk, and a set of gauges to keep track of the boat's bearings. Bob saw this area only when he was passing through it on his way to the control room for his regular watch section—one hour on lookout, one on the wheel, and one manning the controls of the bow planes, the external fins on each side of the shark's snout that maintained the boat's depth.

The boat's every movement, forward, backward, up or down, originated in the control room; it was the *Tambor*'s brain, and above it, atop the conning tower, the periscopes, radar towers, and lookout stations were its sensory organs. The control room, like the forward torpedo room, was a maze of wheels and gauges;

it seemed, in fact, to hold twice as many in half the space. At the forward end was a wheel that was used to steer the boat while it was submerged (when on the surface, the boat was steered by a wheel in the conning tower), a fathometer for gauging the depth of the water, and a large, flat-topped gyro compass to keep the boat on course. An acey-deucey board had been painted on top of the compass to help the men pass the time. A periscope shaft protruded through the room's middle. On the port side was the hydraulic manifold that opened the vents and closed the hull openings during a dive, and above it the "Christmas tree," the panel of red and green lights that indicated which openings had been opened or closed. When they were all closed, every light shone green, and the man on the manifold shouted "green board" to the diving officer, indicating that it was safe to dive the boat. The controls for the bow and stern planes—the winglike rudders that determined the boat's upward or downward motion—were also near the middle of the room, each with a gauge that indicated the depth of the dive and a bubble similar to that in a carpenter's level which showed the boat's up or down angle. Behind these was the ladder leading up to the conning tower, and aft of it was the set of valves that composed the trim manifold. From here the diving officer pumped water into, out of, and between the boat's trim tanks and bilges to control its balance and stability—not an easy task, since the weight of the boat was constantly changing as it consumed fuel, inhaled and expelled seawater, and discarded trash. Even a slight change in water temperature could affect the trim of the boat, and the diving officer had to monitor the changes continuously to ensure that the sub could dive, surface, and maintain a given depth properly at any moment. Aft of the trim manifold were a second periscope, the radar station, the radio shack, and another blow and vent manifold, larger than the ones in the torpedo rooms. The control room sat atop the pump room, which housed the boat's compressed-air, hydraulic refrigeration, and air-conditioning systems. The latter two were necessities, not luxuries, considering the huge amounts of perishable food that had to be stored on each war patrol and the extreme temperatures and high humidity encountered when in the tropical waters of the Pacific and during long periods underwater.

The after battery compartment, just aft of the control room, contained the mess, the galley, crew quarters, head, and washroom on the upper level; storerooms and the other 126 of the boat's battery cells on the lower. Bob rarely ventured aft of this compartment, since he had no duties there and the boat was too crowded for aimless wandering. Most of the *Tambor*'s after half was taken up by its diesel engines—four 1,600-horsepower, V-16 Winton behemoths in the engine room. The development of these new, lightweight, reliable engines had been key to the success of the new fleet-submarine designs. The Wintons enabled the creation of a 310-foot-long, 1,450-ton vessel that could reach a speed of 17 knots on the surface, and, using the power from the storage battery cells to

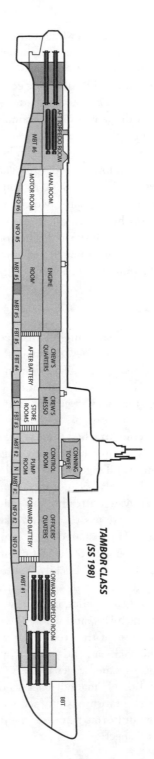

Figure 1. USS *Tambor* cutaway view. (www.geocities.com/Pentagor/1592/tambor.html)

run the electric motors, 9 knots while submerged. At war, the sub was too slow to outrun a Japanese destroyer, but fast enough to run down one of the freighters or tankers that were so vital to the massive importation of raw materials that fueled Japan's war effort and its domestic economy.

Around and atop the engines and batteries were crammed more tanks for ballast and fuel and the maneuvering room, which contained the machinery that controlled the boat's engines. The after torpedo room, similar in layout and function to the forward torpedo room but much smaller, was stuffed into the tail of the boat, with four torpedo tubes and space for storing four reloads. Bunks and lockers for the crew were, of course, jammed into every available space here, as well. The stern planes, which unlike the bow planes could not be tucked flat against the hull when not in use but remained rigidly centered, jutted from the outside of the boat's tail. The boat's massive tubular pressure hull formed a secure enclosure, although sometimes it was hard to figure whether it was more like the snug shell of a turtle or the rib cage of the whale that swallowed Jonah.

~~~~~~~~~~~~~~~~~

Between his duties and studying for his fleet-submarine rating, Bob found time for nights out with his new shipmates. Before the war Portsmouth was wary of sailors and their needs. The women who would have anything to do with them were, like the boat's crew, a rough lot. They weren't prostitutes; they didn't charge for their attentions. But clearly relationships with them were conducted on an economic basis. A girl expected a good, square meal, and the most attractive attached themselves to sailors who bought them not only meals but new clothes and other things. To try to encroach on one of these arrangements was dangerous. Other desirable women who weren't taken were still available only because it was known that they had run off with a sailor's money or watch after he had fallen asleep. Still another class of Portsmouth women were passed around like whiskey bottles in paper bags, and were just as cheerfully shared. Bob sometimes heard sailors comparing notes: "Didn't I see you with Sadie last night?" "How is the old girl anyway?" "A real firecracker, isn't she?" Luckily, a shipmate who had his own car took a liking to Bob, and at night they would drive out of Portsmouth and into the small towns on the outskirts, hamlets where everyone worked in woolen mills and clothing factories, and where the unattached women hadn't been picked over by the rest of the crew. The car provided both transportation and shelter. In the backseat, the young women they met—though they professed inexperience—seemed eager to learn all they could. Many a morning Bob and his friend barely made it back to the boat for muster, but no one seemed to care. Some mornings, in fact, so many of the crew reported still wearing their dress uniforms from the night before that it looked as if they were prepared for inspection.

Bob went to sea on the *Tambor* for the first time on March 6, 1941, for depth-charge tests. No one knew it at the time, but the tests had been personally ordered by President Roosevelt to allay Prime Minister Churchill's fears that the seams in the welded hulls of the American submarines could not withstand depth charging.[2] Two destroyers went out with the *Tambor* to drop the charges on the boat from various distances and at various depths. After each bombardment, the crew assessed and recorded the damage inflicted on the boat, so compartments that didn't hold up well could be shored up or redesigned. These were important tests, and the many improvements made to the *Tambor* would be incorporated into each new boat in its class. For the destroyers it was target practice, and Bob's boat was the target. He realized, too, that the tests were a chance to see how well the new crew members, himself prominently included, might hold up under combat conditions.

As soon as they were out far enough, the diving alarm sounded, and the crew went into the crash-dive drill they had performed so many times before. The hydraulic-manifold watch opened the vents, the electricians put the battery power online and went all ahead full, the engine-room gang shut down the diesel engines, the bow and stern planesmen put both their wheels on hard dive, the trim-manifold watch stood by to pump water from tank to tank as needed, and the blow-and-vent-manifold man flooded the negative tank and stood by for further action, all orchestrated by the diving officer in the control room. The valves on the boat closed one by one, the red lights on the "Christmas tree" went off and the green lights lit up, the crewman at the hydraulic manifold reported "green board," the diving officer gave the order "Pressure in the boat," and the air-manifold man began to bleed air into the sub. When he got a reading on the pressure gauge, it signified that all the openings in the hull were closed, and the dive could safely proceed.

No one was quite prepared for what happened next. Bob had anticipated that the blasts from the depth charges would jar the boat back and forth in the water and that it might feel like being inside a beer can that was being shaken, but when the first depth charge exploded it felt instead as though the outside of the sub had been struck by a gigantic sledgehammer. Paint chips sprang from the bulkheads and dust puffed from the decks. "I wasn't scared, exactly," Bob remembered, "but I wasn't comfortable, either." The charges were dropped at a distance, at first, then gradually closer. As the explosions drew nearer, lightbulbs and glass gauge covers sang out as they popped from the concussion, leaks broke out in packing glands, breakers popped and left the boat without electrical power, and the batteries that were vital to its capacity to run submerged sustained serious damage. The boat itself even became unstable and difficult to steer. After one particularly close hit, Bob heard a crew member talking on the headphones to Captain Murphy.

"Captain, the toilet in the forward head just got blown all to hell. There isn't a piece left that's much bigger than a watch crystal. . . . Yes, sir, we'll save all the pieces. . . . Captain, should we scrape the shit off the bulkhead, too?" One of the first improvements ordered when the boat got back to base was to replace the porcelain toilet bowls with ones made of stainless steel.

For the closest depth-charging tests, a minimal crew took the *Tambor* to the bottom, where it was moored front and back with ropes, anchors, and buoys. It was a cold, windy day, and Bob, as a junior crew member, drew the unpleasant task of taking a small boat out to tie the mooring lines to buoys. Once the sub was in place, its skeleton crew was removed by diving bell. So the *Tambor* sat on the bottom and took its most brutal punishment alone. It was a scene to be repeated during the war, but with the full crew inside, sweating out the bombardment at depth.

~~~~~~

After weeks of training throughout his sub, Bob qualified on the *Tambor* March 31, 1941—a milestone day for him. In May they began the long trip down the East Coast, through the Panama Canal, and into the Pacific, headed for the submarine base at Pearl Harbor, on the Hawaiian island of Oahu. Bob looked forward to warmer weather at last. His favorite time of the day was when he was on lookout and got to see the sights. They traveled close to shore most of the time, within sight of land, but just as he began to enjoy the warm sun and the beaches on the Florida coast, the weather turned stormy, with high winds and very choppy seas. The boat tossed back and forth, making it hard to get from one place to another without being thrown against the bulkheads like a pinball. The boat was taking water through the conning-tower hatch which had to be pumped out of the motor-room bilges, and quite a few members of the crew got seasick. Far worse than that, a sailor sitting on the lower edge of a watertight door was thrown down when a big wave hit the boat. At the same time the jolt dislodged the clamp holding the door, and when it slammed shut the sailor's head was caught. The poor man's skull looked like a broken eggshell, with a bloody groove running along the temple where the door had hit him. Nobody thought he would live long, but the pharmacist's mate did what he could, and the sailor managed to hang on until they were able to transfer him to another ship. Bob never did find out what happened to him.

With the crew at sea, Bob was able to get to know some of his shipmates better. The wildest stories came from the old-timers, like Chesty DeBay, who told Bob about a bar in Panama that had a trough of circulating water under it for spitting and discarding cigarette butts. A friend of his had just brought his new bride to Panama and was showing her the sights, and when he saw his old pal sitting at the bar he rushed up excitedly to introduce his new wife to him. At that moment, however, DeBay, who had been drinking for some time, was attempting to piss discreetly into the trough. But, unfortunately, when his friend grabbed him by the shoulder and spun him around, he besmirched the poor young bride.

Bob got to see Panama for himself when they tied up there, with the old-timers showing the new guys around. Everyone not on watch was given liberty, and the crew went to town en masse. A memorable stop was a big nightclub, with a long bar, tables, and a dance floor. To deal with the tropical heat, an elaborate system of belts and pulleys moved big bamboo ceiling fans back and forth. Still, it was hot. Waiters and waitresses dodged through the crowd, holding their round trays above their heads. They were all native Panamanians, and young local women also moved through the crowd, stopping at the tables to talk to the men. Once the sub's group was seated and had gotten their drinks, one of the women came to their table and started talking to Bob. She was young and beautiful, with shiny black hair fastened behind one ear with a gardenia. As she spoke, Bob recognized a few words, but he must have looked puzzled, because one of the old-timers leaned over. "She likes you," he explained, shouting over the roar of conversation and music. "She wants you to go upstairs with her."

Bob was surprised and a little disappointed; she looked too young to be a whore. But he let her lead him through the crowd and up a narrow staircase at the end of the bar to a tiny room at the top. There was no bedding, just a bamboo mat, but when she took off her gown none of that mattered. Bob was a bit self-conscious when he went back downstairs after only a little while, but at the table his crewmates gave him a rousing reception, asking for a detailed account. As the night continued, most of them took a trip upstairs with one of the women, and Bob noticed that none of them stayed there much longer than he had.

When the *Tambor* passed through the Panama Canal, Bob was on the number-one line near the bow, a perfect spot for seeing the sights. Bob was justifiably proud of his skill and accuracy with the monkey fist, but the Panamanians on the locks at the canal showed him some new tricks. The *Tambor* crew heaved their lines with a simple sidearm motion, just the way they had been taught, but these fellows used a figure-eight windup that was not only beautiful to watch but didn't seem to hinder their accuracy. The progress through the locks took hours, but when they finally got through Bob got his first look at the Pacific Ocean.

Towns on the Pacific side of the canal were wilder than those on the Atlantic side. Moored at the city of Colon, the men were warned to avoid an area called the Coconut Grove. As soon as everyone could get themselves cleaned up, that was where they headed. It turned out to be in a poor, run-down district with dirt streets and an occasional mule cart rolling quietly by, not at all the area the glamorous-sounding name had led them to envision. They walked down a block of small buildings, each with a red light over the doorway, and as they came abreast of each door a woman would step out, take a sailor by the arm, and tell him in broken English just what she would do for him and how much it would cost. When a woman found a taker she whisked him through her door, and the red light went out and stayed unlit until her customer came stumbling back out. It was worth the trip just to see these women operate, but it was dangerous to get separated from your buddies in the Coconut Grove. A number of his crew-mates had their billfolds and watches stolen, a few others got into fights, and the group was lucky to get everyone back to the boat in time for the long sail to San Diego.

~~~~~~~~~~~~~~~~~~~~~~~~~~~~~

"Welcome to the real Navy," one of the old-timers told Bob as they came within view of the harbor at San Diego. It was nighttime, and not only the city but all the boats in the harbor were lit up, glittering on the dark water like a second town. The harbor was so full of ships that the sub had to tie up in the bay, and to get anywhere the men had to travel by boat. The next day, when they needed supplies, the captain made the mistake of sending Bob and a young mechanic out in the diesel-powered boat that was kept under the deck of the *Tambor*. "Go to dock 10-10," they were told, but neither knew where it was. Furthermore, nei-ther of them knew how to drive the boat, a sizable wooden inboard craft. Orders were orders, however, so they climbed down an external ladder to begin their mission. The mechanic somehow figured out how to start the engine, and they threw off the lines and headed for the beach, planning to ask the first person they saw there how to get to the 10-10 Dock. It was around noon, and the wa-ter was filled with vessels headed in all directions, including several roaring PT boats. Bob struggled to steer through the traffic, trying to remember which boat was supposed to turn to port and which to starboard. It must have been clear that he was a novice, because some of the speeding craft circled so they could hurl insults his way. So when Bob spotted a patch of open water between him and the beach, he headed for it, and when he saw a pile of rocks topped with a red flag, he dodged it to the beach side. There was no traffic in the area—a great relief until they felt a jolt and heard the accompanying bang as their boat's bow shot into the air. They came to a sudden stop, the engine cut off, and Bob and his companion sat at an angle, looking up at the sky.

The mechanic sat stunned and silent, so Bob looked over the side and discov-ered that the boat was perched atop a big pipe that ran just below the surface of the water. Once the pair composed themselves they got out, stood on the pipe, and tried to slide the boat off, but the rust and barnacles on the pipe held them fast. They tried rocking and twisting the boat, but this made a rasping sound as if the pipe were a file cutting through the hull. All the while other boats glided past, their occupants yelling and hooting.

"You'd think the sons of bitches would come over and help us instead of just razzing us," Bob said.

"They can't," replied the mechanic, who appeared to be on the verge of tears. "You steered us into a 'Danger: No Boating' zone."

The citizens of San Diego taking their lunch breaks on the beach were kinder, but no less entertained. They shouted suggestions and encouragement, so Bob and his buddy were getting it from both sides.

The only thing they could think to do was to continue rocking the boat, hoping they got free before the pipe filed a hole in the hull. And that's the way they got off, receiving cheers from the crowd on the beach.

On the way back to the sub, with no supplies and a scraped-up boat, they wondered what was in store for them. Bob thought it was just possible they'd be kicked out of the Navy. But at least the other boats were giving them a wide berth; word must have spread about the diesel inboard that didn't know what the hell it was doing. When they reached the *Tambor*, tied up, and climbed aboard, Bob confessed to the deck watch that they hadn't found the 10-10 Dock.

"Didn't they tell you?" the deck watch replied. "When you didn't show to pick up the stuff, they just brought it out here. It's already loaded on the boat."

And that was that. No one ever asked them where they had been all that time or said a word about the scars and scrapes on the boat, and they kept quiet themselves. For a month after the incident, though, whenever Bob and the mechanic passed in the boat, the mechanic gave him a sheepish grin and Bob shook his head in response.

~~~~~~~~~~~~~~~~~~~~~~~~~

Everyone got a few days' liberty in San Diego, and Bob had seen no better place for a sailor to spend free time. Sailors were welcomed everywhere and weren't always being hustled. One night a group of his shipmates went into a bar, saw Bing Crosby himself, and spent the night singing and drinking beer with him—and Bing paid the whole tab. Bob had been occupied elsewhere, however. He had met a woman in another bar. She had stopped for a drink after work, and she and Bob had begun to talk. She was about Bob's age—maybe a little older—and was from a small town somewhere in the Midwest, like Decorah. It was a real conversation. The woman had a good job, was well dressed, and looked great, but weary. She was married, she told Bob, to a man from her hometown, and they had two young kids. He'd joined the Navy during the depression, like Bob, and had shipped out some time ago. At first she'd gotten frequent letters, but lately. . . . Bob came to recognize the situation. A lot of couples had gotten married in a rush when the man had enlisted; often there were children. First they all move to be near his coastal base, and then he's shipped out and the woman is left alone. Maybe when he's been gone for a while he doesn't miss her as much as he thought he would, and the world is full of girls. She finds out that his navy pay—as much as she sees of it—doesn't go very far. And, sure, she's young and lonely.

Her house was not much more than a bungalow, tiny and with a low roof. She called the babysitter on the phone—an elderly woman, she explained, much better with the kids than she was herself—and the woman agreed to keep the children overnight when she told the babysitter that her husband was home on leave. She asked Bob if he was hungry, and he realized that he was, so they went into her kitchen and made sandwiches. She apologized for not having any beer in the house, but he was content to drink a glass of milk. When they went into the bedroom, he saw a framed photo with cracked glass. "I dropped it," she said, "five or six times." Bob looked. The man's hat appeared too big for his head, and somehow that made him feel better about what they were about to do.

The next morning they slept so soundly that neither awakened until it was late, and each had to scramble to get ready, her for work and him to get to the boat. When they were both dressed he asked her if there was anything he could do for her. "Well, there is the babysitter," she said. "I had to pay extra to keep the kids overnight."

"Sure thing," Bob said, and on his way out he left a twenty on the bureau.

He'd told himself when he enlisted that he wouldn't get serious with anyone until he was out of the Navy, but now he felt more certain than ever.

~~~~~~~~~~~~~~~~~~~~~~~~~~

As soon as the *Tambor* left San Diego, Bob understood that the pleasure cruise had ended. On the way to Pearl Harbor the crew ran one drill after another—battle surface, crash dives, silent running, fire drill, submerged approach, surface approach—the whole gamut. And the busy pace continued throughout their first stay at Pearl Harbor. Nearly every day they went to sea, sometimes staying out for several days. In the forward torpedo room, the crew was kept busy loading and firing dummy fish and water slugs at destroyers. The ships also pulled targets for practice by the deck-gun crew. Only when the *Tambor* went into dry dock to repair a propeller bent negotiating a dummy minefield did the crew get a few consecutive days of liberty.

For recreation in port there was a beer garden in a little park between the docks and main buildings. It was only open for a couple of hours late in the afternoon, and the lines were long, so a man was lucky to get two beers before it closed. But, collaborating, Bob's crewmates devised a system for picking up enough bottles for a party. They carried the beer back to the sub in pillowcases and stashed it in the cool of a torpedo tube, so the forward room became the site of evening gatherings. When a junior officer assigned to stay on the sub overnight complained to the captain about the noise, he received little sympathy. As Bob would learn, crew morale in the sub fleet was a high priority.

It was the spring of 1941, and the consensus among the crew was that the United States would enter the war before the year was out. We would probably go into Europe first, the men thought, and since Germany had a pact with Japan, the Japanese would declare war on us after that. The bustle of preparation around the base was undeniable. As a member of the number-one line crew, Bob had been on deck when the *Tambor* pulled into Pearl Harbor for the first time. As impressive as San Diego had been, it did not rival the spectacle of passing Diamond Head and entering the base at Pearl. "It was real exciting," Bob remembered. "We went right through the docks, past Ford Island. I was amazed. I couldn't believe the noise everywhere—hammers working, the big equipment, and the cranes." The show of military might was impressive, and the old China hands on the *Tambor* had nothing good to say about the Japanese ships and sailors they'd encountered in Asian waters. "The experienced guys were very haughty," Bob said. "They said the Jap ships were no good, but that it didn't matter anyway because their crews couldn't sail them straight. But we found out differently."

CHAPTER FOUR

War Fervor

Aftter Bob had witnessed the Japanese bombing of Wake Island, had slept in the *Tambor*'s forward room on the way back to Pearl with a leak bubbling in the corner, and had stood on his sub's bow and seen the devastation of Battleship Row, he wrote to his brother Dick. He sent the letter from San Francisco, where the *Tambor* had been sent for repairs. In it he mentioned Dick's performance in a play, girlfriends, and, with sadness, the death of his sister Marge's newborn child. The letter, which reached Dick at the naval air station in Corpus Christi, Texas, was filled with bravado and euphemism (and colorful spelling), but its main purpose was clear. It was a last will and testament—just in case.

Dec. 30 [1941]
Dear Dick—

I received your last letter o.k. and it was about time you wrote. Bet you made quite a leading man in that play—maybe the movies will put in a bit for you when you get out. Guess they could use a few *men* in the picture business eh. Can't tell you much because of the naval censors—guess it's a good idea. We all get the news out of the papers anyway.

My little red head went back last month so think I'll have to get busy again and find another. Sure hated to see her go as we really had a good one planned for the holidays.

The baby was a boy as you probably know and only lived a couple of weeks. Marg sure can take it as I received a letter from her shortly after and she seemed all-right. I sure wanted that kid to live and be a boy for her sake, but guess that's the way it goes. Maybe she'll have another and we can be uncles anyway. See that you don't knock out any down there— maybe you'd have to marry the gal, she may be a queen, but that family of hers maybe don't want any of those war babies. From the way you talk you must have several standbys for when you get hard up—not bad if they stack up as nice as you say and I imagine they do.

By the way—if I should get a heart attack and kroke one of these days I want you to get half my dust. Marg gets the other half. I didn't tell Marg so don't mention it to her, but Dad knows about it. Take half my insurance, and my savings account is in the bank at home—Dad has a record of it in his safety deposit box. I guess if you get nocked off you have six months pay coming too so get that for you and Marg too. You can do what you want with it—get married—raise hell—or just throw it away. If gram is still living see that she gets something, but you take care of it yourself. All this is just in case my heart goes bad or if I stub my toe and get poisoned or something—maybe my red head will shoot me when she sees me again. I'll sign this letter and you save it in case you'd have trouble collecting. I figure if Dad had any more money he really wouldn't need . . . anyway you guys is me pals.

Don't expect too many letters as all I can say in a letter isn't very interesting. Give 'em hell Dick—and pick off a few of those little guys for me. I think I received your last letter—written about a month ago. I'll write more later.

Your bro—
Robert Russell Hunt

The letter, typed and signed, employs a mix of swagger and self-deprecation that, for later generations like my own, evokes the American 1940s as surely as a swing tune or a Bob Hope road movie. Beneath it all, the letter reflects Bob's state of mind after the outbreak of war and his first wartime patrol. "I didn't figure I was going to make it," Bob told me. We were speaking on the phone one afternoon in 2006. I was in Virginia and he was in Iowa, resting in his apartment after cataract surgery that morning. "I was a poker player," he said. "I knew the odds."

The *Tambor*, the first of the country's twelve new fleet boats, was being readied for the big push in the Pacific, and the crew was granted thirty days of liberty during the refit. So Bob headed for Decorah on the San Francisco-to-New York train, accompanied by many of his crewmates, including Joe Magner, whom he'd fought outside a dance hall at Pearl Harbor.

The fight, which initiated a long friendship, occurred between their first patrol to Midway and their second to Wake. A group of old-timers had taken some of the new crew members to a favorite spot, where the waitresses walked around the tables carrying trays bearing different brands of beer. You chose what you wanted and paid for it on the spot. In a few minutes, another waitress would come around carrying a tray with assorted mixed drinks. One of the new sailors at their table kept jumping up whenever a waitress came near and grabbed drinks off her tray before anyone else had a chance at them. Bob told him to sit down, and Magner, another of the new guys, told Bob to shut up. The rest of the table fanned the flames of rivalry until everyone marched out of the hall and into a dusty clearing near the parking lot. There the group, including a large gaggle of spectators from other tables, formed a ring and shoved Bob and Magner into the middle.

Trained by his boyhood clashes with small-town bullies, Bob struck quickly, though Magner was the taller and heavier man. Bob drove him to the ground and started swinging, but Magner was tough, too, and in less than a minute both men were bloodied. Bob was sitting on Magner's chest, throwing punches, when he heard the shore patrol siren, and a couple of Bob's crewmates rushed into the ring and hauled him to a nearby cab. When the cabbie saw the blood and dirt, he shouted, "Don't bring that mess into my cab!" but the sailors threw Bob inside and piled in after him, directing the driver to a brothel they knew. The ladies, without hesitation, took Bob inside and applied their ministrations. They stripped, bathed, and dried him, tending his cuts and bruises with care, then tucked him between clean sheets to sleep off the damage. In the morning his freshly laundered uniform was spotless—at no charge—and when he arrived back at the sub by cab he looked like he'd just returned from a refreshing vacation. Magner, meanwhile, had been charged with disorderly conduct and dumped back at the boat by shore patrol, his uniform soiled with dried blood and dirt. He hadn't named Bob, however, and according to time-honored convention, the two became fast friends.

Now they were on the train with other crew members on liberty. It was a regular passenger train, not a troop train, and the *Tambor* crewmen rode with civilians. Less than a month into the war, Bob and his mates were the first servicemen from Pearl Harbor these civilians had seen, and everyone wanted to wish them well. It was an extraordinary thing. The sailors had been at Wake and Pearl, the first two spots the Japanese had struck, and now here they were, on a passenger train crossing a country suddenly at war, a country gripped by anger, fear, and patriotism. Unlike their training stints before the war, when they'd taken care to change into street clothes before they went into town, now their uniforms placed them in high regard, and the other passengers went out of their way to be kind. On the train, Bob was surprised at the transformation that came over the men. "On the boat every sentence had a swear word in it," Bob recalled, "but now that was all gone. I could never figure out how they did that. Their grammar wasn't the best, but they were polite. These guys came from many nationalities—from all over the country and all kinds of families—but for the most part they were polite, clean, and good guys."

They also enjoyed a good party. They had carried beer and liquor with them onto the train, and many of the passengers joined in the festivities. The conductor was good to them, but he had his hands full. Of course, there were women on board, several of them quite attractive—a fact not lost on Magner, who styled himself, not without justification, a ladies' man. He was tall and dark and said he preferred "older" women, which to these young sailors meant women in their thirties. When Bob asked him why, he just cocked his head and smiled.

Bob and Magner were sitting together when they noticed a woman who appeared to be about eighty years old staring at them from behind her knitting needles. Bob pointed her out and told Magner that she looked to be about the right age for him. Before Magner could answer, the woman gathered up her knitting and made her way toward them. When she reached their seat, she opened her purse and pulled out a pint of whiskey.

"You boys look a little dry," she said, handing Bob the bottle. "I don't drink much, but I always carry a little along with me when I travel, and I want you boys to have it."

By nightfall a party was well under way, which the conductor managed to contain within a single car. Two young couples heard the noise from their sleeping berths and joined in, still wearing their pajamas and robes. And when the liquor ran out, they volunteered to get out at Reno to buy more. They knew the city and said they could make it back before the train pulled out. So the couples passed the hat, made a collection, and, still in their nightclothes, jumped off as soon as the train slowed at the station. When the train departed, however, they were nowhere to be seen, and the sailors grumbled that they'd been conned. But at the next stop, there were the couples with bags of liquor in both arms. They'd missed the train, taken a cab, and beaten the train to its next stop. So the party continued.

Some crew members met women who liked them a lot, and these men approached the conductor about renting berths by the hour, but he would have none of it. In the party car there was gambling and drinking and lots of friendly banter. The civilians asked questions about the war, but the sailors were discreet. The full extent of the losses at Pearl hadn't been made public, and the crew didn't talk about such things on the train. They were members of the silent service, and their security responsibilities had been driven home to them in no uncertain terms.

One result of this security—and the suddenness with which they'd been given their leave—was that friends and family didn't know they were coming home; therefore, there was no one to greet the sailors when they got off the train. So at each station where a crew member departed, the rest of the men got off first, shouted "Welcome home!" and carried him up and down the ramp on their shoulders, singing "For He's a Jolly Good Fellow."

As the train made its way across the middle of the country, the ranks in the party car gradually thinned. Especially at night, with the lights dimmed and just a couple of poker games continuing under isolated reading lights, it became downright peaceful. So much so, Bob noticed, that Magner was able to have sex with a new acquaintance quite privately at the back of the car under a couple of big railroad blankets.

Halfway across the country, at Cedar Rapids, the train reached Bob's station in the early morning. The remaining crew members jumped off ahead of him, shouted "Welcome home, Bob!" and gave him a quick ride on their shoulders. Then they piled back onto the train and Bob waved as they pulled out.

It was January in Iowa and Bob stood on the platform in his tropical-weight uniform. No one knew he was there, not even his dad, so Bob took a hotel room in Cedar Rapids and called R. C. His dad said he would drive down from Decorah—125 miles to the north—and pick him up the next day, so Bob had time to look up friends from his days at Coe College.

The owner of the bar and grill near the college was a big sports fan and had always loved having Coe athletes in his place. When Bob walked in the owner was overjoyed to see him and surprised by the navy uniform. As they spoke, there was something on Bob's mind. "I think I owe you some money," he said. The owner told him to forget it, but Bob insisted that they square up, so the man pulled out a ledger and found a few charges to Robert Hunt, Coe student. He didn't want to leave with any debts, Bob explained. There was no telling when he might get back.

The owner excused himself for a minute, went back into the kitchen, then returned. It was about noon, and within a few minutes the cook emerged carrying a full steak dinner. "On the house," the owner announced, and told his waitress to take some time off to sit with Bob. In a few more minutes there was a steak dinner in front of her, too. She was an attractive young woman about Bob's age, and they knew each other from Bob's college year when he'd been a frequent patron. Together they enjoyed the good meal and complimentary drinks.

That afternoon Bob ran into some other servicemen and had a few more drinks. The afternoon stretched into the evening, and it was late when Bob returned to the college bar to see who might be there. It was almost closing time, and the help was glad to see him again. But they told him something that made him regret the way he'd spent the evening. The waitress Bob had eaten lunch with had had the night off, but she'd come back in her best dress, hoping Bob would be there. When it got late, though, she'd given up and gone home. He never saw her again.

The next day, driving home with his dad, Bob watched the snowy fields and farmsteads slide past as the road curved through the rolling hills of eastern Iowa. Especially in winter, the little towns they passed through—Hazleton, Maynard, West Union, Calmar—seemed like tenuous outposts with shallow roots. When they descended the long hill into Decorah, the Oneota River Valley produced its familiar sense of enclosure.

The town, situated in a bowl formed by hills and ridges, had been settled

largely by Norwegians in the 1840s, and when the king of Norway visited the
United States he always traveled to Minneapolis and then down to Decorah,
where he stood on the second-floor balcony of the Versterheim ("western home")
Norwegian-American Museum, waving to the crowd below. The Vesterheim
anchored Water Street at one end, and the business district stretched from there
a mere six blocks to the east, lined on each side mostly with two-and three-story
brick storefronts. With a population of about seven thousand, it was a small
town, but the seat of Winneshiek County; and the handsome limestone courthouse, with its Greco-Roman columns and small dome, still features the carved
visage of Chief Winneshiek of the Winnebago tribe over its main entrance. Indian burial mounds dot the county's hills, which were spared during the last ice
age when the glaciers split and left unscraped the "Driftless Area" where Iowa,
Minnesota, and Wisconsin meet. In the middle of town the Upper Iowa River
flows beneath high limestone bluffs on its way to the Mississippi, thirty miles
to the east.

The Hunt family variety store stood in the middle of downtown Decorah,
and R. C. and Bob stayed together in the apartment behind the store. Small as
it was, without his mother Bessie, sister Marge, and Dick, the place felt empty.
Bob's word for the visit, remembered years later, was "uncomfortable." "It was
freezing, I had a bad cold, and everybody got on me for war news," he explained.
"Everybody was all over me and I just wanted to spend some time with my
friends." As with the civilians on the train, the presence of a serviceman who
had been at Wake and Pearl served as a lightning rod for patriotic fervor. Everyone was excited. Just weeks into the war, here was their hometown boy back from
the Pacific where he'd already seen action.

One of the first things R. C. did was march Bob down to the newspaper
offices, where the staff had asked for an interview. "They fell all over us," Bob
said, "but I had to be very careful. We were under strict orders not to talk about
things that could be used by the enemy. Mainly the editor asked me a lot of questions and I didn't answer them."

Then he went clothes shopping. With just his uniforms and one light jacket,
Bob was cold all the time. The men's shop across Water Street from R. C.'s store
was owned by an old friend, so Bob walked over and spent some of his poker
winnings. When he walked out he had the largest wardrobe he'd ever owned: a
suit, a sport coat, two pairs of slacks, three dress shirts and neckties, three sports
shirts, a winter coat, and a fine hat.

When he got home the phone started ringing. There were more dinner
invitations than he could possibly accept, and it seemed that every group in
town—the Rotary club, the high school, and the chamber of commerce among
them—wanted him to speak to them. "The last thing I wanted to do in Decorah
was to give a speech," Bob told me, but he felt an obligation, even if there wasn't

a lot he could say. The events were mostly question-and-answer sessions, and Bob steered them to topics he was free to discuss, everyday matters of life on a sub that would be common knowledge to any submariner.

In the high-school gymnasium the students packed the bleachers, staring at him across the varnished basketball court. They listened so quietly that he heard his voice echo in the big space. Familiar smells—the dry metallic heat from the radiators, the gym's faint scent of rubber and sweat, the smell of damp wool emanating from the student body—brought back his own high-school days. But now he stood behind a lectern, the teachers and principal seated in folding chairs behind him, flanked by the U.S. and Iowa flags. It felt strange to hear phrases like "war effort" and "Pacific theater" come out of his mouth, phrases he had read in the newspaper.

After his short statement, hands shot up. A boy wanted to know how they lived on the boat, where they slept and ate, what the bathrooms were like. A girl wanted to know what it felt like to be underwater. Another boy asked, "Have you killed any Japs yet?" Bob told them what he could, and when he finished, the wild applause and cheering surprised him. It wasn't about what he'd said, Bob understood, but what he represented, standing in front of them in his dress uniform.

The best thing about being home was sleeping late. It was a pleasure to wake up early from habit, realize where he was, and go back to sleep for a few more hours. Only now, back home, did he realize how tired he was. When he finally got up he wandered around town and looked for things to do. Many of his friends had moved away and none had received advance word that Bob was going to be in town. One evening at dusk, when he was walking downtown, dressed warmly in his new suit, topcoat, and hat, a beer truck pulled up beside him and stopped. An old pal of his from high school—Darwin Bernatz—was in the driver's seat, and he called for Bob to hop in. They parked in an alley nearby, and the two of them crawled into the back of the truck. It was a sailor's dream, sitting with an old friend in the back of a loaded beer truck. Considerably later, when the two emerged, Bob discovered that he couldn't walk a straight line. Weaving back to his dad's apartment, he wondered how Darwin was able to drive.

When it was time for Bob to head back to San Francisco, the *Tambor*, and the war, he had few regrets. "I was glad to get the hell out and get back to work," he remembered. "We had a job to do."

Since their attack on Pearl Harbor, the Japanese had moved swiftly in their bid for control in the Pacific. To succeed against the United States, they had to establish a defensive screen west of Hawaii and secure trade routes from Southeast Asia and the Dutch East Indies that would supply their economy and power their military. Oil and rubber were the essential commodities. Nearly coincident with the attacks on Pearl and Wake, they had struck the Americans in the

Philippines and the British in Malaya, Thailand, and Hong Kong. In China they quickly occupied Shanghai. On December 10, in continued landings, they seized Guam, Tarawa, and Makin, forming an arc of occupied territory stretching east from the Philippines to the Marshall Islands and Gilbert Islands. On the same day, Japanese planes sank two British warships, the *Prince of Wales* and the *Repulse*, off the Malay Peninsula. On December 23, the Marines defending Wake Island finally were overwhelmed and forced to surrender. Two days later—on Christmas Day—Hong Kong fell to the Japanese.

While Bob was in Decorah, 1942 opened with the Philippines continuing under siege and the Japanese moving against the Dutch East Indies, beginning a drive that would take them, island by island, through Borneo, Sumatra, Java, Bali, and Timor. When the *Tambor* and crew had assembled back at Pearl Harbor, readying for their next mission, news arrived of the Battle of the Java Sea. On February 27 an Allied fleet had tried to intercept a Japanese invasion force. No enemy ships were damaged appreciably and the Allies lost two cruisers and three destroyers. And on March 11, as the crew loaded the boat with armaments and provisions for a long patrol, Gen. Douglas MacArthur departed the Philippines, declared "I shall return," and left behind a remnant unit of 75,000 Filipinos and Americans to continue the fight. They would hold out into April, then fall and suffer the "Bataan Death March," a forced walk of over one hundred miles that killed thousands.

Against this backdrop, the *Tambor* sailors shipped out on March 15 with grim resolve. Bob remembered his feelings and the mood of the crew. "We had to get back out there and get after them," he said. "I just wanted to kill a lot of Japs. They were being really tough on our guys. I was madder than hell at them."

The sub first cruised northwest the 1,300 miles to Midway, where they topped off their fuel tanks. The base had changed remarkably since their last stop there, before the war had started. Now there were more men and much more bustle and noise. Antiaircraft practice at night made it hard to sleep, so Bob got up, sat on the teak planking of the forward deck, and watched. The island was blacked out—so dark that he couldn't see where the water ended and the sky began—and all he could hear at first was a plane somewhere above. Then there were beams of light shining up, and the searchlights turned in search of the plane. When they found it and converged on the target it pulled behind, the guns started. There were two kinds of concussions, one when the guns fired and one when the shells exploded. The gun flash on the ground was quick, and the flash in the sky almost as quick. Everything lit up with a yellowish red glare, but only for a moment, as if a photo were being taken.

They stayed at Midway for four days. While they were there, one of the crew came down suddenly with appendicitis and they had to leave him behind. He was a lucky man. If his symptoms had started at sea, he might have died before they could have gotten him back to a doctor. Standard instructions in such a case were to put the sailor to bed, pack him in ice, and keep him on a liquid diet until the boat reached port or could rendezvous with a larger ship.

In a famous incident later in the war, however, a pharmacist's mate did perform an appendectomy at sea, having only observed one as a technical assistant. On the *Seadragon*, the captain took the boat down to quiet water at 120 feet, and pharmacist's mate, Wheeler Lipes, placed his patient, S1C Darrell Dean Rector, on the table in the officers' wardroom. Lipes chose knives from the wardroom silverware and fashioned retractors out of bent spoons, sterilizing his instruments with alcohol. The patient was put under with ether poured into a rag in a tea strainer, which, applied too liberally at first, almost anaesthetized everyone in the room. But the operation was a success, and the seaman recovered and returned to duty. Later in the war Seaman Rector was killed in action.[1]

With its fuel tanks topped off, the *Tambor* departed Midway for the heart of its second wartime patrol, a mission that would take it on a southwesterly course, penetrating ever deeper behind the Japanese defensive perimeter that ran from Wake Island south to the Marshall and Gilbert islands. The *Tambor* would go where U.S. surface vessels could not, performing surveillance on Japanese-held ports at Wake, Truk, the Enewetak Atoll in the Marshalls, and New Britain and New Hanover in New Guinea. It was a scouting mission, with the sub instructed to attack targets of opportunity as it went. The boat would work alone. "I never could get it across to anyone how lonely and alone we were out there for the early war patrols," Bob said later. "Everywhere we went was the enemy and no one to help and give us backup."

On March 23 they revisited Wake Island, which had fallen to the Japanese exactly three months earlier. It was the site of their last contact with the enemy, and when they arrived, they found the island relatively unchanged in appearance. Periscope observations showed that the high water towers remained, the hangar near Peacock Point was undamaged, and many land planes were based there. Rounding Peacock Point, Captain Murphy spotted one of the Japanese destroyers hit by the Marines, beached and stripped. Each time the sub raised its periscope Murphy saw planes circling overhead, so the *Tambor* had to perform its surveillance with quick peeks at half-hour intervals. One of these revealed a small *maru*, or Japanese freighter, moored at the island's boat entrance, with a scout plane circling above it. Down in the forward room, Bob and his crew were instructed to stand ready. *This is it*, Bob thought, *our first real shot.*

It was late morning, and Bob was at his battle station, standing between the two columns of torpedo tubes, three on each side. He ran the interlocking system, opening and closing the inner and outer doors of the tubes, making sure they were empty of water before each reload. When he received the order "Make tubes ready for firing," he knew what to do.

At 11:15 AM, after a quick setup, the order came down. From his training,

Bob knew the captain had said, "Fire number one torpedo!" and someone in the conning tower had pushed the electrical firing key and repeated into his mic, "Fire!" The first-class torpedoman relayed the order, and Bob hit the mechanical firing key to make sure the torpedo fired. Then a burst of air shot the fish from the tube, and the sub tugged with the pulse. Immediately the poppet valve opened, venting the tube into the boat, sucking back the air that fired the torpedo so bubbles wouldn't rise and betray its position. Water rushed in, too, hissing as it flooded the tube and adjacent bilges, helping to keep the sub in trim now that the weight of the torpedo was gone. Once the tube was filled with water, the man on its side closed the poppet valve. Then Bob ordered the outer door shut so the tube could be readied for reload. Amid all the action and noise, Bob's training took over. He concentrated on the intricate sequence of steps, getting it all right. Though they'd just fired their first torpedo at a Japanese target, there had been no time for thought, no time for emotions.

As the torpedo headed for the freighter, the plane that had been circling turned and followed its track straight toward the *Tambor*'s periscope. Murphy ordered the sub deep and made an evasive turn. As they went, they heard an explosion, but could not know whether the torpedo had hit the *maru* or the reef behind it. When they tried to return to periscope depth, they heard the sound of screws, and a small patrol craft chased them for hours. When they finally escaped they were too far from the island to see whether or not they'd sunk the freighter.

Before they left Wake, they had a very close call. While they were traveling on the surface, one of the lookouts spotted a plane, and Captain Murphy gave the order to crash dive. The men topside immediately dropped to the conning-tower deck, then slid down the hatch to the control room to man their diving stations. Harry Behrens was the first one down the hatch, and after the last man came down, it was his task to close the hatch and dog it tight as quickly as possible. Tarzan Behrens was chosen for the task because when he closed and dogged a hatch, it stayed shut. But this time, as he made the last turns he heard a tapping noise coming from above. At the same time, one of the lookouts yelled from the control room that two men had not come down. The order was given to blow all the tanks and surface immediately to rescue them. Just as the sea reached the conning-tower hatch, the dive leveled off and the boat began to rise. Harry opened the hatch, dragged the men into the conning tower, and closed and dogged it again. As soon as the two men were safely inside, the word was given to dive again, and down the boat went. The rescued men, shaken but relieved, climbed down to the control room and assumed their stations; they were a lookout and the boat's executive officer, Ed Spruance, the son of Fleet Adm. Raymond Spruance. The tapping noise Harry noticed had been Spruance frantically pounding his Annapolis class ring on the top of the closed hatch. The crown of the ring had been smashed flat, but he refused the machinists' offers to repair it for him. It had saved his and the lookout's lives, and he intended to keep the ring in its misshapen form as a memento.

Departing Wake, the sub cruised on the surface south-southwest. Conserving fuel by using just one diesel engine, the *Tambor* reached the Enewetak Atoll at the far northwest extent of the Marshall Islands two days later. In its harbor they sighted a six-thousand-ton *maru*, and as they waited for it to emerge they conducted their surveillance of the island. After two days the freighter still had not made itself available for a shot, so the sub continued southwest to Truk, where the Japanese had a major base. On the way, however, they received instructions to intercept a target to the north of them. Their *maru* apparently had finally departed, heading back toward Japan. Two days later they intercepted the freighter, sighting smoke from its stacks on March 30 and closing in that night. In a surface attack, the *Tambor* fired three torpedoes. All passed under the ship, which turned toward the sub in an attempt to ram it. A quick dive avoided the danger, and when the boat surfaced the *maru* had steamed into a rain squall and disappeared. Relocating its target the next day, the *Tambor* fired four more torpedoes at long range, but the freighter turned into them and they passed on either side. Murphy wrote in his report: "Having expended 3 days, 7 torpedoes, and 10,000 gallons of fuel on the *Shinho Maru*, we gave it up as a bad job. . . ."

Everyone in the torpedo room was frustrated. Seven fish wasted, and Bob couldn't understand why. Three of the torpedoes had passed beneath their target. Some of the torpedomen were insisting that there had to be something wrong with the fish, or with the Torpedo Data Computer. The mood brightened somewhat when a radio transmission confirmed that they'd hit the freighter at Wake, a *maru* of about three thousand tons. It was their first sinking.

Continuing on their assigned patrol, the *Tambor* headed for Truk, arriving April 3; but patrol boats and planes there inhibited surveillance, keeping the sub down and wary. The same day Captain Murphy pointed the boat south again and steered for the islands northeast of New Guinea. On the way they came upon another target, this one a transport ship. Bob wrote in his diary: "April 6: Crossed the equator at 10:00 this morning. Perfect weather, easy steaming. Sighted transport about 4:00. Made a submerged attack, fired three fish forward and two aft, but didn't hit. Every time we ran up the periscope, he would try to ram us—went right over us a couple of times. At dark we surfaced and went after him again. Chased him all night, but didn't see him again."

Five fish and five more misses. The crew's frustration grew, especially in the torpedo rooms. And to make things worse, the air conditioning had gone out. Operating at the equator with no way to cool the sub was almost intolerable. Especially in a submerged, closed boat, the heat was inescapable. Diving after a surface run, the diesel engines threw off a lot of heat, as did the operation of the electrical motors and cooking stoves. The water outside the hull wasn't much help. In the tropical regions where the *Tambor* was operating, its temperature even at 150 feet was 85 degrees.[2] Inside, the air temperature remained well over 100 degrees and everything was wet. Cigarettes were too damp to light, and everyone, including Bob, suffered from heat rash. He was working in the forward torpedo room one day when his head suddenly began to swim, and the next thing he knew he was flat on his back on the deck. After two days of rest, he was back to work, but another shipmate who had succumbed to heat exhaustion was out of action for the rest of the patrol. The air in the boat smelled foul with sweat, mildew, and diesel fumes. Bob left the plastic cover on his bunk, hoping to keep the mattress dry, and woke in a pool of his own sweat. He raked the puddles off the plastic with his hands, then got up and swabbed the deck with rags. The dangers of slipping on a wet deck were magnified when the nearest doctor was a thousand miles away.

A fellow torpedoman in the front room was a bowlegged Texan named Kennedy, a tobacco-chewing cowboy who used a coffee can as a spittoon. Now Bob noticed that nearly everyone was walking around as bowlegged as Kennedy, trying to keep from chafing the heat rash on their inner thighs. In this condition, he wondered how long it would take them to get to their battle stations. The captain took note: "After two weeks of all day submergence, 11 bunks were wet and stinking. Clothes and locker gear in the forward and after torpedo rooms were mildewed. Practically everyone had heat rash." It was a serious problem, for the boat's equipment as well as the crew, with the extreme humidity corroding electrical contacts and shorting out circuits. Murphy wrote in his patrol summary: "At one time we had both periscope hoist motors and the radio transmitter out of commission and zero grounds in two main motors, all of which casualties are attributable to inadequate air conditioning."

As for the men, Bob remembered the long stretches spent submerged in enemy waters, sometimes fifteen hours at a time, with seventy men breathing the same foul air over and over. The boat carried a white carbon dioxide–absorbing powder, and sometimes in the forward room they spread it on one of the bunks to "fix" the air. Near the end of a long dive, if a man could manage to light a damp cigarette to cut the stench, it often went out for lack of oxygen. Even when breathing wasn't a problem, performing basic tasks was made difficult by the constant flow of sweat, which slickened everything, including the tools in your hands. One crewmate remembered taking off his shoes to pour out the sweat that had run down his legs.

There wasn't much relief. If a crew member's rotation did not include a stint of topside watch he might not get into open air for a full sixty days. "After a long dive," Bob recalled, "the first thing we did when we surfaced was to get the engines online and take a suction of fresh air through the conning-tower

Photo 7. Bob (seated left), Lewis Payne (behind Bob), and Pop Warner (in uniform) in the forward torpedo room. Note crewmate in bunk to left. (Courtesy Robert Hunt)

hatch. You could almost hear a sigh of relief from the whole crew when that fresh air went through the boat." Difficult as these conditions were, somehow they adapted. "It's amazing what a body can get used to," Bob said. "Once after a two-month patrol I stuck my head out the hatch, took a sniff, and said, 'The fresh air stinks!'"

April 7 was Bob's twenty-third birthday, and some of the crew, many of them seventeen or eighteen years old, took to calling him "Old Man" Hunt. Birthday gifts on the boat consisted of things like a stick of gum, a couple of cigarettes, or an old magazine, offered with a laugh. Sometimes the cook baked a cake for the crew to share, but baking was a tricky business below sea level, and no one wanted him to light the stove when the air conditioning was out.

Continuing south to the islands off New Guinea, the *Tambor* was shaken by two bombs dropped from a plane but only suffered a few broken lamps. Going around New Hanover, they evaded two destroyers; then, running on the surface at night, the sound man heard propellers, and at about the same time a watchman on the bridge saw an oil tanker illuminated by a lightning flash. The *Tambor*'s first two fish missed, as did a third. Then the second of two fired from the stern struck home. Bob noted, "Five fish—one hit," and the captain reported: "Ship sank stern first three minutes later, with at least five heavy explosions. She was a tanker of about 7,000 tons, apparently fully loaded."

Running low on fuel, the *Tambor* completed its island surveillance and headed home, refueling at Johnston Island before reaching Pearl May 12. The final count was two freighters sunk, totaling roughly ten thousand tons. The wasted fish and missed opportunities concerned everyone, although no one blamed the torpedomen or the captain. Everyone thought there was something wrong with the fish. It had taken thirteen torpedoes to score two hits, a record that pleased no one, including headquarters.

The Navy had already lost 60 percent of its torpedo supply in the Japanese attack on Manila Bay's Cavite Yard three days after Pearl Harbor. The low store of torpedoes, combined with the low rate at which new ones were being produced, was alarming, and captains were chastised for expending too many fish on minor targets. Guidelines for their efficient use were issued, but it was plain to the crews that too many fish just didn't work right. The captains reported that they ran lower than their settings, that they exploded prematurely, or, most maddening, that they sometimes failed to explode when they struck their target. These complaints were viewed, however, as excuses for the captains' failures. One of the top sub brass in the Pacific, Rear Adm. Ralph Waldo Christie, was the man who had developed the sophisticated Mark XIV magnetic exploder, which sensed the magnetic field created by a ship's hull. Christie was proud of the exploder and could not be persuaded there was anything wrong with it. His superior, Cdr., Submarines, U.S. Pacific Fleet, Robert English, concurred. Both cited improper maintenance and crew failures as probable causes for the high percentage of misses.

Bob, along with everyone else actually on the subs, knew better. "We found out very early on that those damned torpedoes weren't doing what they were supposed to," he told me. "That second wartime patrol was very frustrating because we had ships to hit. We'd set fish for ten feet and they'd run at twenty or go up and down. We all sent back lots of reports, but it was hard to convince the brass." Bob believed the torpedoes, and especially the exploders, were too sophisticated to be practical. "They were highly tuned pieces of equipment, and they couldn't take the bouncing around at sea." In early 1942 the Navy had little more than its sub fleet to take the fight to the enemy, but its captains and crews were fighting a two-front war, one against the Japanese and one against their own brass. SOP !

CHAPTER FIVE

"Point Luck":
The Battle of Midway

I n May 1942, when Fleet Adm. Chester Nimitz huddled with two rear admirals, Raymond Spruance and Frank Jack Fletcher, to go over a plan of battle in response to information that the Japanese would attack the American base at Midway, the three men discussed an ambush to surprise the invasion force. The rendezvous point for the U.S. aircraft carriers, thirty-five miles to the northeast of Midway, they designated "Point Luck." The battle joined in the seas and skies surrounding the two square miles of island territory would prove to be the turning point of the Pacific war, and Bob Hunt, from the lookout station of the *Tambor*, would be one of the few U.S. sailors to actually see enemy ships during that decisive action.

Point Luck was aptly named. Nimitz and his officers prepared for the battle knowing that U.S. forces would be badly outnumbered in surface fighting ships. Four Japanese heavy aircraft carriers—the *Akagi*, *Kaga*, *Soryu*, and *Hiryu*, all of which had launched their planes against Pearl Harbor just six months before—would be met by three U.S. carriers, the *Enterprise*, *Hornet*, and hastily repaired *Yorktown*, which had been badly damaged in the Battle of the Coral Sea. In addition, the Japanese flotilla's advantage included two light carriers and eleven battleships to none in either category for the United States, and ten heavy cruisers to America's six. In light cruisers and destroyers the Japanese advantages were six to one and fifty-three to seventeen, respectively. To balance the odds somewhat, U.S. forces had the advantage of surprise; American code breakers were able to provide Nimitz with a remarkably precise account of the Japanese plan and order of battle. Beyond superior intelligence and a shrewd plan of their own, Nimitz, Fletcher, and Spruance could only hope that the vagaries of battle would fall their way. They could hope for luck.

In the event, the Battle of Midway would turn out to be a contest of airpower, and the adversaries brought roughly equal numbers of planes against one another. The Japanese carriers held torpedo bombers, dive-bombers, fighters, fighter seaplanes, scout seaplanes, and land bombers—a total of 325 craft. The U.S. carriers brought 42 torpedo bombers, 112 dive-bombers, and 79 F4F-4 fighters, but the Americans could also employ the land-based fighters, bombers, and scout planes on Midway, bringing the total number of U.S. aircraft to 348. However, the slight numerical advantage enjoyed by the Midway defenders was more than offset by the technical advantage of the Japanese torpedo bombers and fighters. The U.S. torpedo bombers were old and slow, and some of the dive-bombers, particularly those stationed at Midway, were obsolete, as well. Pilots nicknamed the SB2-U Vindicators, without affection, "Vibrators" and "Wind Indicators." Furthermore, the United States possessed no fighters with the speed and maneuverability of the Japanese Zero.

With only a handful of exceptions, both Japanese and U.S. submarines would prove embarrassingly ineffective in the battle, mostly because of faulty strategy or bad timing. Only two American subs would see major action. The lumbering, outmoded *Nautilus* was commanded with skill and daring by its skipper, Lt. Cdr. William H. Brockman Jr., when it found itself at the right place at the right time. And the *Tambor* would figure in one of the war's most curious submarine encounters, one that, in ironic fashion, affected the battle's outcome.

Neither side underestimated the stakes in the looming encounter. For the Japanese, the Midway strike was essential to its strategy of establishing a mid-ocean picket of island bases, an outer perimeter to defend its "Greater Asian Co-Prosperity Sphere." Tactically, a forward air base at Midway would make Hawaii vulnerable and, perhaps most importantly, would lure the U.S. Navy into the decisive battle sought by the Japanese. If Midway and Hawaii could be taken, and the U.S. Navy neutralized, America and Great Britain would be forced to sue for peace, securing for Japan the empire it wished to fashion out of its holdings in China, Southeast Asia, Indonesia, the Philippines, and eventually Australia, New Zealand, and, ideally, India, as well. So ran Japanese political and military planning. It was crucial, however, that the longed-for showdown with the remains of the U.S. Navy occur as soon as possible, before America's immense industrial capacity could produce a truly threatening fleet. Admiral Isoroku Yamamoto, commander in chief of the Japanese Combined Fleet, knew this well. He had studied and traveled in the United States and was skeptical that Japan could defeat its Pacific adversary militarily. Even before the attack on Pearl Harbor he had declared: "If I am told to fight regardless of the consequences, I shall run wild for the first six months or a year, but I have utterly no confidence for the second or third year."

The Americans, for their part, had no choice but to meet the Japanese at Midway, despite their three-to-one disadvantage in surface fighting ships. Losing Midway would indeed make Hawaii vulnerable. And if the battle were lost and the American fleet overwhelmed, even the U.S. West Coast would be threatened.

~~~~~~

At Point Luck and beyond, the battle would consist of three parts: the search, the fight, and the chase. But before the action itself, two crucial efforts helped to determine the outcome: American intelligence gathering and the planning based on foreknowledge of Japanese intentions. Just two and a half months before the Midway battle, the Navy's "Hypo" decryption unit in Pearl Harbor made crucial strides in reading the Japanese fleet code. Working in a 100' x 60' windowless basement they called "the Dungeon," a staff of forty-seven, under the direction of Cdr. Joseph J. Rochefort, used IBM punch-card machines to analyze a huge backlog of Japanese radio traffic. The Washington, D.C., decryption unit, OP-20-G, where Rochefort had previously worked, had already discerned the basic structure of the Japanese military's coding system. From that point on, the work to finally enable U.S. intelligence to decipher enemy messages consisted of applying sufficient man-hours to the problem of identifying patterns among thousands of intercepted Japanese transmissions. For Hypo, those man-hours sometimes came from unlikely sources. When the battleship USS *California* was disabled in the Pearl Harbor attack and the musicians in its band were left without employment, Rochefort took them on as IBM machine operators, and several of them made careers of decryption from that point on.

The IBM machines required frigid air conditioning to function in Hawaii's tropical heat, and Rochefort took to belting on a smoking jacket over his uniform to keep warm. He also wore carpet slippers to cushion his feet during the long hours he spent standing on the Dungeon's concrete floor. The jacket and slippers earned him a reputation as an eccentric, but those who knew him best described him as brilliant, quietly authoritative, and driven. The task of correlating coded passages from transmissions made over days, weeks, and months was a titanic one, and an organizational challenge. "I was a lousy organizer," Rochefort admitted. "I didn't keep very good files; I carried it all in my head."[1] Especially after the Pearl Harbor attack, the code breakers—mathematicians, linguists, and clerical assistants—labored almost without rest, popping pep pills from a bucket in the Dungeon.

On March 18, 1942, the Japanese fleet code, designated JN-25, was finally broken, and decryption of significant portions of current messages began. Rochefort was in daily contact with Lt. Cdr. Edwin Layton, the intelligence officer for the Pacific Fleet, and had earned Layton's admiration. Both men were fluent in Japanese, and Layton had become convinced of Rochefort's reliability and caution. Therefore, on May 14, when Rochefort telephoned Layton and exclaimed, "I've got something so hot here it's burning the top of my desk!" it commanded Layton's full attention. Stephen Budiansky, in his book *Battle of Wits* tells the story well:

The hot document proved to be a partial decrypt in which the words *kory-aku butai*, invasion force, were followed by the geographical designator AF. *Koryaku butai* had appeared in orders for the invasions of Rabaul, Java, Sumatra, and Bali that Hypo had already read. AF had been tentatively identified as Midway. Rochefort argued that the clincher was an order that air base equipment was to be shipped to Saipan to be in position for the "AF ground crews." AF was obviously an island air base; it was, Rochefort insisted, a matter of simple deduction to see that it had to be Midway.[2]

Layton and, more importantly, Admiral Nimitz, were quickly convinced.

Nimitz acted decisively. Just three days after Rochefort's phone call to Layton, he ordered his three remaining carriers home to be quickly refitted and sent to Midway. The *Enterprise* and *Hornet*—Task Force 16, commanded by Vice Adm. William F. Halsey—sped back from their recently completed mission to launch the daring Doolittle raid against the Japanese homeland. At the same time, the damaged *Yorktown*, under Task Force 17 commander Rear Admiral Fletcher, made best speed back from the Battle of Coral Sea, in which the carrier *Lexington* had been lost. In the meantime Nimitz reinforced Pearl Harbor defenses, sent additional planes to Midway, and recalled all available submarines to patrol the waters around the atoll until further plans for their use in the upcoming battle could be devised.

As Nimitz speedily prepared for the Japanese strike, however, the Washington intelligence command was questioning Hypo's work. Cdr. John H. Redman, in charge of OP-20-G since January, said Rochefort's unit had made decoding mistakes and that the likely target was the Johnston Atoll, a small refueling outpost seven hundred miles west-southwest of Hawaii. Others argued that "AF" designated Hawaii itself, or California. Some thought the whole thing was a massive Japanese disinformation tactic, especially when an uncoded radio transmission to Tokyo from a Japanese seaplane asked that the crew's mail be forwarded to Midway.

To dispel confusion and bolster his conclusions, Rochefort, with the support of Layton and Nimitz, instructed Midway to send an uncoded message saying that its water distillation plant had broken down. Two days later, on May 21, Japanese intelligence sent a JN-25 transmission stating that "AF Air Unit" was short of fresh water. Midway had been confirmed as Japan's target, and to complete its ruse Hawaii radioed Midway the promise of a water shipment.

Yamamoto, aware that he was preparing for a decisive battle, had spent months developing an elaborate plan. A detachment of forces would attack the Aleutians, then a striking force of four carriers and support ships would hit Midway to wipe out its defenses. Finally, the occupation force, carrying five thousand soldiers, would attack and seize the island. At the same time a picket of submarines stationed northwest of Pearl would watch for the American carriers expected to sortie to Midway's aid. When they did, Yamamoto's main body would move forward to pounce on them. Yamamoto's own mammoth super battleship, the *Yamato*, was to be one of seven battleships that made up the heart of the lethal main body. The *Yamato* was the biggest battleship in the world, measuring 863 feet in length and protected by side armor 16 inches thick. It displaced nearly 70,000 tons, more than twice that of the next largest ships in the main body, and its firepower included nine 18.1-inch guns that could accurately throw their 3,000-pound projectiles—nearly the weight of a '42 Packard—over fifteen miles. "Each gun turret," remarked one commentator, "was about the size of a destroyer."[3]

On May 27, 1942, just days before the expected battle, Nimitz held a final staff meeting. Budiansky recounts:

> Nimitz was prepared to stake everything on Rochefort's analysis, but it was a huge gamble. It would mean leaving Hawaii defenseless as he rushed his carriers to Midway before the Japanese arrived. Attending the Wednesday morning meeting would be General Delos Emmons, the Army commander in Hawaii, and General Robert C. Richardson, whom Marshall had sent from Washington. . . .
>
> Rochefort stayed up all the Tuesday night before Nimitz's staff meeting going over the months of messages. Disheveled and beat, he showed up half an hour late but was able to avert the wrath of a room full of waiting admirals and generals when he reported that Station Hypo had broken the last remaining piece of JN-25, a separate code-within-the-code used for dates. He then flourished the payoff: a message dated May 26 ordering destroyer escorts for the troopships to depart from Saipan on May 28, proceed at eleven knots, and arrive at Midway June 6. An earlier decrypt had revealed that air attacks against Midway would commence from a point to the northwest of the island on day "N-12." That fixed the likely day for the Japanese air assault at June 3 or 4.
>
> That same day, May 27, the Japanese changed both the code book and the additive tables for JN-25 and imposed radio silence on the Midway and Aleutian forces. The code breakers were blacked out. But Nimitz had everything he needed already. He knew where the Japanese would strike and with what forces, he knew when, and he knew exactly what he had to do to get there first.[4]

To get there first was no mean feat. The *Enterprise* and *Hornet* had arrived at Pearl the previous day, May 26, with Task Force 16 commander Halsey suffering from an incapacitating rash that covered his whole body. Nevertheless, the task force would sortie just two days later, under new leadership. Halsey, to the surprise of many, recommended his cruiser escort group commander, Rear Admiral Spruance, a man without naval aviation experience. It would prove to be an inspired choice.

The *Yorktown* pulled in on May 27, requiring, according to the most optimistic estimates, two weeks of repairs. In the Coral Sea three aerial bombs had damaged the carrier, one of them scoring a direct hit on the flight deck and penetrating two lower decks before exploding deep inside the ship. The *Yorktown*, for which normal, full repairs would require three months, received heroic around-the-clock ministrations in the navy yard and would depart just three days after its arrival, May 30. Sailing at reduced speed due to unrepaired damage, the *Yorktown* nevertheless was able to rendezvous at Point Luck with *Enterprise* and *Hornet* June 2, one day before first contact with the Japanese attackers. On June 3, two days later than planned, the Japanese submarine picket arrived on station between Pearl and Midway to watch for the American carriers already in place to the north. After the battle Yamamoto would remark, ruefully, "It was a big mistake that the submarine sweep was not well done."[5]

Nimitz's plan was simple but sound. He understood the tenuous situation of his Pacific Fleet and the Japanese desire to finish the job they'd begun with the Pearl Harbor raid, and he planned accordingly. By positioning his carriers beyond the Japanese target, he could use Midway's long-range bombers to scout westward while keeping his naval task forces hidden, and by ordering the carriers to the northeast of Midway, he positioned them for a flank attack against the Japanese Striking Force. Furthermore, an important part of Nimitz's battle plan was contained in a special "Letter of Instructions" given to each task force commander. "In carrying out the task assigned," it said, "you will be governed by the principle of calculated risk, which you shall interpret to mean avoidance of exposure of your force to attack by superior enemy forces without good prospect of inflicting, as a result of such exposure, greater damage on the enemy." The United States badly needed to improve its ratio of forces versus the Japanese navy, and Nimitz was asking his commanders to blend aggressiveness with judgment and restraint, lest they be drawn into the winner-take-all slugfest that the numerically superior Japanese force sought. The judgments to be made would be difficult, particularly since restraint is a trait not usually rewarded in military leaders. Because of seniority in rank, Rear Admiral Fletcher was placed in overall command of both Task Force 16 and 17, but as the battle unfolded Spruance would carry the burden of decision making at the most crucial junctures. And at those junctures Spruance would apply the "principle of calculated risk" with fine discernment.

Rear Adm. Robert H. English provided Nimitz with a submarine battle plan involving all twenty-six subs within reach of Midway and Hawaii. The boats were deployed in screens to the north and west of Hawaii and in a double picket to the west of Midway. Eight subs far to the west formed a surveillance line distant from the U.S. bases, while twelve more were held close to Midway. Of the 12, 10 formed a double arc from northwest to southwest, 150 and 200 miles from the atoll, with 2 "linebackers" situated behind them, to Midway's north and south. The *Tambor*'s assignment was to patrol near the "left end" position of the inner arc, 150 miles west-southwest of Midway.

The *Tambor* departed Pearl Harbor on May 21, and Bob did not make a single entry in his diary until after the sub's return, an indication that this was no ordinary patrol. During the five-day transit to the boat's assigned position, the crew conducted training dives and exercised at battle submerged. Arriving on station May 26, the sub began surface patrol of its sector, and on its first day there practiced battle surface. During the exercise Bob was the first man up, climbing the ladder to his lookout position with one hand and carrying the .30-caliber machine gun in the other. Once he fastened his gun to the lookout rail, it was his job to cover the crew scrambling to man the 3-inch deck gun. Bob knew the drill and his weapon by heart. The gunner's mate, Thaddeus Glebocki, often had come to Bob's forward room to disassemble, clean, and reassemble the machine gun, and Bob helped. He knew all its parts and how they worked, but, to conserve ammunition, he had never fired it. Now, with the Japanese Fleet sailing their way, the exercise went live. "It was so exciting that day," Bob recalled, "because it was the first time I was actually able to fire the gun. It was one of the biggest days of my life." Aboard the *Tambor*, spirits were high in anticipation of battle. Crew members threw glass bottles and other pieces of trash into the sea and Bob squeezed off bursts of machine-gun fire at them. And with impressive booms, the deck gun fired two 3-inch rounds. "We had a ball," Bob said.

The weather was clear and the sea calm, as it would remain throughout the coming engagement. Bob took his turns on lookout, spotting only the occasional Catalina scout plane out from Midway. Then, on May 30, its fifth day on station, the *Tambor* and the other screening subs received a change of orders. Now they were to patrol submerged during daylight and "be ready to surface and pursue enemy units." During the following days of submerged reconnaissance Bob rotated through his stations in the control room, steering the boat and manning the bow planes, ready to take up his duties in the torpedo room when the captain called "battle stations."

On May 31 the *Tambor* radio operator, Bob's friend Red Mayo, intercepted a coded message to Task Force 16 and Task Force 17—the U.S. carrier groups—

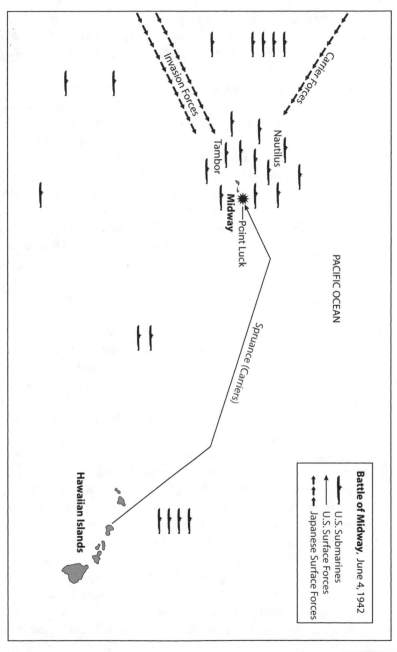

Map 1. U.S. submarine deployment for the Battle of Midway.

Battle of Midway, June 4, 1942

U.S. Submarines
U.S. Surface Forces
Japanese Surface Forces

PACIFIC OCEAN

Carrier Forces

Invasion Forces

Tambor

Nautilus

Midway

Point Luck

Spruance (Carriers)

Hawaiian Islands

ordering them to converge on the latitude and longitude coordinates that designated their ambush post, Point Luck. On June 3, bracing for attack, the command of submarine Task Force 7 sent out crucial instructions, received on the *Tambor* at 0430 and recorded in Captain Murphy's patrol report: "The success of our forces in the coming battle will depend on timely and accurate contact and damage reports," it said, prophetically.

As the *Tambor* patrolled, Red Mayo monitored the radio traffic crackling overhead. Beginning that morning, patrol planes reported sighting ships believed to be part of the Japanese attack and occupation forces, but the carrier striking force remained unseen. Battleships and cruisers were among a group reported to be five hundred to seven hundred miles from Midway, approaching the *Tambor*'s position from the southwest at eighteen knots. The news passed through the boat by word of mouth, each man hearing it in his compartment. The *Tambor* surfaced at nightfall, saw the running lights of two unidentified planes, submerged to avoid them, then surfaced again twenty minutes later. Near midnight it intercepted a report of U.S. B-17 "Flying Fortresses" having struck at the enemy ships that day, leaving a battleship and transport ablaze. It was one of many erroneous reports. Indeed, B-17s from Midway had attacked a Japanese Transport Group that afternoon, but scored no hits. As Spruance was to comment later, "During the Battle of Midway the 'fog of war' was fairly thick."[6] Furthermore, it was a battle fought almost exclusively by airpower, while the opposing ships themselves remained over the horizon, miles apart and out of sight from one another. In a time before surveillance satellites, American and Japanese commanders operated blind until their search planes reported contacts, then pieced together fragmentary information to determine crucial decisions. At the Battle of Midway, then, surface commanders operated under conditions experienced routinely by sub captains when submerged: they had to correlate a series of glimpses to make tactical decisions by inference and deduction.

On the morning of June 4, news came from the radio room that Japanese planes were approaching Midway. Next, word passed through the boat that a patrol plane had spotted the Japanese Striking Force approaching from the northwest, and land-based heavy bombers had taken off to go for the carriers. At 0750, a half hour later, the *Tambor* and other picket subs received orders to make best speed to "attack this force."

By the time the subs received their attack orders much had already happened. That dawn, when Vice Admiral Chuichi Nagumo, commander of the Japanese Striking Force, had begun launching the Midway attack squadrons off his carriers, he had done so with confidence. Nowhere in the Japanese calculations was luck a factor. The navy had enjoyed a succession of victories since Pearl Harbor, sweeping through the South Pacific, and now it brought a massive force against a small island base. Later, seeking to explain a devastating loss, Japanese

Photo 8. The *Tambor*, after refit and repairs at Mare Island, near San Francisco, March 1945. Note the wartime color change from black to gray and the removal of the hull number from the conning tower. The conning tower has also been cut down and a machine gun added. (U.S. Navy)

analysts of the battle would cite the prevalence of "Victory Disease," a malady that infected their high command, junior officers, and enlisted men, leading to flawed planning and execution.[7] The operation depended upon elaborate choreography among disparate forces, and flexibility was not one of its traits. An important symptom of Victory Disease was the planners' overconfidence in their tactical predictions; the success of the plan depended upon the Americans behaving just as expected. But perhaps the key consequence of Japanese over-confidence was the belief that their naval code was unbreakable, a delusion that persisted throughout the war. As their circling aircraft arranged themselves in formations and turned toward Midway, Nagumo and Yamamoto believed they still enjoyed the advantage of surprise, much as they had when their planes appeared suddenly over Ford Island and Battleship Row. It was true that ele-ments of the Transport Group had been located and bombed the previous day, but the attack had been from land-based planes and had inflicted no damage. The Midway base was now alerted, but it was too late for the U.S. Navy to block the invasion, for surely its carriers were still far to the southeast, beyond the Japanese submarine lookouts.

But task forces 16 and 17 were waiting for the attackers at Point Luck. Midway had sent planes out before dawn in directions indicated by the Hypo decryptions, and, as a result, Lt. Howard P. Ady, searching out from Midway in his Catalina, detected a portion of the Striking Force emerging from a rain squall at 0530. He saw two carriers leading a group of cruisers and destroyers and felt the sensation of "watching the curtain rise on the biggest show of our lives."[8] Fifteen minutes later, in what Nimitz would term "the most important contact of the battle," Lt. (jg) William A. Chase, flying in the sector adjacent to Ady, spotted "many planes heading Midway bearing 320 degrees, distance 150" miles. The two reports allowed U.S. forces to locate Nagumo's carriers with certainty, and at 0607 Fletcher ordered Spruance to proceed westerly to attack with *Enterprise* and *Hornet*. Fletcher, meanwhile, held *Yorktown* back to keep from bunching his vital assets.

As Spruance closed with the Japanese Striking Force, he faced an agonizing command decision. He needed to launch his planes as soon as possible to main-tain the advantage of surprise and to strike while the location report on the car-riers was fresh. But he was still beyond the range for safe recovery of his torpedo bombers. He listened to the reports of the air attack against Midway. Beginning at 0630, the Japanese bombed Eastern and Sand islands, knocking out electrical power on Eastern and setting its hospital and hangars on fire. Maybe he could catch the enemy carriers recovering their aircraft. He gave the launch order, and at 0700 *Hornet* began sending up planes, followed immediately by *Enterprise*. The torpedo bombers were at the extreme edge of their range, and of the fliers who survived to return, many would be lost when they ditched in the sea, out of gas. Spruance foresaw this possibility, but made the judgment he thought provided the best chance for overall victory. An hour-and-a-half later, *Yorktown* launched its planes in an intended second wave. The American attack would not proceed as planned.

The first U.S. planes to reach the Japanese were bombers and old Vindicator dive-bombers from Midway, which were met by Zeros and antiaircraft fire sent up by Nagumo's screening ships. High-altitude level bombing by the big B-17s proved nearly useless against swift carriers making evasive turns. As one airman put it, "It's like trying to drop a marble from eye level on a scared mouse." The Midway-based planes inflicted no damage on the Striking Force.

The next planes to reach the Japanese position would be carrier-launched "Devastator" torpedo bombers, but finding the Striking Force, even with coordinates provided earlier that morning, proved to be no simple matter. When the Japanese carriers had nearly finished recovering their attack planes, Nagumo ordered a course change which either went unreported by Midway's bombers or was not forwarded to the U.S. carriers. As a result, the *Hornet's* fighters and dive-bombers failed to locate the enemy and returned home frustrated. Only the *Hornet's* torpedo bombers, led by Lt. Cdr. John C. Waldron, found the Striking Force. When Waldron, who claimed one-eighth Sioux heritage and was an avid student of Japanese tactics, reached the expected contact point and saw empty sea, he made an educated guess. Turning from his prescribed course at just the right moment and in just the right direction, he led his squadron directly to Nagumo's flagship carrier, *Akagi*. But the attack, at 0925, was futile. Zeros shred-

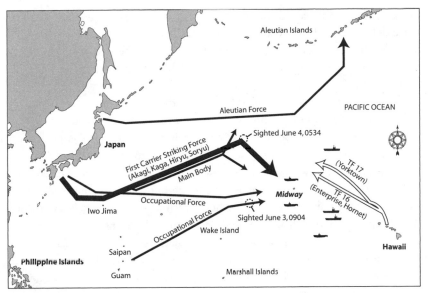

Map 2. The Battle of Midway, June 4, 1942.

ded Squadron VT-8, which recorded no hits. Its lone survivor was Ens. George Gay. After his plane was shot down he treaded water, hiding under his rubber seat cushion until a seaplane rescued him the next day.

The lumbering Devastators from the *Enterprise* and *Yorktown* suffered similar fates. Lt. Cdr. Eugene E. Lindsey's *Enterprise* Squadron VT-6 arrived twenty-four minutes after Waldron. Ten of its fourteen planes were downed by fighters and antiaircraft fire in the attack, which again recorded no hits. Looking on, officers on the *Akagi*'s bridge felt invulnerable. Commander Minoru Genda, the talented air operations officer, was suffering from pneumonia and had recently emerged from his sickbed. Watching the American planes fall, however, he exulted to himself: *We don't need to be afraid of enemy planes no matter how many they are! . . . This is a winning battle!*[9] Fifteen minutes later, when *Yorktown*'s VT-3 came in, led by Lt. Cdr. Lance E. "Lem" Massey, Genda's optimism was only bolstered. In the end, of the forty-one Devastators that attacked the Striking Force that day, only four planes survived, and no American torpedoes found their targets. Besides being slow and poorly armored, the planes carried fuel tanks that were not self-sealing, making them virtual death traps when attacked by the nimble Zeros. Shortly after the Battle of Midway the few that remained were replaced by newer planes, and all remaining Vindicators, like those that had launched from Midway, were retired from combat.

Useless as their attacks had seemed, the pilots of the doomed torpedo planes helped win the Battle of Midway. Persisting as the Zeros struck, then flying resolutely into a wall of antiaircraft fire, they preoccupied the Striking Force defenses, tired the Japanese fighter pilots, and kept the Zeros at low altitude. As a result, when the SBD "Dauntless" dive-bombers from the *Enterprise* and *Yorktown* arrived, they descended upon their targets from high altitude nearly unopposed.

That they arrived at the same time from the two carriers was an almost unbelievable stroke of luck. Through a series of unrelated events, the American fliers achieved, without coordination, a perfectly coordinated strike. First, there had been Waldron's intuitive navigation which had brought the *Hornet* Devastators upon the *Akagi*, followed in succession by the *Enterprise* and *Yorktown* torpedo bombers. Then the dive-bombers from the *Enterprise* and *Yorktown*, having launched ninety minutes apart, nevertheless arrived simultaneously. And when they did, they dropped their bombs on decks covered with planes, aviation fuel, and munitions. This was so because Nagumo had made crucial decisions three hours earlier, and they proved, by luck, to be wrong. When Lieutenant Joichi Tomonaga, after leading the bombing strike against Midway, recommended by radio a second attack wave, the planes on the carrier decks sat armed with torpedoes, a precaution against the discovery of American ships. Now Nagumo ordered these planes rearmed with land bombs for the second strike at Midway. This was at 0715, but thirteen minutes later a Japanese surveillance plane found the American Task Force 16 and reported "what appears to be ten enemy surface ships." Given this discovery, Nagumo ordered that torpedoes be left on the planes not yet switched to bombs. Then, at 0820, when the patrol plane identified one of the U.S. ships as a carrier, Nagumo faced another decision. Should he launch against the U.S. task force immediately, or first collect all planes returning from Midway? At the moment of decision he was under attack by American land-based planes, and some of his fliers were returning in damaged aircraft. Under these circumstances, he decided to get all his planes in before launching against the enemy carrier group. But in the very minute that Nagumo's last plane landed—0918—the *Hornet*'s torpedo bombers arrived. Waves of U.S. fliers would now attack the Japanese carriers with both their flight decks and lower decks fully loaded.

The *Enterprise* dive-bomber squadron VB-6 arrived on the scene after the sacrifice of the torpedo squadrons only because it had failed to locate the Japanese carriers where they were thought to be. Lt. Cdr. Clarence McClusky Jr., leading thirty-two *Enterprise* dive-bombers, reached the supposed contact point with only fifteen minutes of fuel left for searching. He decided that the conventional "expanding square" search pattern would consume too much fuel and cover too little ocean, so he decided to continue on course for thirty-five more miles, then turn northwest, heading into the Japanese ships' last known course. It was "one of the most important decisions of the battle," Nimitz commented later, "and one that had decisive results."[10] On the northwest dogleg McClusky spotted the wake of a single Japanese destroyer heading north and reasoned that it must be trailing the carrier task force. He followed it, and it led his squadron straight to the carriers. This delay in locating the Striking Force lasted exactly long enough to bring his pilots to their targets just as seventeen more dive-bombers, led by Lt. Cdr. Maxwell F. Leslie, arrived on a direct line from the *Yorktown*.

But why was the destroyer *Arashi* there for McClusky to see, hastening north to rejoin the Striking Force? Only because Bill Brockman, captain of the *Nautilus*, had acted with initiative and persistence, attacking Nagumo's force with an old, unwieldy sub that was poorly suited for the job. After the Battle of Midway, in fact, the oversized *Nautilus* was used chiefly as a transport for supplies and guerillas. Nevertheless, when Brockman had sighted smoke and antiaircraft fire on the horizon at 0710—when the first Midway planes were attacking the carriers—he moved quickly to investigate, forty minutes before Rear Adm. English ordered the subs to do so. *Nautilus*, stationed to the northwest of *Tambor*, was the boat closest to the action, and for the next seven hours it would engage elements of the Striking Force. As it dogged the carrier group, planes strafed its periscope, a battleship bombarded it, and destroyers charged in, dropping depth charges. Diving, changing course submerged, and rising again as it was attacked by the screening ships and planes, Brockman managed to squeeze off only a few torpedoes, all of which missed. In his persistence, however, he occupied the *Arashi*, and by the time it managed to force the *Nautilus* down with eight depth charges, the destroyer had become detached from the Striking Force. As a result, it had to speed north to catch up, passing beneath McClusky's planes and showing them the way to the carriers.

The action that followed, when the *Enterprise* and *Yorktown* dive-bombers descended on the *Kaga*, *Akagi*, and *Soryu*, has come to be known as "The Five Minutes of Midway." McClusky, approaching from the southwest, split his group, sending the squadron led by Lt. W. Earl Gallaher against the *Kaga* and Lt. Richard H. Best's planes against the *Akagi*. At virtually the same time Leslie's *Yorktown* Dauntlesses dove upon the *Soryu*, while the *Hiryu* lay slightly detached to the northeast. At 1020, on board the *Kaga*, Commander Takahisa Amagai heard a lookout call, "Dive bombers!" and looked up. Reacting first as a fellow professional, he thought: "*Splendid [is] their tactic of diving upon our force from the direction of the sun, taking advantage of intermittent clouds.*"[11] The first three bombs missed, then Gallaher hit the flight deck filled with planes, igniting their aviation fuel. Damaged and tipped at odd angles on the deck, they burned like torches. Two more bombs missed, then three more struck, and the *Kaga* stood in flames, doomed.

Meanwhile, the *Akagi* crew worked frantically to launch its second wave, and as Best fixed the carrier in his sights he saw the first plane take off from its deck.

Moments later that deck was pierced and twisted, when two of three bombs dropped by his group scored. Normally, two hits would not be fatal to a big carrier, but the flight deck of the *Akagi* was covered with planes and fuel lines, as well, and the hangar decks below held piles of land bombs that had been removed in favor of torpedoes. As fuel burned and ignited the armaments, a series of induced explosions stopped the *Akagi*. From its bridge, air operations officer Genda looked to the northeast, placing his hopes now in the Second Carrier Task Force, the *Soryu* and *Hiryu*. But what he saw shook him. A plume of white smoke rose from the *Soryu*, and for the first time he felt "really shocked."[12]

At the same time that McClusky and Gallaher's Dauntlesses had attacked the *Kaga*, Leslie's *Yorktown* planes screamed down on the *Soryu*, with Lt. (jg) Paul "Lefty" Holmberg scoring the first hit. In minutes the carrier was struck three times, and within a half hour the *Soryu* sailors—those who had not been killed or thrown overboard by the blasts—heard the order to abandon ship. From 1022 to 1026 American pilots from two ships, meeting accidentally over their targets, had left three Japanese carriers burning. Ensign Gay, the only survivor of torpedo squadron VT-8, had watched the action from the water, peering from under his rubber seat cushion as Japanese ships maneuvered all around him. Now he saw three columns of black smoke rising from the *Kaga*, *Akagi*, and *Soryu*. Amid the same scene, Nagumo and other officers from the bridge of *Akagi* sat in a lifeboat, while sailors rowed them to the cruiser *Nagara*. Among them, Genda boldly uttered the word "calamity," and a fellow officer replied: "The outcome will surely decide the fate of Japan."[13]

In the action, the *Enterprise* lost fourteen of its thirty-two dive-bombers, a number of them ditching in the ocean for lack of fuel. The *Yorktown* lost no planes, but when its pilots returned they found their carrier under attack and had to divert to the *Enterprise* to land. Leslie and Holmberg, however, had to ditch near the cruiser *Astoria*, which quickly picked them up. The *Hiryu*, escaping notice to the northeast, had launched its planes, and by 1200 they had found the *Yorktown* and hit it. The crew managed to put out fires and quickly repair the flight deck, but the ship was damaged badly and Fletcher was forced to transfer his flag to the *Astoria*. While scout planes searched for the remaining Japanese carrier, the *Hiryu* launched another wave. At 1443 its pilots again found the *Yorktown* and set it ablaze, thinking they had damaged a second carrier. At 1455 the *Yorktown* crew was ordered to abandon ship. Fletcher, aboard the *Astoria*, now recognized that he was in no position to oversee the battle, and he graciously transferred command. His message to Spruance stated simply: "Will conform to your movements."

Meanwhile, Spruance had finally received a position report on the *Hiryu* and sent up an attack. McClusky, his air group commander, had returned from the first strike with a bullet wound to his arm, so Earl Gallaher now led twenty-four planes off the *Enterprise*, including fourteen diverted *Yorktown* dive-bombers. By 1701 they were over their target, and in ten minutes the *Hiryu*, like the other Japanese carriers, was engulfed in flames.

Admiral Yamamoto, to the west with the Main Body in his flagship *Yamato*, had absorbed that morning the news of his three disabled carriers. Then, at 1730, Nagumo informed him that the *Hiryu* was burning, as well. It was a devastating blow, and reactions among the staff officers ranged from stoic to operatic. Nevertheless, amid conflicting reports of the enemy's strength and position, Yamamoto and his chiefs developed plans to assemble their remaining surface power for a night attack against the U.S. fleet. The stages of their intricate plan had been reversed. First they must deal with American naval power, and only then invade Midway. But the counterattack was not to be. Wisely, Spruance retired eastward, remaining within range to support Midway, but avoiding a nighttime engagement in which his chief asset—the carriers and planes—would be ineffective.

While the fighting of June 4 was taking place, the *Tambor* was attempting to reach the action. They had far to go from their southern position, but as they went the radio shack picked up encouraging reports. At mid-afternoon the news was almost too good to believe: "All four [Japanese] carriers badly damaged." (In fact, it wasn't true; the *Hiryu* had not yet been located.) Now, more than ever, they itched to get into the battle, but they were receiving contradictory reports on the location of enemy ships. It was frustrating, but worse was the news that arrived that evening: the *Yorktown* was badly damaged and dead in the water. Later, however, there was reason to cheer again. Red Mayo intercepted information that a sister sub, the *Nautilus*, had scored three hits "on a damaged *Soryu* class carrier" earlier in the day. Again, the report was erroneous, but no one would realize this until after the war.

What had actually happened, if known, would have provided more evidence of serious problems with the U.S. torpedoes. Brockman, having shadowed the Japanese Striking Force all day, and having been attacked repeatedly, climbed to periscope depth yet again and sighted a burning carrier eight miles off. Creeping forward submerged at three to four knots, he closed on the motionless ship, then set up carefully for his shot. At 1359 he ordered four torpedoes away. One failed to leave its tube, but the remaining three sped toward their target. Through the periscope Brockman watched his fish cover the 2,700 yards between him and the carrier, then observed: "Red flames appeared along the ship from bow to amidships [and] many men were seen going over the side." Then destroyers charged him and he took his boat down to three hundred feet, satisfied that he'd sunk his carrier. After the war, however, when American and Japanese records were correlated, the sinking was erased. The ship had been the *Kaga*, and surviving crew members recalled that two near misses had passed the bow and stern. Only the middle torpedo struck the ship, but it failed to explode and broke in two. The warhead sank and the after body bobbed to the surface, where sailors thrown into the water by the dive-bomber hits used it as a life buoy.[14] One climbed up and straddled it like a cowboy, making the others laugh despite their peril.

The *Tambor* had experienced a frustrating day, hearing reports of a battle they couldn't reach. But overnight that situation changed. At 2115, Sub Task Group 7.1 received new orders. All twelve boats were to redeploy in a protective arc to the west of Midway, one hundred miles out, with "all units to arrive on station and dive before dawn." The *Tambor*, once more, was directed to the line's left end, and further instructions specified caution: "Encounters with friendly surface forces during night possible."

As the *Tambor* patrolled on the surface, Bob manned his port bow position, leaning against the rail of the lookout platform, scanning the sea with binoculars. It was 0200, June 5, and the night was clear, the weather calm. But it was a tense night, with the precise locations and strengths of Japanese task groups uncertain. And no one could be sure of the enemy's intentions. English's orders to reposition the subs around Midway suggested that an invasion was still possible. And if an invasion were to be prefaced by a naval bombardment, it would most likely occur by darkness that night.

Yamamoto had, indeed, ordered such a bombardment, and the four fastest ships in his navy had been racing toward Midway at thirty-two knots to make it so. They were the heavy cruisers *Kumano*, *Suzuya*, *Mikuma*, and *Mogami*, each carrying ten 8-inch guns, and they were accompanied by two destroyers. By 12:20 AM they were within ninety miles of Midway, but had separated from the slower destroyers, which couldn't keep up.

At 0215 Bob scanned his lookout quadrant with powerful binoculars. There was a particular way to do it, systematically, covering the sea and sky in his area. "What you look for," Bob explained, "is any change in the shape of the horizon line and anything else that looks just a little different than normal. I thought I saw a small, dark bump on the horizon, but couldn't be sure and asked the lookout aft of me to check it out. He thought he could make out something, too, so I reported the sighting to the officer of the deck, and everyone on the lookouts and bridge confirmed that there was something out there. Then we sighted more bumps. We couldn't make out what they were, but there were several of them, so the captain was called to the bridge."

Soon it was clear that there were four ships distributed across the *Tambor*'s bow, slightly to port. But whose were they? The subs had been warned that friendly surface craft might operate in the area that night, so Murphy ordered a change of course to stay in contact with the mystery ships until he could identify them. Only a few minutes later, however, contact was lost, and the sub maneuvered to regain it. And this time, to the lookouts' surprise, the ships appeared to the starboard side and had changed course. What had happened was this: Yamamoto's staff had calculated the cruisers' position and decided they were too late to complete their bombardment on time. If the ships could not destroy the base before daylight, they would make easy targets for Midway's land-based planes. Yamamoto, therefore, cancelled the mission and recalled the ships, which turned north. So, at 0238 the four cruisers traveled in a line at twenty-eight knots, sailing to join the Japanese Main Body, with the two destroyers and an oiler trailing somewhere behind.

The *Tambor* made a 180-degree turn to parallel the ships, keeping them to the port stern side, adjusting course as the still-unidentified ships steered to the northwest. As the sub made eighteen knots on the surface, the ships turned inside the *Tambor*'s wide arc. Running ahead of his quarry, Murphy then ordered a turn due west, crossing the ships' bows and working to catch them in the moonstream, the better to identify them by silhouette. But at 0306 the lookouts again lost contact momentarily, and Murphy took the opportunity to radio Midway, reporting "many unidentified ships."

Five minutes later the ships appeared again and the *Tambor* turned its stern to them on a parallel course, heading northwest. Soon, however, they disappeared again and remained out of sight for a full half hour. Who were they and what were they doing? Everyone was eager to get into the fight, but Bob and his shipmates fully supported their captain's caution. They and their fellow submariners on other boats had been bombed by their own planes, and having been on the receiving end of friendly fire, they weren't eager to dish it out. Murphy's immediate problem, however, was to decide which way to maneuver to find the ships again: They had turned only left since first contact, so the *Tambor* began turning that way, feeling its way for contact. And at 0342 the guess was rewarded when Bob and the other lookouts reported two ships to the eastward, traveling now on a southerly course. With only a few minutes of darkness left, the *Tambor* made best speed on a parallel course—235 degrees—attempting to get ahead of the ships before daybreak.

At 0400 dawn approached and visibility improved. The ships were no longer mere blobs on the horizon—their general shape was clear—and Bob judged them to be larger than destroyers, but still he could not make out the gun placements that would tell them what they needed to know. At this point Murphy decided to find out who they were, and he ordered a signalman topside. When Harold Moore appeared he carried the heavy signal light—the size of a large snare drum—and Bob helped him bolt it to the same railing where he'd fastened the machine gun for battle surface. The captain ordered an identifying signal, and the light's shutters clattered loudly as Moore spelled out the code in short and long flashes. Then they all saw a light flashing on the lead ship.

"What did he send?" Murphy asked.

"Damned if I know, Captain," answered Moore.

Then Murphy yelled, "Dive—Dive—Dive! Take her down and rig for depth-charge attack!"

Bob remembered: "I dropped from the lookout station to the bridge, then did my usual no-step slides down the ladders, first into the conning tower and then to the control room. I may have used a couple of steps on the way down, but on a crash dive it was mostly a free drop." In the control room he took his diving station and put a hard dive on the bow planes. When the hydraulic-manifold operator called a "green board" to the diving officer, the stern planesman angled the sub down.

They were submerged for twenty-five minutes, but heard nothing—no screws, no splashes, no explosions—so they came up to periscope depth to take a look. Standing immediately behind Bob, Murphy now saw two Japanese *Mogami*-class cruisers maneuvering away from them, signaling each other with brilliant all-directional lights. The big cruisers had been much closer than he'd thought when challenged—in his patrol report he said he'd thought they'd been destroyers, distorting his estimate. Then Murphy reported a further surprise. Still peering through the periscope, he exclaimed: "On the far cruiser, about forty feet of the bow is sheared away! That's slowing her down—one of our planes must have found her."

The captain then ordered a change of course and best speed to pursue the targets. Bob recalled: "The daylight was starting to come out now, so we had to stay down or they would blow us to pieces with their guns. But you can only run submerged at full speed for a short period of time before you exhaust the batteries." Submerged, the *Tambor* made, at best, nine knots, and Murphy estimated that the cruisers were making seventeen, despite the damaged bow on one of them. "So we had to let them go," Bob said. "When they got out of sight we surfaced and sent headquarters their course, position, and speed, so our planes would know where to find them." After cruising with the Japanese ships half the night, losing them was a bitter disappointment. They had been prized targets, and the men cursed their luck. "There were some 'sons of bitches!' and things like that said," Bob remembered.

What the crew didn't realize was that they were responsible for the damage Murphy had seen. It had occurred when the four cruisers, sailing in a line, sighted the *Tambor*. The lead ship, the *Kumano*, had spotted the sub and immediately signaled the ship behind it to take evasive action. As the *Kumano* signaled "Red! Red!" to the stern, it turned sharply away from the *Tambor*. The *Suzuya* followed suit, also turning hard to port and signaling to the cruiser behind it. So the maneuver and the signal proceeded down the line. But traveling at high speed without lights made a sudden echelon turn a dicey maneuver, and the *Mogami*, bringing up the rear, plowed into the *Mikuma* ahead of it. The glancing blow cut gashes into the *Mikuma*'s hull and punctured a fuel tank. It was not a

Photo 9. *Tambor* bow on, 1943. (U.S. Navy)

serious injury, but the *Mogami* fared far worse. Its bow up to the first gun turret was compressed and jammed to the side, nearly perpendicular to the rest of the ship. Admiral Takeo Kurita stopped his group, assessed the situation, and gave orders. The two lead cruisers would proceed back to the Main Body to join up with Yamamoto, while the damaged ships were to stick together for mutual protection. Without firing a torpedo the *Tambor* had, unwittingly, damaged two of the enemy's heavy cruisers.

But when had this happened? Bob only learned that the collision was caused by his boat—and not by planes—when he read about it in *Life* magazine after the war. And he naturally assumed that the event had occurred after the light signal, while the *Tambor* was submerged awaiting a depth-charge attack. More likely, however, the collision had occurred earlier, when the *Tambor* lost contact with the ships shortly after 0311. The sub had just completed a run across the ships' bows and had turned to stay ahead and slightly to the port of the oncoming cruisers. After that turn, however, contact was lost for thirty minutes, and the next contact, recorded at 0342, reported two—not four—ships. The lost contact was, in all likelihood, due to the collision, with the group making its damage assessment and splitting up during the ensuing half hour. Kurita detached his flagship and the *Suzuyo*, departing to the northwest to rejoin Yamamoto's Main Body. The two ships seen by the *Tambor* at 0342 would have been, then, the *Mikuma* and *Mogami*. Slowed by the *Mogami*'s damage, they were heading southwest to meet up with the trailing destroyers. Even a badly damaged bow may not have been apparent through binoculars in dim early light, and Bob remembered, "I wasn't paying attention to the number of ships then—I was tracking the nearest one." Only after the dive, given the approach of dawn and the periscope's higher magnification, did the *Mogami*'s damage become apparent.

Still submerged, the *Tambor* made best speed to intersect with the cruisers' track and get off a shot, but the ships escaped to the west. There was nothing to do now but surface and report. The time was 0617, June 5, and, partly due to Murphy's earlier vague report of "many unidentified ships," preparations were still under way to repel an attack on Midway. An hour later all subs of the *Tambor*'s Task Group 7.1 were ordered to surface and pull back to assigned sectors near the base. But after a long day of vigilance, near midnight the *Tambor* received word that enemy forces seemed to be retreating. The report from headquarters included a caution, however: "The retirement may be temporary. All forces must be alert and prepared for further enemy action."

The next day American planes, using the *Tambor*'s report and the oil slick trailing the *Mikuma*, tracked down the fleeing ships. Dive-bombers from the *Enterprise* and *Hornet* carried out waves of attacks on the cruisers and their two accompanying destroyers, *Arashio* and *Asashio*. Both destroyers were hit by single bombs but were able to continue navigation. Between them, they lost fifty-nine men and claimed two U.S. planes shot down. The *Mogami*, remarkably, not only survived the loss of its bow but absorbed six bomb hits, and eventually limped home to Japan, having lost nine officers and eighty-one men. In the process, its antiaircraft gunners claimed ten downed American planes. The *Mikuma*, however, was ravaged by fire and explosions after many bomb strikes and sank shortly after noon, June 6. Excluding the four carriers destroyed two days earlier, it was the largest Japanese ship sunk since the beginning of the war.

The encounter had consequences beyond the sinking of the *Mikuma* and the casualties on the other ships. After the search and fight, the Battle of Midway was in its third phase—the chase—and Spruance faced a new challenge. How far and how quickly should he move his ships westward to pursue the withdrawing opponent? The Americans had already won a decisive victory, but now they had a chance to pursue the enemy and deal an even more devastating blow to the Japanese navy. There were considerable risks, however, and much that Spruance did not know, including the location and movements of

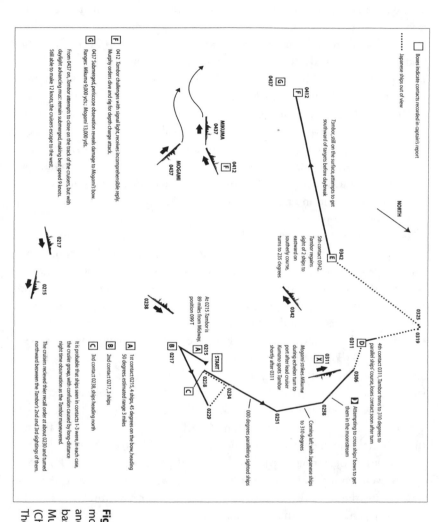

□ Boxes indicate contacts recorded in captain's report

····· Japanese ships out of view

NORTH

A 1st contact 0215, 4 ships, 45 degrees on the bow, heading 50 degrees, estimated range 3 miles

B 2nd contact 0217, 3 ships

C 3rd contact 0238, ships heading north

It is probable that ships seen in contacts 1–3 were, in each case, the cruiser group, with confusion caused by long-distance night time observation as the *Tambor* maneuvered.

The cruisers received their recall order at about 0230 and turned northward between the *Tambor*'s 2nd and 3rd sightings of them.

At 0215 *Tambor* is 89 miles from Midway, position 095T

000 degrees paralleling sighted ships

Coming left with Japanese ships to 310 degrees

Mogami strikes *Mikuma* during echelon turn to port after lead cruiser *Kumano* spots *Tambor* shortly after 0311

D Attempting to cross ships' bows to get them in the moonstream

4th contact 0311, *Tambor* turns to 310 degrees to parallel ships' course, loses contact soon after turn

E 5th contact 0342, *Tambor* regains sight of 2 ships to eastward on southerly course, turns to 255 degrees

Tambor, still on the surface, attempts to get southward of targets before daybreak

MIKUMA 0437

MOGAMI 0437

F 0412 *Tambor* challenges with signal light, receives incomprehensible reply, Murphy orders dive and rig for depth charge attack.

G 0437 Submerged, periscope observation reveals damage to *Mogami*'s bow. Ranges: *Mikuma* 9,000 yds.; *Mogami* 13,000 yds.

From 0437 on, *Tambor* attempts to close on the track of the cruisers, but with daylight advancing must remain submerged, making best speed 9 knots. Still able to make 12 knots, the cruisers escape to the west.

Figure 2. June 5, 1942, movements of USS *Tambor* and Japanese heavy cruisers, based on Lt. Cdr. John Murphy's war patrol report. (Chart by Robert Schultz and Thomas Carter)

many Japanese elements. Confirmation that the carrier *Hiryu* had sunk was not received until days later, when a boatload of survivors from its engine rooms was recovered by American searchers. And Japanese intentions were uncertain. Was the withdrawal westward a temporary movement to regroup or a full retreat? Had Yamamoto called off the landing on Midway or not? In this context the *Tambor*'s encounter with a bombardment task group near the base was extremely significant. But Murphy's initial contact report of "many unidentified ships" had been maddeningly incomplete. He had reported the ships' position, but not their course, speed, type, and number. It was possible, for four crucial hours, to think that he'd spotted the full Japanese invasion force poised to strike Midway. Murphy later wrote: "We should have made an opportunity . . . to amplify our initial report, but we didn't."[15] It added one more element of confusion to an already murky situation and was enough to make Spruance pause at a crucial moment of decision.

Some officers in his carrier task force were furious that Spruance was not more aggressive, concluding that he was no charging "Bull" Halsey. Nimitz took a different view, commenting years later that Halsey's hospitalization might have been another stroke of American luck.[16] Among the most important reasons for the U.S. victory in the Battle of Midway was Spruance's judgment: he displayed all-out aggression and prudent caution at just the right moments. He sent everything he had at the enemy as early as he could, even imperiling his torpedo pilots; but after knocking out the Japanese carriers he refused to chase blindly and put the victory at risk. In these judgments he kept his purposes clearly in view: to protect the American base at Midway and, with his outnumbered forces, to heed "the principle of calculated risk."

Later, commenting on his post–June 4 decisions, Spruance wrote: "The fact that Admiral Yamamoto with seven battleships, one [light] carrier, cruisers, and destroyers was operating to the northwestward of Midway was not known to us for several months after the battle. . . . Had we continued on to the westward during the night of 6–7 June, we would probably have run foul of . . . his superior Japanese forces the next morning."[17] These forces included the super battleship *Yamato*, and the American carriers, for the sake of speed, were lightly armored. To blunder upon the big Japanese guns would have given Yamamoto a chance to salvage a draw from his defeat. That this did not happen was due to Spruance's wise caution, perhaps bolstered by the fog of war June 5 and 6. In this context, the *Tambor*'s nighttime encounter and Murphy's vague contact report can be seen to have added a final point of luck.

Already the United States had lost one of its three carriers. The *Yorktown*, set ablaze twice by Japanese planes, had been stabilized after its June 4 evacuation. There was still the prospect of towing her home for repairs when the Japanese sub *I-168* made a painstaking, daring approach and fired its torpedoes. They hit

Photo 10. This photo of the *Mikuma* shows the gashes in the cruiser's hull suffered when, surprised by the *Tambor*, it collided with the *Mogami*. (U.S. Navy)

the *Yorktown* and its accompanying destroyer *Hammann*. The *Hammann* broke in two and sank immediately, but the tough carrier lingered with a severe list for over fifteen hours before it finally went down the morning of June 7. After delivering its blow, the *I-168*, captained by Lieutenant Commander Yahachi Tanabe, dove and absorbed a severe depth charging—the crew counted sixty near misses. The sub took serious damage, but eventually made its escape. It was the only Japanese submarine to contribute meaningfully to the battle, and before its pursuit of the *Yorktown* it had surfaced near Midway to make a nighttime bombardment against the Eastern Island base.

For the American subs, the morning of June 6 again brought new orders. They were to leave their picket and make best speed westward. "Expect some cripples this morning," said task force command. That afternoon and evening the *Tambor* responded to position reports but was unable to reach the enemy ships. They saw B-17s from Midway pass overhead, also seeking targets, and at 2200 that night heard that one of them had dropped two 1,600-pound bombs on a cruiser, which sank in fifteen seconds. Attack photos and stories by shaken American submariners would later reveal that the bombs had fallen on the *Grayling*, which made a crash dive and survived.

Through the night of June 6–7 the *Tambor* cruised the surface in response to periodic radio reports of enemy ships. Its only sightings, however, were distant green flares rising from the sea's dark surface. Murphy surmised that they were being fired by Japanese sailors in lifeboats. It was a big, dark ocean, and survivors, both Japanese and American, would be collected for days. The destroyer USS *Ballard* would save thirty-five *Hiryu* sailors on June 18. And two American fliers, Albert Winchell and Douglas Cossett, ditched their torpedo bomber during the June 4 attacks and languished in a raft for seventeen days. When their emergency rations ran out they captured an albatross and ate it raw. Finally, they were spotted and picked up by a Catalina seaplane on June 21.

The *Tambor* had no room to take on prisoners and was still under orders to patrol for enemy ships. As the night wore on, however, more flares constituted its only sightings. The next morning, June 7, Bob lay in his bunk in the forward room, trying to catch some badly needed sleep. It had been hard to rest, even between shifts, with action reports circulating through the boat, and he knew that at any moment he could be called to his battle station between the torpedo tubes. But now, at last, he slept, though his slumber would soon be interrupted. "We were running on the surface and the diving alarm went off," he recalled.

"So everyone wakes up and waits, because we know it's either an enemy plane or ship. I was tired, so I just rolled over in my bunk and waited for the bombs or depth charges—whatever they would throw at us. I guess we got down to about eighty feet when the bomb went off and I dove out of my bunk and raced in the dark to the back of the room to slam and dog the compartment door, then ran forward to the torpedo tubes to check for damage and leaks. On my way back from the forward part of the room I felt my feet burning. After I phoned in my damage report, I sat on my bunk and checked my feet. Then I realized that the explosion had shattered all the lightbulbs in the room and that I'd been running around barefoot over broken glass. So I wiped the blood off, put on a pair of sandals, and started in on the cleanup. That bomb shook us up pretty good, but soon we were able to surface and continue our mission."

At the same time that Bob made his run across broken glass, a crewmate in the control room was shaking glass out of his hair and brushing it off his shoulders. He'd been manning the stern planes, staring at the big depth gauge in front of him—shirtless in the heat—when the bomb struck and shattered its cover. When he opened his eyes he discovered that he was unhurt and the gauge still worked, so he and the bow planesman kept the boat in trim as they swept the glass from their bodies.

"Before this incident there had been a lot of grumbling from the crew about the dives we made on radar contacts," Bob said. "They didn't believe in the radar. But this time we dove on radar without seeing an approaching plane, and it probably saved us. After that, everyone thought the radar was great." Like the *Grayling*, the *Tambor* had probably been bombed by a U.S. B-17, and before long a Navy spotter was placed on each bomber to assist with ship identification.

On June 9 the submarine task group was ordered back to Pearl Harbor. The Battle of Midway had been won, and the damaged *Tambor* and Bob limped home. Not until two weeks later did Bob make the next entry in his diary. Then he wrote:

WAR PATROL NO. 3

Cruised with Jap force—was bombed with very large bomb—very close—dove on radar & got to about 80 feet—both periscopes out—broken air compressor pot base—battery blower casings smashed—lots of broken glass—scared hell out of the crew.

Two days liberty—the rest working—off to sea again—what a life.

CHAPTER SIX

"Hot, Straight, and Normal":
At Liberty in Hawaii

A t Pearl Harbor, as the Battle of Midway underwent analysis, one conclusion was inescapable: the American submarines, taken as a whole, had contributed little to the victory. Admiral English reacted by shaking up his staff and replacing several skippers. Four successful sub captains were reassigned to staff jobs or shipped to the States to oversee production of new boats and the training of new crews; Hap Lyon of the *Gudgeon* complained of failing eyesight and was replaced; and three captains were sacked based on performance.[1] The *Tambor*'s John Murphy was one of the three.

Murphy, like nearly all who had fired the Mark XIV torpedo equipped with the Mark VI magnetic exploder, had complained about its performance. After the *Tambor*'s second patrol he had recommended that the torpedoes be set to run shallower than specified, and was rebuked. Al McCann, the supervising officer, countered: "The Squadron Commander does not concur in the *Tambor*'s recommendation regarding depth setting of torpedoes. Specific instructions in this regard have been issued and must be followed." On that second patrol, the *Tambor* had fired eighteen fish at nine targets, and claimed just two sinkings. Bob thought several misses were due to torpedo failure. Nevertheless, McCann blamed Murphy's shooting. "There was an excessive expenditure of torpedoes," he wrote. "With the supply of torpedoes available, such unproductive expenditure cannot be justified." The brass would not entertain the possibility that equipment failure was undermining their captains and crews.

After Midway, Murphy was blamed for his performance the night the *Tambor* encountered the Japanese cruisers. Bob and his crewmates thought their captain had behaved with admirable restraint, given the warning that American ships might operate in their area overnight. Having been bombed by their own planes, they were sensitive to issues of friendly fire. The issue for the brass, however, had less to do with matters of aggression than with the ambiguity of Murphy's contact report. After his replacement, Murphy reflected, with modesty:

I think I had bad luck to the extent that some warheads didn't explode as they were designed to do. I also think that some of my attacks were not well conducted and that my judgment was faulty more than once. However, I believe that the principal reason I was not kept on . . . was that *Tambor*'s report of contact in darkness with Japanese cruisers and destroyers at the start of the Battle of Midway was misinterpreted as a report of contact with the Main Body. . . . I was told that Admiral Spruance directed Admiral English to have me transferred because of this incident. I really cannot find much fault with the decision.[2]

Bob Hunt and the rest of the crew admired Murphy and presented him with a certificate of appreciation when he departed. Given their experience with the torpedo fiasco, their general view of "upper management" was that they tended to pass blame downward.

~~~~~~

The Pearl Harbor to which the crew returned after the Battle of Midway was far different from the prewar Pearl that had greeted them when the *Tambor* had first arrived there in May 1941. At that time it had been the headquarters for the Pacific Fleet for only a year, President Roosevelt having positioned the fleet there to warn Japan against further aggression in Southeast Asia.

In those prewar years Pearl Harbor was in no way ready for all the ships and sailors that descended on it in May 1940. Previously it had housed only a submarine base and a small cruiser squadron, but now it found itself home to three aircraft carriers, nine battleships, twelve heavy cruisers, nine light cruisers, fifty-three destroyers, twenty-three submarines, and the ships' crew members, most of whom had been separated from their families due to lack of housing space. There wasn't enough room to strategically disperse or maintain all the ships either, so they were crowded together in the harbor, and overhauls still had to be performed in California. The Army was responsible for air security on the island of Oahu but lacked both the resources and the leadership to do the job properly. Commander in Chief Pacific Fleet, Adm. James O. Richardson, objected to the move to Pearl Harbor so vehemently that Roosevelt replaced him with Admiral Kimmel, who was a capable leader but also a victim of what Adm. Ernest King termed the Hawaiian commanders' "unwarranted feeling of immunity from attack." As Kimmel himself said: "I never thought those little yellow sons of bitches could pull off such an attack, so far from Japan."[3] Yamamoto would take ruthless advantage of this mindset on December 7.

When Bob Hunt had gotten to prewar Pearl, however, the only problem on his mind was how soon he would get to meet the "White Russian" prostitutes he'd heard so much about from the *Tambor*'s old-timers. Ever since the boat's departure from San Diego they'd been telling stories about the women who, according to the old navy hands, were the most beautiful, intelligent, and classiest working girls to be found. And the brothels in which they worked, the men said, were the most luxurious and accommodating in the world. Bob wasn't sure what a White Russian was, but he was eager to learn.

In those days, the main streets in downtown Honolulu had been so crowded with sailors on liberty that it seemed every time he turned a corner Bob ran into a solid wall of blue and white. But the old-timers led Bob and his buddies down a little side street lined with palm trees. Every house on the modest street, Bob's guides told him, was a brothel. When the sailors rang the doorbell of the first house on the block, an older woman—sedate and proper—greeted them and led them inside. Although the old-timers hadn't been to Pearl Harbor in a couple of years, she called them by name and asked them where they'd been since their last visit. The living room was large and tastefully decorated with expensive-looking furniture, fancy drapes, and paintings on the walls. The young women sitting on the fine furniture were well-dressed and attractive.

Turning to Bob as a newcomer, the madam conducted a kind of interview, asking about his background, his interests, and his sexual preferences. It was an odd conversation, but no matter what the woman asked, she did so with such a sweet and motherly air that the entire transaction seemed irreproachably wholesome. It was like a visit to the USO, but with sex instead of doughnuts.

When he was finally paired off with one of the girls, Bob felt sure she must be a White Russian. He had no idea how to tell, and he wasn't going to ask, but if beauty and intelligence were their distinguishing traits, as he'd been told, she had to be one. She instantly became and would always remain Bob's favorite—and not just because she knew her way around a bedroom. Bob came to consider her a great friend, and each time he returned from a war patrol, he sought her out. "She would hold me in her arms," he remembered, "and say to me, 'Was it bad this time, Bob?'" It was an important comfort. The house, in the early part of the war, became one of the first places Bob went when he got off the boat. It had a domestic air about it, the madam always remembered his name, and the ladies had even cleaned him up after his fight with Magner.

That hadn't been Bob's only Pearl Harbor fight. As the war had approached, the teeming streets of Pearl had gotten more and more crowded—and tense—with the buildup of sailors and soldiers. Anyone who followed the news could hear the clock ticking as U.S. involvement in the war became more likely. With more bodies and more tension overfilling the island, emotions erupted regularly on the streets and in the bars. Every night the MPs' sirens wailed, and early every morning the trucks drove up to the dock at the sub base and dumped a bruised heap of sailors, sometimes including Bob, at their boats. On some nights there were two truckloads. The deck watch ordered them all to quarters, and the men in the *Tambor's* forward torpedo room continued the party with beer they'd stashed in a torpedo tube or the emergency food locker. All the combatants were put on report, but no one ever got into real trouble. The brass knew that submariners were too valuable a commodity to court-martial, and the submariners knew it too.

Pearl Harbor seemed dedicated to the care, feeding, and entertainment of the military, and it was easy to forget that people other than prostitutes, madams, and bartenders actually lived and worked there. Even though the ratio of men to women seemed to be about a hundred to one, it was still possible, with a little luck, to meet a regular, nonprofessional woman, like the one named Dorothy who occupied much of Bob's time, to his peril, in the summer of 1941. She was the "redhead" he'd referred to in his last-will-and-testament letter to Dick, and her driving may have threatened his life as much as the war.

He met her at a posh, horseshoe-shaped bar on an outing with Harold Moore, the *Tambor's* short, stocky signalman. She sat directly across the horseshoe from them and quickly attracted their attention with her shoulder-length dark hair and cute pug nose. She noticed the two men soon enough, as well. Moore went over, talked to her for a while, then brought her over and introduced her to Bob. She joined them for a drink, and then another, and another after that. When they went to the men's room, Moore said to Bob, "This girl wants to go out and party, and she has her own house. If we play our cards right, we could have a home away from home."

"That's fine for you," Bob told him, "but two guys and one girl—that doesn't add up."

"She says she'll find a girl for you at the dance hall. She knows all of them over at the dance hall."

Bob was easily convinced, but things did not go according to Moore's plan. Dorothy, true to her word, found a Hawaiian girl for Bob, and they all took a taxi back to Dorothy's house. She immediately took Moore to her bedroom, and Bob and his date sat on the couch in the tiny living room. Bob made advances, but the petite Hawaiian told him she didn't know him well enough to let him do what he had in mind. Then Moore came out of the bedroom. "Dorothy wants more to drink," he announced and left on his errand. Bob got up to use the bathroom, but met Dorothy coming out of the shower, an encounter that she took entirely in stride, standing before him without clothes or towel. And then, somehow—a lot of alcohol had been consumed that night—Bob and Dorothy found themselves in the kitchen, on the floor. Bob's date was in the next room on the couch, and Moore could return at any time, so Bob and Dorothy tried to be both discreet and quick, but when Dorothy's leg struck a cupboard door the steel pots and pans tumbled out. Suddenly discretion was no longer an issue, and haste was irresistible. Dorothy's leg kept hitting the cupboard door, and

Photo 11. Bob's Honolulu friend in front of her bungalow. When she bought a car and insisted on driving even after a night on the town, Bob felt his life was in greater danger on leave than on war patrol. (Courtesy Robert Hunt)

the pots kept clanging. It was like having sex to the accompaniment of a Gene Krupa drum solo.

When Bob and Dorothy finished they returned to the shower. It was quieter there but equally satisfactory. Then, clean and dressed, the pair returned to the living room where they found Moore and the Hawaiian girl sitting glumly together on the couch. Moore held a pint of whiskey, however, so they all had a nightcap together before Moore returned to the boat and the girl left for home. Since Bob was off duty for the weekend, he stayed and crawled into bed with Dorothy for some much-needed sleep. They spent the weekend together, the pair became companions, and Dorothy's tiny house became Bob's new home away from home.

She was from the mainland and had followed her navy boyfriend to the island. She found a good office job right away and rented the bungalow, but soon her boyfriend was shipped out for two months. She was lonely and she enjoyed Bob's company. When he was in port and she had a free weekend, they always got together. She could never be sure exactly when her boyfriend would return, and she was reluctant for her neighbors to see Bob hanging around, so there were complications. They went out a lot. And when they did, Bob's first impression was confirmed. This girl liked to drink, but she had little tolerance for alcohol. Sometimes this could be a problem, especially after she bought a used car.

The new mobility provided by the car allowed the two of them to visit outlying nightspots, but the more Dorothy drank the faster she drove. One night, on the way back into Honolulu after an evening of bar hopping, she was scraping curbs, driving onto sidewalks, and leaving a wake of honking traffic along her path. Bob clutched the dashboard and hung on as they careened down a hill and around a curve, sending a spray of gravel from under the tires. It was like riding a runaway truck, and Bob considered the irony of surviving sub duty, only to die in Dorothy's car. He was relieved when a patrolman finally pulled them over.

At the City of Honolulu police station, Dorothy was charged with going forty miles an hour in a twenty-five-mile-per-hour zone and driving the wrong way down a one-way street. She was indignant. Deep in her cups, she became so loud and unruly that the arresting cop called in a policewoman to cart her off to the city jail. Bob remained behind with the desk officer, who sat behind a typewriter and asked Bob to explain what had happened. He was lucky that he didn't get thrown into jail himself; when he leaned his elbow on the desk he inadvertently pinned the typewriter carriage in place so that the officer's keystrokes piled on top of each other, making his report into an inky mess. Only the fact that he was in uniform saved him from receiving the same treatment as Dorothy.

They were told to appear in district court the next morning for sentencing, and Bob wasn't sure what to expect, but luckily, most of the others in the crowded courtroom had been charged with more serious offenses and were much less respectable-looking than he and Dorothy. The harried judge merely fined them both, Dorothy twenty-five dollars and Bob only five. Bob kept a copy of the receipt for his fine payment in his wallet, as a remembrance and a warning: "District Court of Honolulu, City and County of Honolulu, Oct. 27, 1941, No. 36146." Soon it also became a memento of a more innocent time, for it was only nineteen days later that Bob went out on his first war patrol, and only twenty-two more days before Yamamoto's plans for Pearl Harbor achieved their awful fruition. The island would never be the same. After December 7, 1941, there was a total blackout every night, and the civilians lived in constant fear that the Japanese were coming back to finish what they'd started.

Dorothy went back home with her boyfriend after he returned from his tour of duty. It was just as well. Bob had begun to suspect that the guy wasn't just her boyfriend but was actually her husband. He was also beginning to think that it was too much to expect to survive both Dorothy on leave and the Japanese on war patrols.

~~~~~~~~~~~~~~~~~~~~

It was at Pearl Harbor, not in the middle of the Pacific, that the *Tambor* suffered its first casualty. In mid-May 1942, after the war patrol that had sunk two ships but ended in such frustration over missed opportunities and erratic torpedoes, a mechanic named LaRoux fell off the boat, hit his head on the side, and drowned. The black gang (as everyone called the mechanics) had been working around the clock overhauling one of the boat's engines, and that night they had broken out the alcohol and fruit juice and had a party. The boat's heads were out of commission, so LaRoux went up the hatch to take a leak off the side, but he must have lost his way in the darkness. Harry Behrens and Jake Schultz both dove into the cold, oily water to try and rescue their crewmate, but by the time they found him, it was too late.

The accident saddened the crew, but the parties continued. "Some of the crew were married guys or seriously religious and walked the straight and narrow," Bob recalled. "Not everybody did what me and my buddies did. But a lot of guys were pretty wild." With the price of whiskey at Pearl Harbor steadily rising and the storage of large amounts of contraband alcohol on board a risky business, the crew's attention turned longingly toward the two fifty-five-gallon tanks of pink lady in the forward torpedo room. It wasn't needed for the fish anymore; the torpedoes now came aboard fully fueled. The oil that gave pink lady its color and name made it undrinkable, but thirsty sailors are not easily deterred. They mixed it with strong fruit juices or blended it into milkshakes, but the oil made them sick. They tried straining the stuff through loaves of bread, but that didn't work, either.

One day, as the *Tambor* returned from a test run of an overhauled engine, Bob was at his usual station on the number-one line. While he was helping to moor the boat, one of the sailors on the dock, a fellow Bob had never seen before, sauntered up. He was wearing a big smile, something not seen much around Pearl Harbor since the attack.

"Any of you gentlemen work in the forward torpedo room?" the man called out. He talked like an officer, but Bob could see from the insignia on his sleeve that he was only a seaman 1st class.

"I'm a forward torpedoman," Bob answered. "What about it?"

"What's your name?"

"Who wants to know?" The man introduced himself amiably enough, so Bob softened a bit and told him his name.

"I'd like to talk to you for a minute, Torpedoman Hunt," the man said, and as soon as the gangplank was in place he stepped aboard. He walked straight up to Bob, flashed him a conspiratorial grin, and asked him: "Do you have, by any chance, any of that pink lady in the forward room?" He was a square-jawed, dark-haired guy about Bob's size. He looked Bob full in the face. He had the confidence of an officer, even if he lacked the rank.

"Sure we do," Bob said. "Why the hell wouldn't we?"

"How much?"

Again, he sounded so authoritative that Bob answered him before he had a chance to think. "A hundred and ten gallons. We're full up. What do you know about pink lady, anyway?"

"I know how to get the oil out of it." The man smiled. He looked like a recruiting poster, his teeth perfectly white and straight.

"Okay, now you've got my attention," Bob said.

"I've got a little operation going that I thought you might be interested in." And then the man described the network of stills he had running all over the base, and the trade in alcohol and other commodities of interest that he managed. "There's demand for things," the guy said, "and I'm in the supply business."

For every five gallons of pink lady Bob gave the guy, he'd get back a pint of purified alcohol. It was a proposition Bob didn't have to think about for very long, and soon he had a business partner. After that, every few days the guy drove up in his jeep to pick up his pink lady and drop off the pints of hooch. From then on, whenever the boat left on another mission, Bob made sure the two fifty-five-gallon drums were topped off, and when the boat returned "The Supplier" was there to meet them. Soon he and Bob were fast friends.

One night after the man picked up his pink lady, he asked Bob to come along with him. "You look like you could use some fresh air," he said, flashing his recruiting-poster smile. As tight as security was on the base, he seemed to come and go as he pleased and never seemed to have anything to do other than run his "little operations." Bob was impressed, especially because every gate on the base was manned by marine guards who looked as if they were chosen for their size and surliness. Most of them bore so strong a resemblance to Frankenstein that he was surprised not to see bolts coming out of their necks. Their standard greeting was "Where the hell do you think you're going?" But when The Supplier pulled his jeep up to the gate with Bob beside him, these monsters turned into lapdogs. They put their guns on their shoulders, strolled over to the jeep, and jawed with him as if he were a long-lost brother. He propped himself up in the seat with his feet on the dashboard and held court with them for a while, and when he was finished they waved him through the gate, even though neither he nor Bob had a pass.

"One hand washes the other," Bob's host explained as they pulled onto the main road. "They do me a little favor, I do them a little favor. Whatever they want—booze, three-day passes, hard-to-find supplies."

Bob wanted to ask him where he got his goodies, but decided he was better off not knowing. He wasn't even sure he wanted to know where they were headed. There was no moon out, so the blacked-out island was pitch dark. The headlights on the jeep were hooded to keep them from being seen from the air, so Bob could hardly see the road, but The Supplier whizzed along as if they were driving in broad daylight. After executing a series of gravel-crunching turns without once applying the brakes, he steered into what appeared to be a residential area, parked, and turned the engine off. The houses, as far as Bob could make them out, all looked alike.

"What's this?" Bob whispered to his host.

"Married sub sailor housing. Wait here," the man said, and jumped out of the jeep.

He disappeared into the dark, and Bob, alone, thought about all the things that could happen to him if he were found here. He wondered how far The Supplier's influence extended. Could he keep the two of them from being court-martialed? Minutes passed. The darkness was total. It was like sitting in a cave.

Bob jumped when a shadowy form appeared beside him, but then he saw his host's smile gleaming in the darkness. "Not a good night, I'm afraid," he said. "Too bad. We both could have had a fine time." Then he swung back behind the wheel and they were off again. As they went, Bob added this man's smiling face to his mental list of reasons not to get married until he left the service.

The drive back to the base was as harrowing as the trip out. "You've been a good partner," The Supplier shouted to Bob over the sound of the engine and the rushing wind. "I'm going to do something for you." Bob wondered what was coming next. A bottle of contraband liquor? A woman in some out-of-the-way place?

"How would you like to have your own still?" he shouted. "I'll give you the plans. It wouldn't take up much space on the boat."

Bob turned to look at the man in the dark. Their own steady supply of cost-free alcohol? Was it really possible? "You'll just give us the plans?" Bob shouted back, "And we keep all the product?"

"Sure, why not. It's a simple design. Two one-gallon cans, copper tubing, copper fittings, and a hot plate are all you need."

"That's no problem," Bob yelled. There were plenty of empty one-gallon juice cans on board, and the black gang used a hot plate to heat the pistons when they were working on the engines. The mechanics would surely be able to scrounge up the tubing and fittings as well, especially when they learned it was for such a good cause.

The Supplier reached into his breast pocket and pulled out a neatly creased square of paper. "Here's a drawing. Nothing to it." Bob took the paper, tucked it in his own breast pocket, and buttoned the flap securely.

Soon they were back at the base, and Bob was worried that he might not be let in without a pass. But, although they were at a different gate and the guards were just as tough looking, they turned from pit bulls to puppies when they saw who was driving. After another leisurely chat with the marine guards, they drove to the boat. When The Supplier roared away the jeep's tires squealed and its driver threw up his hand in a valedictory wave. It was the last time Bob ever saw him. However, the *Tambor's* machinists used his diagram to construct their own still, which stayed in more or less continuous use for the rest of the war, either in a hotel bathtub or on the boat itself. Whenever they pulled into Pearl for R and R, Harry Behrens carried two five-gallon tins of distilled pink lady to the Royal Hawaiian in his sea bag, and in exchange for providing this vital service, his shipmates stuffed his personal items into their bags.

~~~~~~~~~~~~~~~~~~~~~~~~

After the Battle of Midway, the crew's liberty in Pearl Harbor would be the last they spent there for nearly a year-and-a-half, apart from a brief stop on their way to Bethlehem Steel in San Francisco for a major overhaul in September 1943. The upturn in U.S. fortunes after Midway and the concomitant change of strategic priorities would take them to Western Australia for overhauls and liberties from September 1942, to December 1943. When they finally got back to Pearl after the long absence, everything had changed. Whiskey was up to thirty dollars a quart, which made Bob and his shipmates even more grateful for their still. More servicemen were on the streets than ever, but most of the wives and girlfriends had, like Dorothy, shipped back to the States. And on the quiet street where the old-timers had shown Bob the genteel brothels, lines of servicemen snaked to the front doors. Inside, a woman sitting at a table in the parlor took their money and gave them a little ticket, as if they were going to the movies. The customer went down the hall and into one of the rooms, which was divided now into six areas by makeshift partitions that didn't reach the ceiling. One girl worked parallel rows of three small chambers, moving back and forth between the two middle rooms. While one man undressed behind a partition, he heard the man ahead of him with the girl, and when that man finished he was sent on to the third small space to get dressed. The girl didn't even get dressed between customers; she just threw on her robe and went to the adjacent middle cubicle where the next man waited. When she arrived the customer had to be ready. If he was too drunk or too inhibited, the girl handed him a rain check, like at the ballpark. Gone were the fine décor, the motherly madam, the remembering of names—all replaced by hardcore, assembly-line sex work. Bob visited once, saw the change, and did not return.

All change was not for the worse. The crew now got to stay at the Royal Hawaiian Hotel, known as the "pink palace of the Pacific." It sat on Waikiki Beach, with a view of the water out every oceanfront window, and, true to its name, the sub sailors got the royal treatment when they stayed there. Room service brought up meals and snacks at any hour of the day or night, the beer garden was open every day, and a volleyball game ran nonstop on the beach.

Vice Adm. Charles "Uncle Charlie" Lockwood, who had succeeded Bob English as commander of Pacific subs when English died in a plane crash in February 1943, understood the extreme needs of the sub crews for rest and recuperation between missions if they were to remain effective in their demanding service. After two months at sea, nearly all of it spent below decks in the subs' cramped compartments, the men came ashore in rough shape. Bob remembered: "When submariners returned, they looked different. They were pale, sometimes with long hair and beards, and a faraway look in the eyes, as if hypnotized. They said very little, kept to themselves, not comfortable. If they stayed with their own group, it was because they had a bond of common experience." They also had to keep quiet about where they'd been and what they'd done, and that was easier among fellow submariners.

Despite the rising fortunes of the Allies in the Pacific war, anxiety ran high on Oahu that the Japanese might yet attempt a desperate thrust against Pearl Harbor, including an invasion with land troops. Even in front of the Royal Hawaiian you could see the barbed wire buried in the sand. The total blackout was still in effect at night, and every door on the island was locked as soon as the sun went down. If you didn't get back to the hotel, you had better have another place to spend the night, or you'd end up sleeping on the beach, chilled by the cool night breezes off the water.

It was after the Midway battle that Jake Schultz introduced Bob to a couple of local women whom he and Bob's old buddy Joe Magner used to run with. True to form, Magner, who had been transferred to the *Trout*, had been spending time with a woman in her thirties. With another girl, she lived just three blocks from the Royal Hawaiian. She worked at a local tavern and had access to a steady supply of beer, which otherwise had become hard to find on the island. Once Bob got to know Magner's former girlfriend he began to really like her—although he was taken aback the time she answered the phone while they were having sex and had a long conversation with her boss about her work schedule without missing a beat.

The arrangement fell apart the night Bob brought Ed Spruance and one of his fellow *Tambor* officers to her place. The young officer knew Bob's friend had a house, and he asked to bring a date there for some privacy. When he arrived with another officer and his date, the small place became crowded. Bob's girl was upset—she told him she didn't like officers, let alone two of them with dates—and it didn't matter to her that one of them was Admiral Spruance's son. Then the night took a turn for the worse. After a lot of drinking, the officers decided to induct their girls into what they referred to as the "A.B.A." They talked the girls into baring their behinds and letting their dates bite them hard enough to leave a mark, which, they explained, was the badge of membership in the Ass Biting Association. Bob's girl stormed off to bed, the girl with Ed's friend decided she didn't want to sleep in the house with the rest of them and took her date off to sleep in his car, and Ed crawled onto the davenport in the living room with his girl. Bob retired to the bedroom, but when he tried to get into bed, his girl shoved him away. "Now you know why I can't stand officers," she said. He knew he wouldn't be able to get back into his room at the Royal Hawaiian, so that night he slept on the floor.

As complicated as rest and recuperation became sometimes, it was little wonder that Bob had fond feelings for his bunk in the forward room, where he was lulled to sleep by the sound of water outside the hull and the whir of the motors that shifted the bow planes. For a few days, at least—before they entered enemy waters—there was quiet and order.

CHAPTER SEVEN

"Moving Haven":
Mission to the Philippines

aptain Murphy's removal from command of the *Tambor* after only three war patrols was by no means unusual. In the first year of the war alone, forty submarine commanders were relieved of duty—most for unproductive patrols, others because they wilted under the stress. Command decisions made in the heat and confusion of battle were endlessly and ruthlessly dissected after the fact by the top brass. These analyses, called "endorsements," were the means whereby the U.S. submarine fleet was gradually transformed into the effective—even decisive—force it eventually became.

The early sub commanders were hamstrung by the extreme conservatism and lack of imagination of the Navy's tactical "book," which often seemed to view any risk as excessive. Such caution contradicted not only the best use of the submarines, but also the venturesome temperaments of the captains and crews. The captains were advised that the preferred mode of attack was to locate their targets by sonar and to fire their torpedoes while deeply submerged, ignoring the fact that the loud pings of their sonar would give away the subs' own location to enemy ships. A postwar analysis of U.S. submarine attacks found not a single instance of a successful sonar attack. The potential of the sub fleet as commerce raiders was still not fully grasped, and submarines were often ordered to abandon their pursuit of slow-moving cargo ships to give futile chase to battleships, cruisers, and carriers.

Gradually, however, tactics and strategy evolved, due mainly to a bold group of sub skippers who rewrote the book. Even in the gloom and frustration of 1942, a few tallied impressive results: Burt Klakring of the *Guardfish* and Charles Kirkpatrick of the *Triton* both sank merchant ships totaling over 15,000 tons; Chester Bruton of the *Greenling* and Robert Rice of the *Drum* topped them by racking up over 20,000 tons; and Creed Burlingame of the *Silversides* outdid them all with almost 28,000 tons. It was in the following year, however, that the tide decisively turned. In 1943 the capabilities of the fleet submarine were finally put to full use by such skippers as Dudley W. "Mush" Morton of the *Wahoo*, whose boldness and tactical brilliance revolutionized the accepted ratio between aggression and caution. Morton favored surface attacks under the cover of darkness and perfected the tactic called the "end around," in which the sub used its high surface speed to outrace its quarry on a parallel path and lay in wait for its approach. And once the night surface attack became standard, its efficacy was improved by changing the color of the submarines from black, which was easily seen at night against the surface of the ocean, to a mottled gray.

On the *Parche*, Cpt. Lawson P. "Red" Ramage and his torpedo officer discovered that the new hydraulically operated outer torpedo doors made it possible to safely reload their boat's torpedoes while it was traveling on the surface at top speed, another significant advance. Such aggressiveness was not without its dangers, however, as is demonstrated by the fates of the war's most productive sub skippers and the equally courageous men who served under them: Morton of the *Wahoo*, Howard Gilmore of the *Growler*, and Samuel D. Dealey of the *Harder* were all killed in action. Richard H. O'Kane, executive officer under Morton on the *Wahoo* and then captain of the *Tang*, was captured by the Japanese after his boat was blown up by a circular torpedo run; he came within days of dying in captivity before he was rescued. Eight other *Tang* survivors were also taken prisoner, but, remarkably, all survived the war. Among them was Henry Flanagan, who had put the *Tambor* into commission and served with Bob on its early war patrols. There was no denying that submarine warfare was an exceedingly dangerous game.

Another major reason for the failure of so many of the early sub commanders was the failure of their prime weapon, the torpedo. Again and again, a skipper would patiently maneuver into position for a clean shot at an enemy vessel, only to hear what Mush Morton sardonically called the "thud of the dud." Even before the war had ended analysts had concluded that the early handling of the subs' torpedo problems was a scandal. Captains and crew were ill-served by their superiors, who refused to acknowledge the evident flaws in the design of the Mark VI magnetic "influence" exploder, so called because the keel of its target was supposed to trigger the magnetic needle that controlled the torpedo's detonation. If the magnetic exploder failed, contact with the target was supposed to detonate the torpedo. The Bureau of Ordnance had tested the exploder only once, shortly after its development in 1926, sinking an obsolete submarine on the second try. Despite this indifferent performance, however, the Mark VI was not tested again and was defended fiercely by Bureau of Ordnance officials and the Navy high brass alike.

For months, the sub captains' claims that the torpedoes were running too deep for the exploder to activate were dismissed as excuses for their own poor performances. But when Red Coe, captain of the *Skipjack*, returned to Australia from a war patrol in a fury over a succession of missed targets at point-blank range, he finally found an ally in Rear Adm. Charles Lockwood, who had replaced Cpt. John Wilkes as commander of U.S. Asiatic Submarines in April 1942. Lockwood organized a test firing in King George Sound, using a large fishing net—the first time in sixteen years that the Mark VI had been tested. The holes made in the fishing net by the test torpedoes proved that the sub skippers had been right all along: the fish were indeed running too deep. Subsequent design modifications corrected this flaw, but also made the torpedoes more likely either to detonate prematurely or not at all. Further improvements were resisted by Rear Adm. Ralph Christie when he replaced Lockwood as commander of U.S. Asiatic subs; Christie had helped design the exploder mechanism and was one of its most ardent defenders. But Lockwood's reassignment to the U.S. sub command in Pearl Harbor in February 1943 put Uncle Charlie in position to hasten a solution to the torpedo problem.

A year later, a test of the contact exploders in Australia by Swede Momsen, the inventor of the Momsen lung, proved them defective as well. After a brave diver retrieved a torpedo that had been fired against a cliff and bounced off, it was discovered that the firing pin was not striking the fulminate mercury caps in the booster with enough force to explode them. The 90-degree angle which sub commanders had been taught was ideal for a hit turned out to be the one at which the firing pin was least likely to initiate an explosion. Finally a complete overhaul of the torpedo design was ordered, and in October 1943 it took a team at Pearl Harbor only three weeks to produce a safe and reliable contact exploder. For the first time in the war, almost two full years after it had begun, submarine commanders and their crews could go into battle fully and reliably armed.

While the *Tambor* was being refitted in Pearl Harbor in preparation for its fourth war patrol, its new captain, Steven H. Armbruster, arrived. The patrol began eventfully on July 23, 1942, when the *Litchfield*, performing its usual duty escorting the sub out of the harbor, sighted a periscope and dropped a depth charge, while the *Tambor* raced out of the area on all four screws. After a five-day trip to the Marshall Islands, the sub and crew spent a week feinting around the atolls of Wotje and Moloelap, tracking freighters, but were forced to evade planes and patrol boats before they could maneuver into firing position. Finally, on August 7, they found an armed passenger freighter sailing in the clear and took it out with a single torpedo, the explosion rumbling through the boat. The next morning they spotted a tramp steamer, sank it with a single fish, and sped away before a patrol boat could do anything more than drop one badly aimed depth charge at them.

So far, so good—two torpedoes fired, two ships sunk—but their luck took a turn on August 17, as they pursued six big *maru* in the harbor near Kwajalein during a driving rain. A patrol boat screened them from their targets and forced them to submerge for three hours. All they could do was sit, wait, and listen as the pinging of the patrol boat's sonar sounded through the sub, speeding up as it moved closer to them, slowing down as it ventured farther away. For some reason it never dropped any depth charges on them, but the longer the *Tambor* stayed submerged, the more battery power it used. As the hours wore on it became clear that the boat would have to surface to recharge, no matter the situation above. "The weather was so bad that we couldn't see them through the periscope," Bob wrote, "but we knew they were still there because we could hear them on the sound gear. There was no question that they knew we were still in the area, and if we surfaced they would blow us out of the water. So the captain decided to make a battle surface, and if they were still in sight we would fight it out with them. Not a good situation for a submarine to be in," he concluded, with characteristic understatement.

During a battle surface, the first two men to go topside were those assigned to the two .30-caliber Lewis machine guns. It was their task to take the guns from the gunner's mate in the control room, climb the ladder to the hatch, fasten the guns on the two mounting plates on each side of the conning tower at the lookout stations, and cover the crew manning the 3-inch deck gun while they made it ready to fire. Bob's station was on one of the machine guns, and he had dashed into the control room fast enough to be first in line to go up the ladder. But the man assigned to the other gun never showed. Gunner's mate Glebocki handed Bob both guns, but it was difficult enough to climb the ladder holding just one, and the entire operation came to a halt, like a busted handoff in the backfield, as the two of them stood at the foot of the ladder puzzling over how to proceed. Glebocki finally took one of the guns back from Bob, who darted up the ladder as fast as he could manage with the heavy gun in one hand. "I think what happened," he commented later, "was that the other guy decided he didn't really want to charge to the top side and take on the whole Japanese navy with that little peashooter."

After Harry Behrens opened the conning-tower hatch, Bob climbed to the lookout station, mounted the machine gun, locked it in its holder, and chocked the action to throw a shell into the barrel. It wasn't until he crouched over the gun and started a sweep with his finger on the trigger, ready to blast away, that he realized he couldn't even see the bow or stern of the *Tambor*, let alone the patrol boat at which he was supposed to fire. The storm that had kept them from seeing the enemy boat through the periscope had intensified into an opaque white sheet of rain. At almost the same moment, Captain Armbruster realized that the same heavy weather that kept them from seeing the patrol boat also provided the perfect cover for their escape, and yelled a quick order to the engine room: "All four engines online and all ahead full—let's get out of here!" Bob scrambled down from the lookout station to the bridge and slid down the conning-tower ladder back into the control room, where Glebocki, still waiting at the ladder, took Bob's gun. Before the boat's next run—to everyone's satisfaction—the Lewis guns were replaced by .50-caliber machine guns, which, in Bob's words, "packed a much greater wallop."

The next day they sank a five-thousand-ton freighter off the Micronesian island of Ponape, near the main Japanese naval base at Truk. That was the high point of the patrol. The boat's air conditioning expired on August 21, and, suddenly and decisively, so did their luck. They repeatedly spotted enemy ships but were chased away by patrol boats and destroyers or lost their targets in bad weather. And as the mission wore on the temperatures climbed to well over a hundred degrees in most of the boat's compartments during the day and cooled down only a little at night. In the engine room, where temperatures of 130 degrees were recorded, two firemen passed out from heat exhaustion. In every compartment the decks stayed wet and dangerously slippery from the high humidity. Sleeping was nearly impossible in such heat, but became even more difficult when virtually everyone on board, Bob included, came down with severe heat rash. It was hard for him to sit still long enough to play poker, even though it was practically the only thing he *could* do when he wasn't on duty. Itchy blisters erupted all over his body, then broke as he surrendered to the overpowering urge to scratch them, in an endless cycle of misery. He was lucky, though, that he wasn't one of the many crew members who also got a fungus infection. The pharmacist's mate stayed busy dispensing a makeshift ointment of pink lady laced with oil of menthol and handing out cotton compresses to apply it. Some of the officers slept in the torpedo-room bilges where it wasn't quite as hot, but there wasn't room there for anyone else. Conditions were so bad that most of the crew swore they would never go on another war patrol.

Instead of returning to Pearl Harbor, the *Tambor* was sent to the main U.S. sub base in Fremantle, Western Australia, arriving on September 19. The Japanese were bombing Darwin, at the northern tip of the continent, and the brass thought they might try to hit Fremantle as well, so the boat was rerouted to Albany, where the crew spent eighteen days before going back out to sea. Despite their vows during the previous patrol, Bob and almost all of his shipmates—their moods brightened by a couple of weeks of R and R—went back out. This time they carried thirty-two mines to plant in the Hainan Strait, a finger of water separating Indochina from the island of Hainan, west of the Philippines and just south of China. The mission was part of an extensive mine-laying campaign conducted by U.S. submarines in the fall of 1942, in which four Pearl Harbor–based subs planted minefields along the Japanese coast, and five Australia-based subs, including the *Tambor*, laid mines near Indochina. Although the load of mines left room for only eight torpedoes, they were ordered to hunt Japanese ships in the Gulf of Tonkin as soon as they had dispensed their mines.

The mine plant was made on the night of November 2—"a very touchy four hours," as Bob explained in his diary, "as we lay in shallow water and can't dive. About halfway through, one of the mines exploded. Too far away for any damage— about four thousand yards—but gave us a good scare." Two days later, relieved of the mines and free to hunt, they sank a 12,000-ton freighter, although they spent five of their eight torpedoes in the effort. On November 6 they fired two more in a futile attempt to sink another ship that, when it was sighted again later, was revealed to be a passenger-cargo vessel with a French flag painted on the side.

With only one fish left, they headed home, but on the way they confronted an unarmed sampan, took its occupants prisoner, and sank it with machine-gun fire and three rounds from the 3-inch gun. The boat may have been unarmed, but Japanese fishermen had been known to alert enemy warships to the presence and position of American vessels, so the crew wasn't taking any chances. There were ten fishermen, ranging in age from an old man to a boy of about ten, all from Formosa. The crew immediately put them to work cleaning the boat and washing the dishes. They did good work—the boat had never looked so good at the end of a patrol. None of them spoke a word of English, however, and they had to be watched continuously, even when they used the toilet—a duty made even more objectionable by the fact that most of them had intestinal parasites.

Two days later, Captain Armbruster used their last torpedo on a clear shot at a ship that looked suspiciously like a Q-boat—a high-speed, heavily armed vessel disguised as an ordinary freighter or steamer. If a sub engaged one in an attack, it might have a hard time getting away, but Armbruster fired anyway and missed. The ship turned and bore down on the *Tambor*, using the wake from the torpedo to guide it, but the *Tambor* crash-dived and managed to evade it, then headed back to Fremantle, armed only with its guns. Marines took the Japanese fishermen away at gunpoint as soon as they stepped off the boat, and the crew never heard anything about them again.

Four weeks later, on December 15, they left Fremantle and headed north on yet another war patrol, the *Tambor*'s sixth, and the fifth commenced in 1942. After March 15, Bob and his crewmates spent 208 of the remaining 292 days of 1943 on or under the waters of the Pacific. It was a grueling, hectic pace, but the war would not wait, and they might have spent even more time on patrol had it not been necessary to repair and refit. While the sub sailors went off to rest and recuperate after each patrol, the relief crew, composed of men who had been or soon would be going on war patrols themselves, worked on the boat. The relief crews and their supplies were housed on the submarine tender *Pelias*, which serviced not only the *Tambor* but all the other subs in squadron 6, divisions 61 and 62 (the *Tautog*, *Thresher*, *Triton*, *Trout*, *Tuna*, *Gar*, *Grampus*, *Grayback*, *Grenadier*, *Gudgeon*, and *Grayling*). The relief crews were always the first to greet the subs when they came back from patrol, running out to help cleat the lines, ask how things had gone, pick up dirty laundry, and hand out beers. The men in charge of each compartment gave them a list of needed repairs, and the relief crews were usually very reliable in getting things correctly fixed, not merely because it was their duty but also because they never knew when they might be assigned to a patrol on the same boat.

The patrol they had just completed—the *Tambor*'s sixth—had been plagued with problems from the very start. The *Pelias* itself had almost sunk trying to cross the Pacific during a long stretch of foul weather, and the 5-inch deck gun it was transporting to install on the *Tambor* had bounced all over the tender ship, threatening to crush everyone aboard. Problems also had developed with the new SJ radar system that the relief crew installed on the *Tambor* before the patrol. SJ radar was a more directional system than the SD radar they had been using; instead of merely warning when a plane or ship was in the area, it gave distance and bearing. On a test dive three days before the boat left the harbor, however, the SJ radar mast leaked badly, and the relief crew spent the next two days working on it. But during a trim dive the day after they left Fremantle, the mast began to leak again at a depth of just sixty feet. A hole was discovered on a flange in the hull, so they headed back to port, where the desperate relief crew pirated a replacement flange from the hull of the *Trout*, which was in dock being refitted, and transplanted it to the *Tambor*.

For all the rush to get back out on patrol, nothing much happened once they were there. They spent Christmas day around Christmas Island; cruised past Flying Fish Cove but, much to everyone's disappointment, saw neither a flying fish nor any signs of life other than one little building on the shore with a Japanese flag flying over it; and passed between Princess Island and Krakatau, where the great volcano had once erupted. Summer had just begun in the Southern Hemisphere, and again it was extremely hot. Then early on the first morning of 1943, they sighted a Japanese destroyer and fired four torpedoes at it. All of them missed, and the boat was forced to submerge under a barrage of eighteen depth charges, one of which came so close that the crew heard it scrape lightly against the hull as it dropped. By the time they ascended to periscope depth once more, the destroyer had left, and they pulled clear of the straits to surface and inspect the boat for damage. Both antenna insulators on the foremast had been broken, and the antenna itself was found lying on the deck. A gasket had been blown off the safety vent, which was leaking badly. The SJ radar, which the relief crew had labored over for so long, no longer worked. Worst of all, the air conditioning was again sputtering from leaks in the joints and valves.

They stayed on the surface while repairs were made, but never saw another ship. Captain Armbruster ordered up a shot of brandy for the entire crew, and they headed back for Fremantle along the bombing-restriction lane that had just been designated in the area to keep U.S. planes from attacking their own ships. All U.S. submarines were surrounded by a "moving haven"—a fifty-mile-long, ten-mile-wide rectangle of water that advanced in lockstep with the boat, in which it was supposed to be safe from friendly fire—but trigger-happy U.S. pilots were still firing on their own subs far too often, so bombing-restriction lanes were established as additional protection.

As they approached Fremantle, an enemy submarine was sighted near the port, so they had to enter the harbor without an escort, zigging and zagging to confuse anything that might be out there. It had been Bob's third patrol under Armbruster, and "we got along just fine," either because of or despite the fact that "I do not remember ever having a conversation with him." Whether due to personal temperament or orders from his superiors, Armbruster was noticeably more aggressive than Murphy, though with mixed results. They sank three ships on his first patrol, but had also been forced by dwindling batteries to come up for what could have been a disastrous battle surface, and were saved only by surfacing in the heavy rain squall. On his second patrol Armbruster executed the mine-laying operation flawlessly and sank a 12,000-ton freighter, but it took him five of his eight torpedoes to do the latter. Then he had not only fired on what turned out to be a French ship but also got suckered into attacking the Q-boat, leaving them stranded without torpedoes in the middle of the Pacific. Clearly Armbruster was not out there to play it safe and was determined to get results, even if it meant taking chances—which was, after all, the same line the most successful sub commanders had been taking.

Armbruster's most distinguishing physical characteristic was not any feature of face or voice but the fact that his hands would begin to shake whenever they made an attack. This trait did not go unnoticed by the crew, who soon nicknamed him Shaky Jake, despite the fact that many of them—Bob included—had begun to suffer from the same malady, and not just when the boat was under fire. After one attack, a crew member who had been in the control room told Bob that the only time Armbruster's hands weren't shaking was when he had a firm grip on the periscope handles. "Right," Bob replied. "And he grips them so hard the whole boat shakes."

~~~~~~

The *Tambor*'s seventh war patrol was shrouded in secrecy from the beginning. As Bob wrote in his diary on February 18, 1943, "Off again with a full load of fish and some landing equipment. Have three Filipinos on board and a couple of extra officers. Don't know why yet." The "landing equipment" consisted of Tommy guns, cases of ammunition, radios, a small wherry, and demolition equipment. The three Filipinos were stationed in the forward torpedo room, and they spoke English, so Bob soon learned that they were guerrilla fighters and that the *Tambor* was taking them home. The two officers, they told Bob, were named Smith and Parsons. Bob thought Parsons was an Army man, since he was wearing khakis with no insignia; it wasn't until many years after the war that he learned Parsons was a lieutenant commander in the Naval Reserve. Then again, Charles "Chick" Parsons was a somewhat mysterious figure. He'd been managing a stevedore company in Manila when he was taken prisoner after the Japanese occupation of the city on New Year's Day 1942. Somehow he talked the Japanese into allowing him to leave the islands on the repatriation ship the *Gripsholm,* on the pretext that he was a neutral. The feat had impressed General MacArthur enough to put him in charge of the effort to coordinate guerrilla forces on the islands, an operation nicknamed Spyron (for Spy Squadron). Since then he had been bouncing back and forth between the Philippines and Washington, organizing the guerrillas in the former location and winning them support among military brass and politicians in the latter. He was a daring character—he had caught the imagination and won the devotion of the guerrillas by helping them steal an old power boat and steering it all the way from the Philippines to Darwin, in Western Australia. And he was so devoted to his boss that he carried matchbooks imprinted with the legend "I SHALL RETURN."

Both the Americans and the Japanese realized the importance of the Philippines and were willing to expend considerable resources in the struggle to control them. Scattered in the Pacific just north of the equator and just east of Indochina—about twelve hundred miles south of Japan—the 7,107 islands of the Philippines were Japan's gateway to the material and strategic riches of the Southeast Asian islands and, if retaken by the Americans, could serve as the base for air assaults on the Japanese mainland. As Admiral Soemu Toyoda, chief of the Japanese Naval General Staff, bluntly declared, "Should we lose in the Philippines operations, even though the fleet should be left, the shipping lane to the south would be completely cut off so that the fleet, if it should come back to Japanese waters, could not obtain its fuel supply. If it should remain in southern waters, it could not receive supplies of ammunitions and arms. There would be no sense in saving the fleet at the expense of the loss of the Philippines." War Plan Orange, devised by the U.S. Navy around the turn of the twentieth century, also recognized that the Philippines were the key to control of the Pacific. The plan forecast that Japan would conquer the islands as the prelude to invasions of China and Southwest Asia and that the final showdown in the Pacific between the U.S. and Japanese navies would center on the Philippines. War Plan Orange was, in fact, the main reason that the Panama Canal had been built—it was completed in 1914—as a way to get American warships from the East Coast to the Pacific for the decisive battle.

War Plan Orange proved remarkably prescient in predicting both Japanese ambitions and tactics; the bitter irony was that, by the time the Japanese began actively to pursue their ambitions, the attack on Pearl Harbor had rendered the U.S. Navy powerless to stop them. The submarine fleet, having survived the attack and using its ability to maneuver in enemy-controlled waters, played a major role in the desperate efforts to thwart the Japanese assault on the Philippines. That effort, however, was hampered by the destruction of 60 percent of the American torpedo supply in the Japanese annihilation of Cavite Navy Yard on December 10, 1941. It was also during the Cavite raid that the *Sealion* was sunk and five of its sailors killed—the first sinking and first fatalities of the war for the American sub fleet.

Half of the U.S. subs in the Pacific were rushed to the defense of the Philippines, including six 1920s-vintage S-boats; they performed miserably, not so much from any shortcomings of their commanders and crew but from the inability of the top brass to shake the fog of prewar complacency. Just a day after the attack on Pearl Harbor, for example, a squadron of Japanese aircraft from Formosa caught MacArthur's entire air force bunched together on the ground at Clark and Nichols fields and wiped it out. Included in the wreckage were thirty-five B-17 bombers, the fabled Flying Fortresses, which had been rushed to the Philippines and were a vital cog in the plans for defense of the islands. In contrast to the harsh treatment submarine commanders would soon receive for their failures, MacArthur was never required to answer for his inaction.

The submarines themselves were continually sent either to the wrong place to intercept the Japanese forces or too late to the right place. The late arrival of seven submarines at Lingayen Gulf on December 21 allowed the Japanese to land 43,000 men there: the bulk of the invasion force that would capture Manila on January 1 and chase MacArthur's forces into the Bataan Peninsula. The subs were late again to Davao, allowing the Japanese fleet to sail off unimpeded to the Dutch East Indies. Typical of the strategic futility of the time were Captain Wilkes' attempts to repel the next Japanese attack in January 1942. He had massed his seventeen subs at Java, then moved them to Timor Island, where he guessed the Japanese would strike. After his subs departed, however, a hundred transports and their warship escorts sailed through the now-unguarded Karimata and Makassar straits and into Java, and by the time the subs made it back to their original position, the Japanese were firmly entrenched and easily repelled their attacks. On February 27, the Japanese crushed the Allies' last remaining cruiser force in the area in the Battle of the Java Sea. By March the Philippines and Dutch East Indies were both firmly in Japanese control, and U.S. forces had been evacuated at Corregidor, including MacArthur himself, whose parting verbal shot at the Japanese now graced the covers of Parsons' matchbooks.

Only the guerrillas were left to pick up the pieces, and they mounted a spirited resistance to the Japanese occupation, their ranks swelling to a quarter million. Information on Japanese troop and ship movements transmitted to U.S. forces by the guerrillas would help save American lives and doom Japanese ambitions throughout the war. The first of what would be forty-two supply missions to the guerrillas by U.S. submarines had been made by the *Gudgeon* in December 1942; the *Tambor*'s was the second, commanded by the guerrilla leader himself.

The *Tambor* crew did not like Parsons. They sensed that he considered himself better than them, perhaps because he was an officer, perhaps because MacArthur's officious command style had rubbed off on him, or perhaps because he found the environment of a submarine nearly intolerable. Aboard the *Tambor* he complained about everything, and especially the heat, although for once the air conditioning was functioning properly. Even the forward bilges were too hot for him to sleep in, so an electric fan was installed next to his bunk. The loud whirring of the fan kept Bob awake all night, but his comfort, of course, was of secondary importance. The night before they were to reach their rendezvous point with the guerrillas off Mindanao, the southernmost and largest Philippine island, Bob was jolted out of his bunk by a loud yell—then Parsons bolted out of the bilges with blood coursing down his arm. He had rolled over in his sleep and stuck his hand into the fan. At first everyone was worried that the mission would have to be scrubbed, but the pharmacist's mate was able to patch Parsons up to an acceptable degree.

On the evening of March 4, the *Tambor* surfaced and proceeded toward Pagadian Bay. The wherry was taken off its skids and lashed to the deck, a noisy operation that had to be finished before they got too close to the beach. Early the next morning they arrived just south of the town of Labangan, in the province of Zamboanga. The rendezvous with the guerrillas was to take place on the beak of a protuberance of land shaped like a buzzard's head on the west coast of Mindanao. Visibility was poor—good for the secrecy of the operation but bad for navigation, which had to be executed mainly by SJ radar. Just after 5:00 AM Parsons, his fingers splinted and bandaged, sailed off in the wherry with two of the guerrillas, and the *Tambor* submerged to await their return that afternoon. The small boat would fly a white flag if all was clear, a black flag if there was trouble. The only thing anyone on the boat could do was sit and wait.

Finally, around 4:30 in the afternoon, the returning craft was spotted through the periscope, its white flag whipping in the rain. Minutes later, they also saw a small power launch towing a native lighter, flying both a white flag and an American ensign. As soon as it could be confirmed that Parsons was in the wherry, the boat surfaced and approached, the rain pelting down so heavily that the beach was not visible. Again the bad weather was good cover for the transfer of supplies, especially since it took over an hour to get everything loaded into the lighter. Bob didn't think that the rickety boat could possibly bear the weight of all the supplies—not only did it settle deeper into the water with every box they loaded onto it, but one of the guerrillas was bailing water with a bucket all the while. Somehow, though, it stayed afloat.

After the transfer was finished, there was another excruciatingly long wait while Parsons completed and transmitted his report. The *Tambor* crew stood in the rain and chatted with the American guerrillas who had come along to help their Filipino comrades. The Americans were staying on the Japanese-occupied islands willingly, and to honor their commitment the crew loaded them up with canned peaches and other delicacies from the galley. Bob talked to a navy radioman who had escaped into the mountains when the Japanese overran Mindanao. Bob invited the man to come finish the patrol and then go back to Australia with them, but he was not about to go anywhere. He explained to Bob that he couldn't afford to leave Labangan—not only were his officer-grade paychecks being held for him stateside, but the guerrillas on Mindanao had started their own currency system, since they had nothing else with which to buy or barter. All the villagers accepted the homemade bills as legal tender. He gave Bob one as a souvenir of the mission. It was nothing fancy, just a strip of tan paper about the size of a bank check, with "P.50" stamped on one side and on the other, typed across the top, "THE MUNICIPALITY OF LABANGAN, PROVINCE OF ZAMBOANGA, WILL PAY TO THE BEARER ON DEMAND THE AMOUNT OF THIS PROMISSORY NOTE—FIFTY CENTAVOS." Bob gave the radioman extra cigarettes in exchange for his fifty-centavo note and watched as he climbed into the motor launch for the trip back to the island with the overloaded lighter in tow.

To avoid revealing its presence in the area, the *Tambor* hadn't fired on the enemy ships they'd seen on the way to Mindanao, but now that the mission was completed hunting season was again open. They cruised into the Davao Gulf, a finger of water in the center of the island, in search of freighters and made a couple of dives in the vicinity of the Marianas Trench, the deepest depression in the world. They then circled Mindanao's east coast and threaded their way through the narrow passageways between the islands of Leyte, Bohol, Cebu, and Negros. On March 14, they almost ran aground in the rain and fog at the northern tip of Mindanao, when the navigator, between keeping an eye out for mines and trying to keep track of all the boat's twists and turns, got lost. Bob was on the forward port lookout, squinting through the rain and searching through his field glasses for anything that might momentarily become visible, when he heard a roar in his ears and realized that it was the sound of crashing surf. At almost the same moment the starboard watch heard and reported the same sound on his side of the boat, and they both yelled down to the watch officer on the bridge, who shouted "EMERGENCY! EMERGENCY! ALL BACK!" Bob waited anxiously for what seemed like an eternity before he felt the boat slow as its reversed screws bit into the water. If they had run aground and gotten stuck or had damaged the screws on submerged rocks, they would have made a helpless target for the first Japanese ship or plane that happened along.

Once they got the boat stopped, however, there was another problem: the channel they had blundered into was too narrow to turn the boat around in. Their only option was to back out—very, very slowly. It was a tricky and tortuous process, but at least the weather was on their side, as it had been for the entire patrol. The rain and fog continued to obscure their location while they were vulnerable to attack. As soon as they got out of the channel, Armbruster abandoned the planned route and headed for the open water of the South China Sea until the weather cleared. Of the incident in the channel Armbruster made no mention in his log. Obviously he had learned from the experiences of Captain Murphy and many other submarine commanders the importance of a clean patrol report.

The bad weather continued for the next week. Even when they managed to spot an enemy ship through the unremitting rain and fog, they could not get close enough to take a shot. Their only relief from the monotonous frustration was the discovery of an intruder in the forward torpedo room. At first they only heard the noises it made at night, when the room was dark and everyone who wasn't on duty was trying to sleep. It wasn't a mechanical noise like air in the line; it was more of a skittering, scurrying sound—the sound of something alive. Then Bob found gouges nibbled into the binding of his diary, tooth marks appeared in one of the Momsen lungs, and droppings were found in the mess storage area. The creature was finally spotted one night—a rat—waddling across the forward-room deck. That was the only appearance he made, though they continued to hear him padding around from time to time. Apparently he possessed the nervy flair of a true submariner, for he weathered all the dives, extreme heat, bad air, and depth charges without complaint.

They finally got close enough to a naval auxiliary ship on March 22 to fire three fish at it and watched with relief and satisfaction as it went down bow first. It was the first ship they had sunk in over four months, since the 12,000-ton freighter on November 4 the previous year. A week later, before dawn on the morning of the 29th, they spotted two dark objects on the horizon which were soon identified as a freighter and its escort. Three more fish were fired, with two possible hits, but they couldn't stay around long enough to confirm the sinking, since the escort dropped fourteen depth charges on them. An air-compressor base was smashed and a sound head was knocked out, but no major damage was inflicted; subsequently their sinking of the freighter was confirmed.

On the way back to Australia they made so many dives—"about forty-five on this trip," Bob estimated—that "we even have seaweed growing on deck." His twenty-fourth birthday came and went on April 7 with no commemoration other than a terse notation in his rat-chewed diary. On April 11 they pulled into Exmouth to refuel, and Bob noted that it "sure feels good to get out on the deck and stretch." While there, however, Bob saw a group of his shipmates throwing tin cans and bottles toward the water and shooting at them with their .45s. The shots were spraying in all directions, and each time one of them fired, he stepped back, directly into the line of fire of the others. After lunch some of his other shipmates decided they wanted to go swimming, although they had been warned that the area was infested by sharks. A man with a rifle stood at a lookout station to shoot any sharks that might come by, but Bob had little confidence that his marksmanship would guarantee he'd hit the shark and not the man. Disgusted, he wandered toward the bow of the boat, where he saw another group of ship-mates leaning over the side and pointing excitedly. One of them was holding a line in the water, and when he brought it up Bob saw a red hunk of beefsteak stuck into a big fishhook on the end of it. *A swimming party at one end of the boat with an armed lookout to protect them from sharks*, he thought, *and a fishing party at the other end trying their damnedest to attract them*. The combined effects of fatigue, reckless overconfidence from their many near escapes, and fatalism from their continuous exposure to sudden or lingering death were beginning to show. Six war patrols, with almost three hundred days on or beneath the water in just a little over a year—it took a toll. The crew needed some rest, and needed it badly. *Good thing*, Bob thought, *we're on our way back to Fremantle.*

CHAPTER EIGHT

"Pirate Poetry":
At Liberty in Australia

In the six months before the *Tambor*'s arrival in Western Australia in September 1942, the area had become one of the Allies' main bases of naval operations, a development which the Australians welcomed. The country had been shocked two days after the Pearl Harbor attacks when the Japanese sank the *Prince of Wales* and *Repulse*, two British warships sent to the South China Sea by Winston Churchill to protect the island continent. As the Japanese rampaged through the South Pacific in late 1941 and early 1942, destroying Allied bases and overrunning islands and atolls with virtual impunity, the Australians felt increasingly vulnerable to a Japanese invasion, and abandoned by the British. Australian prime minister John Curtin bitterly declared that his countrymen "would now look to America, free of any pangs as to [her] traditional links or kinship with the United Kingdom."

It was, ironically, the Japanese who did the most to make Curtin's prediction come true, by pushing American forces relentlessly to the south. After the Cavite Navy Yard was destroyed, the Asiatic Fleet and its submarine command moved to Surabaya, in the Dutch East Indies, and from there to Tjilatjap on the southern coast of Java; after the Japanese navy drubbed the Allies in the Battle of the Java Sea, the closest port available was in Fremantle, a small town near Perth on Australia's western coast which Admiral Lockwood once compared to "a typical Kansas boom town." Captain Wilkes set up a sub base there and established his headquarters in nearby Perth, the largest city in Western Australia. One of Wilkes' first orders was to send the submarine *Permit* to evacuate General MacArthur from Corregidor after the Allied disaster there in March 1942. Always the showman, MacArthur stood up the *Permit*, preferring a more theatrical departure on a PT boat to an underwater exit, but the *Permit* did evacuate thirty-six code-breaking experts from the island. On its way to the new Fremantle base, another U.S. sub, the *Sailfish*, sank a 6,400-ton *maru* near Bali on

March 2, and two days later the S-39 sank a large fleet tanker in the Java Sea. Eleven of the old S-boats patrolled the Solomon Islands for a time from a base in Brisbane, on Australia's east coast. Although they weren't equipped for the heat and humidity of the South Pacific, they proved surprisingly effective, sinking several Japanese ships, including the heavy cruiser *Kako*. By the end of 1943, with the Japanese driven out of the Solomons and Allied fortunes on the upswing in the South Pacific, the Brisbane base was shut down and all U.S. submarines were based in either Pearl Harbor or Fremantle. The main task of the Fremantle subs was to hunt down the tankers ferrying oil to Japan, so that any warship that escaped Allied firepower would eventually die of thirst.

At first the move to Australia was not popular with the *Tambor* crew. The fourth war patrol had left them exhausted and frustrated, and it was also their bad luck to arrive in Australia just as the Southern Hemisphere winter was changing to spring, inaugurating the rainy season. Albany, down the coast from Fremantle and Perth, wasn't comparable to Pearl Harbor as a liberty site, and there wasn't much to do there but sit around and watch the rain. Wine was just about the only type of alcohol available, provided by an ex-*Tambor* crew member stationed at Albany who moonlighted as a bootlegger. "We didn't like it much," Bob commented, "but we didn't let it go to waste, either."

The crew found the area around Fremantle, which they saw for the first time in November 1942, after their fifth war patrol, much more hospitable. For one thing, the people seemed to have a special fondness for American sub sailors, who were just about the only young men the Australian civilians saw in those days. Most of the Australian soldiers and sailors were stationed in the northern part of the country in anticipation of the Japanese invasion that still hadn't come. Around the same time that American subs showed up in the western ports and American sailors appeared on the streets, the bombing of Darwin and the Japanese move to the south seemed to stall; whether it was fully justified or not, the Aussies seemed to believe it was the American subs that had kept them from being invaded. The sailors were greeted with open arms, and the U.S. Navy arranged for their exclusive use of two of Perth's most luxurious hotels, the King Edward and the Ocean Beach. The bars were well stocked and the women seemed pro-American, as well. Soon Western Australia was as popular with the sailors as Honolulu.

After unloading in Fremantle, the *Tambor* crew lined up at the base to get their mail and their pay. Bob seldom got any letters because he seldom wrote any. Anything interesting he could write to his dad, Dick, or Marge would be cut out by the censors, and he saw no point in writing to anyone else, especially women. With everything uncertain—where the boat would harbor next, not to mention whether they would survive their next mission—Bob chose not to pretend that it was possible to make promises and keep them. It didn't seem fair

Photo 12. A two-sided propaganda leaflet dropped by the Japanese and given to Bob by a British soldier he met in Australia.

to the women he met, and he didn't like having his mind tugged around in the midst of circumstances he couldn't control. Look at what had just happened to him and his shipmates: they'd been sent from Pearl Harbor to Australia without any warning. For all he knew, he would never see Hawaii again. So, when he left a port, it was good-bye and good luck—no letters, no phone calls, no dates or plans for the future. If he did show up there again, great, but if not, no hard feelings either way. Everybody had his own way of dealing with the uncertainties of war, and this was the way that made sense to Bob.

During the last patrol he'd had his usual good run at the poker table, and after he collected his own pay (bumped up a few bucks after a promotion in November 1942 to torpedoman 1st class) he stationed himself at the end of the line to collect the money that was owed him. He had learned that if you didn't collect from your shipmates the minute they got the money, you might never collect at all. As usual, everyone had a sob story—they needed the money for leave, they owed someone else, they had to send it home to their sick mother—but Bob would have none of it. "A loan is a loan," he told them, and he told himself that if they had a sick mother at home who needed money, they should have sent it to her in the first place instead of gambling it away and then hitting him up for a loan so they could gamble some more. There was a lot of grumbling, but he knew from experience that the hard feelings would last only until they needed another loan, and he would again become their best buddy, and their banker.

After collecting his pay and his loans and adding it to his winnings, he had over a thousand dollars in his pocket, and he took it directly to the bar at the King Edward Hotel. The months and the miles at sea were beginning to wear on the crew, and he had a lot to wipe clean from his mind. Since the victory at Midway, the Allies had the Japanese on the run at last, and the top brass were eager to press their advantage, which meant more frequent war patrols and less time off between them. On the last patrol Bob had seen more of his crewmates brooding silently over their coffee mugs in the mess compartment or lying on their bunks staring at the ceiling. Silence was almost as much the enemy as the Japanese, because in silence you had the chance to think about where you were, what you were doing, and what could happen to you. When Bob saw someone like his normally genial shipmate Alfred sitting in silence, he tried to snap him out of it, talk to him, get up a game of acey-deucey, hand him a wrench and give him a job—anything to get him back into the world of specific, present dangers and out of the host of imagined ones swirling in his head. Sometimes it worked, but sometimes it didn't, and when the boat went out again, Alfred had vanished from the crew, never to be seen again.

Near the end of the fifth patrol, one of Bob's crewmates had begun to recite pirate poetry. He walked around the boat chanting the words "pieces of eight, pieces of eight" over and over, and when they got back to Australia and checked into the King Edward Hotel, he grabbed a fire ax off the wall and shattered the doors of several rooms. Bob never saw him again either.

Two of the stewards also had gotten into a scrape at the end of the last patrol, and Bob had to help break it up. At first all of the stewards on the *Tambor* had been Filipinos, but as the submarine fleet expanded some of them were transferred to other ships and replaced by African Americans. There always seemed to be bad blood between the Filipinos and the blacks, for reasons Bob never understood, and one night when he was trying to sleep he heard someone yelling near the back of the torpedo room. He snapped on the light and saw one of the black stewards pressed against the watertight door, waving a straight razor in one hand and shouting. From the other side of the door came the voice of a Filipino steward. They were threatening to cut each other to pieces, slit each other's throats, and stick knives in each other's bellies. Bob calmed down the man on his side, and one of the officers came running from his quarters on the other side to wrestle a butcher knife away from the Filipino.

So Bob thought a few drinks were in order. The King Edward's bar was large and comfortable, and most of the crew was there. Bob bought a round of drinks for everyone, then another, and after the crowd began to break up, he kept buying rounds for himself. Soon he was filled with warm feelings for Australia, the

King Edward Hotel, and its handsome bar. His pockets were filled with money, more was piled on the bar for the kind, wise bartender, and life seemed filled with wonderful possibilities. This is a very good place, Bob thought, and he resolved to buy it. When he told the excellent bartender his intentions to purchase the hotel, the man smiled doubtfully, so Bob spread his money out on the bar in a show of good faith. Then, as if taking him up on his offer, a barmaid stepped up, swept the bills into a linen sack, and led him by the hand to the hotel lobby, where the hotel manager counted the money, gave him back a couple of hundred dollars, handed him a receipt for the rest, and put the sack in the hotel safe. Facing him and speaking slowly, the barmaid explained that she had seen more than one sailor come through, flash a wad of money, and leave with empty pockets. The next day Bob sent his winnings back to Decorah for safekeeping.

The comings and goings of the subs were supposed to be top secret, but the Perth residents always seemed to have anticipated their arrival. Every time the *Tambor* pulled into the sub base, for example, a cab driver named Louie was waiting outside the base to take Bob into downtown Perth and serve as his personal chauffeur for as long as he was in town. How he knew Bob was arriving was as much a mystery as how he kept his long-sleeved shirt so spotlessly white. Gasoline was in short supply, so all the cabbies and bus drivers had attached big charcoal burners to the backs of their vehicles and rigged the engines with converters so they could run on charcoal fumes when the gas ran out. The charcoal didn't last long, so Louie had to stop periodically and reload the burner, his shirt getting a little dingier every time. The next morning, however, his shirt was gleaming white again. Either Louie had an endless supply of white shirts or a very good laundry.

Departing the *Tambor* to go on liberty, Bob roomed with Harry Behrens at the King Edward, but then the pair were invited to the Ocean Beach Hotel for a party thrown by the torpedoman in charge of the forward room, Ernie Costa. Ernie, an affable Italian, had been nicknamed "Wop" by the crew until he patiently explained that the word was an insult. His party was a lively one, and Bob and Harry quickly noted that the Ocean Beach, unlike the King Edward, was right on the water, and, more importantly, at this point in the war allowed women in its rooms.

The next day Bob and Harry moved out of the King Edward and into the Ocean Beach and discovered that it was the site of a more or less continual party that included every room in the hotel. Room service brought up trays of drinks and food in what seemed like regular shifts. The parties frequently got noisy, and young women would come out onto the balconies of the apartment house across the way to see what was happening. As soon as one of the sailors spotted them, he would wave them over, and they often joined in. If a sailor and a friendly Aussie girl hit it off, all they had to do was open the door of a vacant room with an Australian coin, which worked just as well as a key.

Things were so lively in Perth that Bob and some of his crewmates eventually decided they needed to find places to rest from the rigors of their recuperation. A couple of old-timers who had been stationed in Australia before recommended a little town about 170 miles to the east, reached easily by train, called Katanning. It was, Bob discovered, hardly a town at all—just a couple of blocks of shops and offices with a train line running through its middle, hauling cargo and cattle and occasionally a few passengers. Set in the midst of rolling green hills, wheat fields, and a few widely scattered farmhouses, Katanning was not much different from the midwestern towns of Bob's childhood. The only significant differences were the temperature—it was midsummer in Australia and almost as hot as it was on the *Tambor* when the air conditioning went out—and the sheep. The sheep in Katanning must have outnumbered the people by a hundred to one, and every patch of green in the fields was dotted with them. There were stockyards just outside of town, and when the wind blew from a certain direction the town took on the scent of a submarine at the end of a long patrol.

The day after Bob arrived in Katanning, he took a walk around town to get his bearings. It didn't take long; the town was small and its one main street was unpaved and dirt-caked. But that main street presented a surprise. Moving in his direction from the other end of the small downtown district he saw a girl on the back of a quarter horse. It seemed out of place, even in an out-of-the-way place like this one, and Bob had liked horses since his family had raised and sold them back in Colby, Wisconsin. So he waved, and to his surprise, the girl steered the horse right over to him and leaned down over its neck to talk. She was small and compactly built, wearing a blouse and shorts, swirls of blonde hair escaping from the flowered kerchief knotted under her chin. She had a more delicate face than he expected for a girl riding a horse down Main Street—high cheekbones faintly streaked with sunburn, a straight, small nose, and a friendly but slightly demure smile. "You know, I'm nuts about horses," Bob said. "I used to have ponies." The girl smiled at him and introduced herself and her horse. Bob patted its neck as they talked, and it was all he could do not to reach out and pat the bare leg clinging to the horse's flank, as well. He noticed as she chatted with him that she had a faint, sibilant note in her speech, not the Australian accent that turned every "i" into an "oi." It made her seem an even more exotic creature, and he was sorry that she didn't stay and talk to him longer. The next day he walked the same route through town, hoping she would show up again, and she did. He knew then that she must be interested in him too, and sure enough, she invited him to her parents' ranch for Sunday dinner.

Her name was Greta and her family was German—that was the accent he hadn't immediately identified—and as Germans they were automatically figures of suspicion in Australia. They were required to meet with local authorities at

Photo 13. Greta, Bob's friend in Katanning, Western Australia. (Courtesy Robert Hunt)

regular intervals to explain their activities and assure everyone that they were not Nazi spies. At the ranch, Bob met Greta's parents, shared a meal with the family, and saw their part of the countryside. He must have made a fair impression, he thought, because the visit resulted in a second invitation, this time to a neighbor's ranch. At that outing a few days later, Bob and some shipmates went rabbit hunting with the ranch's owner. Then, just before dinnertime, the rancher led Bob to a corral that held some very nice-looking quarter horses and asked him if he'd like to ride one. Perhaps he thought all Americans were born cowboys, but for Bob it had been a long time since he'd sat a horse. Greta was looking on expectantly, and Bob had been a good rider as a boy, so he picked a brown and white pinto and the ranch hands saddled it up.

Perhaps he had not chosen wisely. The rancher had said something about the horse not having been ridden for a while. Apparently there was a reason. The moment Bob climbed aboard, the pinto bolted out of the corral and flattened into a full gallop. Bob had barely gotten his hands on the reins and his feet into the stirrups, and now he hung on for dear life. Out of memory or instinct, he bent low over the horse's neck, but this made him feel only slightly more secure. Pulling back on the reins and shouting "Whoa!" had no effect on the charging animal. It ran like its tail was on fire. Bob thought of saving himself by jumping off, but the view rushing past—shaking and jolting with the clatter of hoofbeats—was of potholes and stones. *Eventually this animal has got to tire out*, he thought desperately, *but I may not be on it by then.*

Out of the corner of his eye he could see his shipmates standing on the rails of the corral, whooping and laughing. *Maybe if I can steer him back to the corral.* Bob pulled the reins to the left as hard as he could and the horse's path bent

Photo 14. Bob rides his pony on the farm his family owned in Wisconsin before their move to Iowa. (Courtesy Robert Hunt)

into a wide leftward trajectory. He had to hang on like death, and his arms were tiring, and still the stony ground rushed past in a blur. Finally, after swinging in a wide arc, the pinto was headed back toward the corral, still at a full gallop. But it missed the gate and was pointing, instead, at the ranch house, where a clutch of family and guests watched the spectacle from the front porch. As the house rushed toward him Bob tried everything he knew but could neither slow the horse, nor turn it to the right or left. As the house loomed up Bob saw the folks on the porch startle and begin to scatter. Oddly, he seemed to have time to study each figure as some ran into the house and others bolted to the right and left, leaping off the porch. The porch was elevated, with four wooden steps leading up to it and was covered by a roof supported by white-painted wooden pillars.

The front of the house was constructed of lapped siding, also painted white. They were galloping straight for it. They were going to hit it.

The horse stiffened all four legs and dropped its rump, skidding now toward the porch steps in a sudden cloud of dust. The horse hit the steps and suddenly disappeared from under Bob, who flew through the air. Bob skipped once on the porch floor and slammed into the front of the house.

He lay still on his back. In the sudden quiet, he was afraid that if he tried to move he would discover that he couldn't. Then he heard the others running to him, shouting his name, and then he moved his arms and legs. When he sat up he realized, to his surprise, that he was not badly hurt, just bruised, scraped, and shaken. Even more miraculously, the pinto was already back on its feet, panting and snorting but also unharmed. And once it became apparent to everyone that Bob and the horse had survived, everyone clapped him on the back and laughed. Then the dinner bell clanged and everyone left Bob to go inside and eat.

He turned to follow, still vibrating like a struck gong. He wasn't the least bit hungry; what he really wanted was a stiff drink. But he stepped inside and went through the motions with the rest of them, making sure to pass the dishes and lift his coffee cup with both hands. All through the dinner, Shaky Jake had nothing on him.

After the meal they all took a tour of the ranch and watched the cowboys—mounted on the tamer horses—herd the sheep, aided by a pair of border collies that looked and acted more intelligent than many of the naval officers Bob had known. He stood by Greta, and she seemed glad to have him there. Back inside, during a long series of drinks and parlor games, they sat near one another. In one game involving instructions and poses, there was an opportunity to lean against Greta and hold the pose. The physical contact soothed Bob's still-jangled nerves, but it also made him long to be alone with her, something that looked increasingly unlikely as the afternoon stretched into evening. When the party finally broke up, the rancher offered to drive Greta home, and Bob rode along. He'd given up on the possibility of being alone with her, but if he accompanied her home at least he could say good-bye to her under more private circumstances. A couple of miles along the way, however, the car veered off the side of the road and into an empty field, and the rancher announced that he was going to walk up to a tavern just ahead and have a couple of beers before they went the rest of the way. As soon as he had disappeared into the darkness, Greta turned to him and they had their private moments. This wasn't the kind of girl you had sex with, Bob knew, but she was tender and sweet, and she soothed his nerves in ways she probably didn't suspect. The rancher's gesture was even kinder than any of them realized at the time, for the next day Bob and his shipmates were called back from Katanning to go on another war patrol.

After weeks at sea Bob returned to Katanning and walked down the same street where he'd met Greta, hoping to see for a third time that lovely vision of the girl on her horse. But it wasn't to be. This time a lady emerged from the town's only department store, stopped, and spoke to him. He wasn't sure why she did; he didn't feel particularly forlorn, but maybe he looked sadder than he felt. Then again, it wasn't unusual in such a small town for a stranger to strike up a conversation as if she'd known you all her life, and American sailors were popular in Katanning.

"Why are you alone on such a fine afternoon?" she asked. He couldn't think of a reason, and before he could voice a reply, she told him that a girls' football game was going on at the fairgrounds and that it was just a short way down the street. When the information didn't immediately stir him into action, she added. "I would advise you to take a look." It seemed as good a way to pass the time as any, finally, so he headed down the dirt road toward the fairgrounds.

As he found a seat on one of the rickety wooden bleachers and sat down to watch the game, he realized why the woman thought he would find this game so appealing. The field was filled with young women in jerseys and shorts chasing a white and black ball, shouting and calling to one another, their ponytails bouncing after them. They were all deeply tanned and appealingly long-legged in their white pants and high white socks. One team was clad in white shirts, the other in dark blue. It really wasn't much of a game, but Bob's eyes were immediately drawn to an especially long-legged girl on the blue team who moved with particular grace and athleticism. He soon found himself ignoring the game and focusing on nothing but her. He had been at sea for several weeks and couldn't help but imagine what wonders those long, tanned legs might perform in another setting. "I would advise you to take a look." *Yes, indeed,* Bob thought. *Thank you very much.*

When the game was over he left the bleachers to introduce himself. The young woman was almost as tall as Bob—most of it those wondrous legs—and although she didn't seem to mind his attention, he had to walk quickly to keep up with her. Her skin glistened with sweat, and she smelled clean, like an athlete, and very much unlike the inside of the *Tambor* at the end of a patrol. You weren't allowed to take a girl into a barroom in Katanning, so he offered to buy her a malted at the local ice-cream parlor, and she accepted. Bob felt like taking her straight to his hotel room, but she wasn't that sort of girl. She lived in Katanning with her parents, she told him over their malteds. Her father worked for the railroad, and her name was Shirley. Sitting with this girl in an ice-cream parlor on the far side of the world, the cool of the malted in his mouth, her dangerous legs tucked primly out of sight beneath the table, he felt as if he had been dropped into the middle of an Andy Hardy movie. He was Mickey Rooney and she was Judy Garland.

It did seem like a typical small-town courtship for a while, despite all the circumstances to the contrary. She took him home to meet her parents, and they
took an immediate liking to him, especially her mother. It didn't hurt, of course,
that he was an American submariner, one of those who had saved them—so the
Australians thought—from invasion by the Japanese. It was easy to forget that
this wasn't real life, just a brief vacation from the wider world and its war. Even
when the untidiness of reality intruded, the effect was usually comic. There was,
for example, the time Shirley's mother invited Bob's shipmates to her house for
a party. They brought plenty of liquor along, which in itself wasn't so bad, but
late in the day Shirley's mother stormed into the living room and announced
that she was going to swing her frying pan at the next sailor who peed in her
flower beds.

The party finally broke up, Bob's friends left, and Shirley's mother went
upstairs to bed. Her father was out of town, traveling for his job with the railroad. It was the first time Bob and Shirley had been alone together, and it turned
out that she was a very friendly girl. Just as they were getting to know each other
better, however, Shirley's mother came back downstairs, turned on the light, and
announced that she couldn't sleep. "It's dreadfully lonesome in the bedroom,"
she said. "Could you two come up and keep me company?"

Bob didn't know what the mother had in mind—it sounded a little strange
to him—but Shirley seemed to understand what was happening. She stood to
follow her mom, and Bob fell in line as they made their way to the stairs and
climbed in single file to the second floor. In the mother's bedroom there were
no chairs—only the rumpled double bed. And then Shirley's mom climbed into
it, pulled back the covers, and looked at Bob.

And that's how Bob finally got Shirley into bed—her on one side, Bob in the
middle, and her mom on the other side. Once he resigned himself to the fact
that Shirley's legs were tucked away for the night and adjusted himself to the
sudden change in his fortunes, it really wasn't so bad. They lay quietly in a row,
chatting for a little while, then Shirley's mother turned out the bedside light and
they fell silent. It was dark and warm and Bob relaxed in a way he hadn't been
able to do in a very long time. *Any port in a storm*, he thought, then fell asleep.

Soon enough, the real world and the war asserted itself again when the
inevitable call came for everyone to get back to Fremantle for another war patrol.
Not only was Bob's domestic idyll disrupted, but there was a practical difficulty,
as well. He still had almost a thousand dollars in the safe at the local hotel. All
the banks in Katanning were closed for the weekend, and there wasn't time to
reach one anywhere else. He couldn't take the money back on the *Tambor* with
him. It wasn't that he mistrusted his shipmates, but if the boat was sunk all that
cash would go to waste at the bottom of the ocean. He could think of only one
thing to do. Before saying good-bye to Shirley, he wrote his father's address in
Decorah on a slip of paper, wrapped it around the wad of bills, and handed her

the package. He could never recall trusting a woman other than his mother so much before. But if you couldn't trust Judy Garland, who could you trust?

Judy Garland or not, she turned out to be eminently trustworthy. When the *Tambor* returned to Fremantle, Louie was there as usual, white shirt gleaming and charcoal-powered cab billowing smoke. And once more Louie chauffeured Bob back to Perth, dropping him in front of the King Edward. But before Bob got inside, another *Tambor* sailor ran up to him on the sidewalk. "There's a girl looking all over for you," he said. That sounded ominous but before Bob had time to consider the problem another cab pulled up to the curb, and out jumped Shirley. So not only Louie had anticipated the boat's arrival; Shirley had, too. It was as if the entire city of Perth had broken the naval code.

"You got me into quite a peck of trouble," she told him. As he recalled it, he had never gotten the chance, thanks to her mother, to have gotten her "into trouble," but before he could protest she handed him a slip of paper. It was a receipt for a draft from one of the Katanning banks to R. C.'s bank in Decorah. "I had to answer a lot of questions about your money," Shirley said. When she'd walked into the bank with a thousand American dollars in her hand and told the teller it belonged to an American sailor, there was quite a stir. She'd been grilled by one bank officer after another as to how she'd gotten the money, and by the time it was over she had begun to wish that she had just kept it for herself. As relieved as he was to learn that the money had gotten safely to his dad—and that the "trouble" had not been terribly bad—he was even happier when she told him she planned to spend the week in Perth with him. This was especially good news since there were now 170 miles between Shirley and her mother.

All the hotel rooms in Perth were full, so she ended up staying with her aunt and uncle, which wasn't so bad for Bob. Shirley's relatives lived near the Ocean Beach and their house had a screened porch with a rollaway bed and a door through which one could enter and exit without going through the house. Bob and Shirley spent their days at the beach, their evenings being squired around the local bars and restaurants by Louie, and their nights in the rollaway bed on the porch. Finally, Bob had those beautiful legs all to himself, and he took full advantage of the privilege, observed only by her aunt's big green parrot, which Shirley kept in her room for company.

Shirley's aunt and uncle threw a party for his shipmates the night before Shirley left to go back to Katanning, and once again they embarrassed Bob. This time, after a couple of hours of steady drinking, they decided that the parrot looked thirsty and fed it a shot of whiskey. Moments after the bird lapped it up, he fell off his perch, rolled over on his back, and could not be revived. It was a sad note on which to end what had been an idyllic leave. Soon Shirley was gone and the crew was ordered back to Fremantle.

Each return to Australia brought new encounters. The cities and towns were vir-tually empty of young Australian men, most of whom were fighting the Japanese, and Australian women sought out the Americans on leave for companionship. On the eve of a departure, Bob met a woman in Perth who turned his head. She was a blind date, arranged by his friend Red Mayo, who had been seeing an Australian nurse during the leave. Red's girl had a friend, another nurse, and Bob remembers her as the most beautiful woman he met during the war. The two couples went out for drinks and dinner, then Bob and his nurse went to the beach for a sunset swim. They got along so well that Bob was tempted to violate his principle about making plans for future leaves.

Upon the boat's safe return from its patrol the crew was greeted with the usual cold milk, fresh fruit, ice cream, and mail. Included in Red Mayo's mail packet was a letter from his Australian nurse. In anticipation of his return, she'd taken time off and rented a cottage down the coast in Bunbury with her friend— Bob's blind date. The letter contained explicit instructions for the two sailors. They were to bring towels, blankets, and silverware, and, in an underlined sen-tence, they were admonished: "Don't get drunk before you get here—the drinks can come later."

The two men had gritted their teeth through several close calls on the patrol, but now they were back in the sunlight, alive, and their liberty had been arranged for them by two attractive women who had planned for their arrival. What's more, the owners of a local brewery, in gratitude to the American subma-riners who were defending their country, had promised each *Tambor* sailor a free case of beer. Bob and Red packed their bags, Bob summoned Louie, and the two sailors made flank speed for the brewery in the charcoal-powered taxi. The beer bottles were the big one-pint, six-ounce size, and the only way to fit everything into the taxi was to pile all the luggage on the front seat next to Louie and stow the beer cases on the floor of the backseat. Red and Bob, in back, sat with their feet on the beer and their knees at their chins. It was a tight fit, but they were hardened submariners who knew how to deal with cramped quarters.

The drive to Bunbury, in fact, seemed paradisal. Charcoal power made for a slow ride, especially up hills, but that only provided more time to enjoy the sun on their arms and the wind on their faces and to anticipate the company of the two women waiting for them in the rented cottage. Also contributing to the sense of well-being were the two cases of beer under their feet.

Before long the two men agreed that one beer apiece would not violate the letter's instruction. It was good beer, and strong. Bob remembered his feelings: "Feet up, head back, bottle of beer in hand. Life gets better all the time."

When they pulled into Bunbury, they spotted two sub sailors who turned out to be Harry Behrens, the *Tambor* quartermaster who had stayed behind on the relief crew because of an infected leg, and another relief-crew sailor they knew as Longears because, Bob recalled, "he had funny-shaped ears." Bob and Red decided to wait with their friends and swap stories while Harry and Longears waited for the bus. They sat on the stone steps of the courthouse, next door to the bus depot, and, with the storytelling, more beer was broken out. They didn't have an opener, but Bob had become expert at hooking the cap of one bottle on another and jerking it down so that the cap of the upright bottle popped cleanly off.

Harry and Longears explained what had attracted them to this quiet, little resort town for their leave. A couple of nights before, in Perth, they'd gone to a pub and met a pair of friendly nurses. The four of them had had fun together, and the women invited them along to a cottage they'd rented in Bunbury.

Bob and Red looked at each other, and Red fell silent. Harry and Longears continued. The day before had been the best day of their leave. They'd gone fishing and swimming with the nurses, then showered in a beachside community shower with partitions between the men's and women's sections that didn't reach all the way to the ceiling. There was only one bar of soap, so they tossed it to each other over the partition, an intimacy that led to an evening in the cottage with popcorn, beer, and a cozy fire. Harry and Longears had spent the night.

Red was visibly disgusted now and stormed off in the direction of the cottage. Then the bus arrived and Bob's two friends departed, leaving him alone with Louie, who was becoming impatient to return to Perth. When Red returned he was fuming. "I'm finished with that girl," he declared. "You can stay if you want, but I'm leaving."

Bob persuaded Red and Louie to wait while he made a quick trip to the cottage himself. He wanted to know if "his" nurse would still welcome him. When he arrived, the two friends complained about Red's jealous anger. "Red's" nurse exclaimed, "He chased me around the kitchen table with a butcher knife!"

Bob sympathized the best he could, then explained that he had to go back to the courthouse and have Louie drive him to the cottage with his things. Would that be okay with them? It would.

Back on the courthouse steps, Red was suffering. He'd thought he'd had something special with this girl. Bob felt it was only right to spend a few minutes with his friend before he had Louie drive him to the cottage. He grabbed another beer, sat next to Red on the stone steps, and hooked its cap to the cap of another. He jerked down on the lower one and its cap popped off—but he'd jerked too hard. The bottle shattered against the step and Bob's hand plunged into the broken glass, slashing a finger. The deep cut bled fiercely. It also hurt, and Red opened another beer to administer general anesthetic.

Now Bob wanted to go to the cottage, but Louie worried about his taxi. Finally he agreed to let Bob lie across the wooden beer cases and bleed into them rather than onto the seats. So Bob crawled in.

He must have passed out, because when he awoke there were two nurses standing over him, but they were in uniform and Bob was in the Perth hospital. As one of the nurses bandaged his hand, she said to the other: "There are two things these Yanks can't do. Ride motorcycles and open beer bottles. I'm getting tired of broken legs and bleeding hands."

The next day Bob returned to Bunbury, but without a second sailor to entertain the second nurse, "Red's" girl complained of loneliness. And the beach life was less fun than it could have been; with a heavily bandaged hand, Bob could not go into the ocean. After a single night at the cottage, they returned together to Perth.

What had started as a promising leave had become a great disappointment, leaving Bob with two mementos. The first was a permanent scar on his finger. It would be his only war wound, and he would not put in for a Purple Heart. The second was a set of three photos given to him by the beautiful Australian nurse. In one she sat on a wall, smiling into the camera. In the other two she was nude, once alone and once with her companion. It was, she said, a gift to remember her by. But after the next war patrol, the *Tambor* was sent back to Pearl Harbor, and he would never see her again.

CHAPTER NINE

Close Calls in the South China Sea

On the first day of May 1943, between the *Tambor*'s seventh and eighth patrols, Lieutenant Commander Armbruster was replaced as captain by Lt. Cdr. Russell Kefauver, the boat's former diving officer and one of the signatories, along with Davy Jones and Neptunus Rex, of Bob's Deep Submergence Certificate back in 1940. Although Kefauver's dark, mournful eyes and laconic nature made him resemble a basset hound more than anything else, he was just as much a sea creature as the other signers of that certificate, completely at home in the close confines and tense atmosphere of a submarine. With his slender frame, he even seemed built for the job. His first act as skipper was to order the crew to cut their leave short and report back to Fremantle to complete the boat's overhaul. Bob and Harry Behrens, who received the news in Katanning, ignored the order. They figured they had earned their two weeks off and were taking it, no matter what any new captain said, and were not convinced otherwise until the MPs came to town and told them to report back to the boat "or else." Bob and Harry weren't quite sure what "or else" meant, but decided it would be best not to find out, so they bought train tickets, got drunk, and crawled aboard for the trip back to the base.

When they stumbled off the train and got back to the boat, still redolent of the shaving lotion they'd tried to drink on the train after their booze ran out, they discovered they weren't the only *Tambor* sailors who had refused to report and had been rounded up from all over Western Australia. All fifteen or twenty of them appeared to be in various stages of inebriation or hangover as they slouched on the dock, but when Kefauver strode out briskly to address them, he fixed them all with a single glare from those dark eyes. "You men have deserted ship in time of war," he said calmly, "and I could have you all lined up and shot." So that was what "or else" meant. Despite his knowledge that the Navy couldn't afford to be shooting its submariners, Kefauver's demeanor made Bob feel, just for a moment, as if execution were a possibility. But Kefauver quickly went on: "Our boat is in terrible condition and I want every one of you to get aboard right now and go to work. You'll fix everything that's screwed up and I don't want you to stop until our boat is ready to go on war patrol." Every man on the dock ran to his station at once, and Bob worked until he could no longer hold his eyes open, two days and nights later. For as long as Kefauver stayed on the boat, he had the crew's full attention.

He was right about the boat. The relief crew, uncharacteristically, had done a bad job. Two of the eight valves on the blow and vent manifold were leaking, so the relief crew had taken it apart and ground the valves, but when they put it back together, all eight valves leaked. The firing valve on one of the tubes in the forward torpedo room wouldn't work no matter what they did to it. They had also received a load of torpedoes which needed extensive overhauling, or "routining," before the crew could be confident they would travel "hot, straight, and normal" when fired. Bob found himself suddenly in charge of these and all other operations in the forward room when Ernie Costa decided to stay in Australia with his girlfriend. When Kefauver put Bob in charge of the room it was a testament to the captain's confidence in his abilities and evidence that he held no grudges. Somehow, through long days and nights of hard work, the crew got the boat ready on time for its sixth war patrol.

As this work went on, the *Tambor* was moored next to the *Trout*. One afternoon the crew saw that a ceremony was forming up on its neighbor's deck. The crew of the *Trout* was being awarded the Presidential Unit Citation for an action in February 1942 that included delivering 3,500 rounds of ammunition to the beleaguered island of Corregidor and evacuating gold bars, silver pesos, securities, mail, and State Department dispatches from the Philippines. The *Tambor* crew had received no special recognition for their own recent mission to the Philippines, and, what was worse, they spotted on the deck of the *Trout* a former *Tambor* sailor. There, wearing a big grin on his face and a medal on his chest, was Bob's old buddy and one-time sparring partner Joe Magner, who had been on the *Tambor* as late as February 1942 and had transferred to the *Trout* only a few months earlier. "Don't give him a medal!" someone shouted, and someone else yelled, "Yeah! He just got on the boat!" But despite their jeering the ceremony went on, although Magner cast a couple of nervous glances their way. Bob watched silently, the whole scene confirming his opinion that the Navy always gave the medals to the wrong people and that if he were ever offered one he would reject it, with some choice words for whoever made the offer.

~~~~~~~~~~~

Never was a submariner's status as a member of the silent service more manifest than when his boat left port on a mission. There was some note of ceremony when the boat came back in—the relief crew rushed out to meet you, congratulated you for getting home in one piece, asked you how the hunting went, brought you fresh food and beer and mail, and picked up your laundry. And one of the high-ranking officers on base came out to greet the boat's officers and escort them to their quarters. But when you went out, there was no one to see you off except the two or three men from the relief crew who were needed to throw off the lines and haul in the gangplank. They wished you good luck and good hunting, and when you were on the line crew you replied: "If we don't come back, tell it like it was, and when the war's over, wave the flag for me on Market Street." It was a kind of ritual, and it was a way of looking forward to the end of the war and a big celebration in San Francisco—even if you might not be there. Then the boat slid quietly out of the harbor and you were gone, for who knew how long—maybe for good. Bob always found it a bit spooky, a bit lonely, and thrilling.

As the *Tambor* prepared to depart on May 7, Bob was at his usual station on the number-one line, and he was worried—not about the war patrol to come, but about the disposition of the sixteen pints of whiskey he had bought from a bootlegger the night before. Since he had nowhere to store it while he was gone, he would have to take it on the boat with him. He knew there would be enough room for it in the emergency food locker in the forward room once he took the food out of it, but the bootlegger hadn't shown up at the dock with the booze yet. Luckily, a new junior officer, fresh out of Annapolis, had been put in charge of the boat's departure, and since he didn't know what he was doing, things were moving very slowly. Bob had begun to worry, though, that Kefauver would lose patience with him and come down from his post on the bridge to supervise the departure himself. He didn't worry about pulling the wool over the eyes of a green junior officer, but he knew he couldn't con Kefauver.

The lines were finally singled up, the gangplank was hauled in, the number-two and -three lines were thrown off, and the boat had just begun to drift away from the dock when Bob spotted a figure running toward them with a paper sack cradled in his arms. When he reached the sub, Bob tossed him the money, but by now the boat's stern had swung too far from the dock for Bob to grab the sack, even when the bootlegger held it out at arms' length. Some of Bob's forward-room shipmates had noticed what was going on, however, and produced a big leather valise. Before Bob had time to wonder where they'd found it, Ole Clausen had flung it to the dock and the bootlegger had stuffed the bottles of whiskey into it. Then Ole threw him a heaving line, and the bootlegger ran it through the handle of the valise, which began to slide along the rope toward the boat. With sixteen full bottles of his finest inside, though, it sank to the middle of the rope and stuck where no one could quite reach it.

"Hold my feet!" Ole yelled, and the line crew grabbed him by the ankles and lowered him over the side. Dangling head downward, Ole pushed down on his end of the rope and the valise slid toward him—fast. When it reached him it hit the side of the boat with a loud clank. On the bridge, standing next to the captain, Harry Behrens heard the sound, but Kefauver was speaking with another officer and didn't notice. Quickly, they hauled Ole up, valise in hand, and hustled both to the hatch that led to the forward torpedo room. As they did, another newly assigned *Tambor* officer spotted his valise, loped forward, and demanded to know what the sailors were doing with his luggage. A row of sailors quickly blocked his path and explained that he could go no farther because he was not assigned to the number-one line. When he tried again to find out what they were doing with his valise, they assured him they were just taking it to storage in the forward torpedo room. The explanation puzzled him because he'd already taken the bag to the forward room himself for storage, but he couldn't get past the sailors and his valise wound up in its proper place again, so eventually he let the matter drop. In the meantime, the bootlegged liquor had been safely stowed in the forward room's emergency food locker.

As the *Tambor* departed on its eighth mission, the Japanese had not yet acknowledged the grievous loss they had suffered on April 18, 1943. Five days before that date the American code breakers had learned that Admiral Yamamoto would make a flight in the Pacific theater. Quickly, a plan was developed to go after his plane. U.S. P-38 Lightnings out of Guadalcanal intercepted the G4M bomber carrying the Admiral and, in a strike that lasted fewer than thirty seconds, sent it down over Bougainville. The loss of Japan's supreme naval commander and chief strategist was judged so traumatic and demoralizing that the Japanese government did not announce it publicly for a month.

Back in Washington, mid-May saw the Trident Conference, at which the Americans and British fenced over the issue of invading Europe in France or Sicily. The British urged a thrust from Sicily, through Italy, to the Balkans at the earliest possible date, and they complained that the Pacific war was distracting the United States from its responsibility to protect vital shipping in the North Atlantic. In the end, however, the American position prevailed. The Pacific effort would proceed unabated, and a date in the following year—May 1, 1944—was set for an invasion in France.

~~~~~~~~~~~~~~~~~~~~~~~~~~~~~~~~~~~~~

"Arrived at Exmouth today and stayed all night," Bob wrote in his diary on May 11. "Left this afternoon, headed for Lombok again. We think the next run will take us back to the States. Had a couple of air-raid warnings while we were here—the Japs bombed Darwin again." Exmouth was as far west as one could go in Western Australia, perched at the tip of a finger of land in the Indian Ocean pointing at the precariously narrow Lombok Strait between the Indonesian islands of Bali and Lombok. It was the *Tambor*'s point of entry into the Java Sea, and from there they would proceed through the Makassar Strait, between the islands of Celebes and Borneo, into the Celebes Sea, then northwest to the South China Sea. There, between Indochina and the Philippines, they would hunt the Japanese merchant ships passing back and forth between Japan and the resource-rich islands of the South Pacific.

Between Fremantle and Exmouth, Bob got acquainted with the new members of the crew. He made fast friends with a fellow named Fred Richardson, who worked in the engine room but dropped by the forward torpedo room regularly for a visit. Fred was tall and so skinny that his uniform looked like it was still on a hanger in a closet, but he told good stories and even recited poems that he claimed to have written himself. Fred was a valuable addition to the crew. He lifted everyone's spirits with his cheerfulness and gab. Also new on the boat was a junior officer named Alan Bergner, an ex-football player from Annapolis with a rock-solid physique. Bergner had brought on board a pair of the biggest and heaviest dumbbells anyone had ever seen and they were stored, of course, in the forward torpedo room. They nearly gave hernias to the guys who lugged them onto the boat, and once the *Tambor* was at sea they had to be tied down so they wouldn't roll around and injure the crew. When the torpedomen weren't busy, Bergner came into the forward room and did his exercises, and he usually left the dumbbells out for the men to tie down again.

In their first two weeks out of Exmouth they saw nothing but a few scattered planes and sailboats. Since Bob was now in charge of the forward room, he spent most of his time there and in the control room instead of at his old lookout, wheel, and bow-plane stations. His watch station was in the forward room, wearing a pair of headphones, ready to call the shots. He had also been ordered to train as the diving officer on his watch section—Kefauver's old duty. He enjoyed the training, as well as his other duties in the control room, but he didn't like being stuck below deck all the time.

The monotony of the patrol was relieved on the fourteenth by an unexpected guest—a goldfinch that landed on the arm of one of the lookouts. No one could figure how the little bird got so far out to sea. The lookout cradled it in his hand until his watch was over, then took it into the control room to show it to everyone on duty there. The bird was promptly dubbed "Sailor," and the mechanics in the engine room built a cage for it out of wire and spare parts. It was hung in the control room, and everyone spoke to Sailor on their way to topside lookout. Everyone was afraid that the pressure in the boat would kill the mascot when the boat dove, but he chirped happily on the makeshift perch in his cage as the boat went down.

On May 16, they spotted three patrol boats, none of which gave them any trouble; on May 18, in the Celebes Sea, they made two surface runs on what they thought at first were sampans, but which turned out, on closer inspection, to be logs. It wasn't until the twenty-sixth, when they reached the Hainan Strait—the passageway between the South China Sea and the Gulf of Tonkin—that they finally saw enemy ships. Following a trail of smoke, they submerged and spotted two freighters and a tanker. They made an end around and positioned themselves for a nighttime attack. When the time came, they made a surface approach under cover of darkness. They got close enough to see men on decks manning 6-inch guns, but all three torpedoes fired from the forward room missed. Early the next morning, they tried a submerged approach and fired four fish aft at the same targets, but again all missed. Both times the Japanese ships responded with depth charges, but the *Tambor* got away safely each time.

Entering the Gulf of Tonkin, the crew hoped for better luck with the torpedoes. They got it on May 29 when they scored three hits on a freighter and sank it. A second ship chased them away with depth charges, and all through the action Sailor sat in his cage in the control room and chirped merrily.

While the fish in the after torpedo room were being moved around, a loading line got entangled with a starting lever and the torpedo started running while it was still inside the boat—a "hot run." The ignition of alcohol and high-pressure air in the torpedo's combustion pot filled the room with acrid smoke and fumes, and before the crew could close the compartment's watertight door, smoke filled the boat. They had no choice but to surface so the hatches could be opened and the air exchanged. The Japanese support ship had left, luckily, and since they were already on the surface, Kefauver decided to look for survivors from the freighter they had sunk. They found two lifeboats crowded with sailors; some immediately held their hands up in surrender, while others jumped out and tried to swim away. The crew soon discovered that the sailors who remained in the lifeboats were the ship's Chinese crew and the ones who swam off were the Japanese officers. In enemy waters and with little room for prisoners, there was nothing they could do for the Chinese. With any luck they would be picked up by a patrol boat. But the *Tambor* was under orders to bring back Japanese officers, when possible. So they chased the swimmers but were able to capture only one, who wouldn't surrender until they sprayed the water around him with Tommy-gun fire.

One of Bob's shipmates marched the prisoner into the forward room, sat him on a stool, and aimed a .45 pistol at his head. The prisoner looked tiny and shriveled, and he shook with cold or fear, or both. Captain Kefauver entered the compartment, accompanied by the pharmacist's mate, who carried a tumbler and a bottle of whiskey. The prisoner began to jabber excitedly, then, realizing that they couldn't understand him, gestured elaborately and slid from the stool onto his knees. Kefauver explained that he was going through his death ritual.

Bob had never heard of such a thing, but when the prisoner pointed his finger at his temple, his meaning was clear enough. They waved their hands and shook their heads, the guard lowered his pistol, and the pharmacist's mate poured a glass of whiskey and offered it to the prisoner. He looked at the glass, then at Bob, who grabbed the tumbler and took a big belt out of it, then offered it again to the prisoner. This time he took the tumbler and downed the rest of the whiskey in one gulp. *There are some things we all understand,* Bob thought.

After the prisoner-taking, things were quiet for two weeks. Then, in the South China Sea, for two weeks there were Japanese ships, patrol boats, and airplanes everywhere. The SJ radar went out again, so they received no advance warning of enemy vessels or planes, and the lookouts had a lively time. The crew was kept so busy shuttling back and forth from their regular watches to battle stations that no one could get a decent night's sleep. The only good thing about it was that all the activity made the time go faster. May passed into June almost without notice, and early on the morning of June 2, just past midnight, the lookouts spotted a white light shining through the darkness. Following it for nearly three hours, they finally drew close to a seven-thousand-ton Japanese freighter. With the freighter less than a thousand yards away, Bob stood in the middle of the forward room, his crew at their stations, awaiting the order to fire. When the order came down through Bob's headphones, he relayed it to the men at the switches. They fired one fish, which missed, then another; Bob waited to hear the explosion, but instead heard a panicked lookout shout into the phones: *"Circular run and here it comes!"*

The torpedo they had just fired had missed its target, made a wide turn, and was coming back at them. It happened more often than anyone liked to think about, usually due to a faulty gyroscope. Bob braced himself for impact as the boat pitched sharply to the right.

"It missed us," he heard the lookout mutter over the phones. Kefauver had ordered full right rudder quickly and dodged it. Bob hardly had time to relay the news to the crew before he heard another hoarse shout from the lookout: *"Captain, here it comes again!"*

Bob couldn't believe it. The fish was making a *second* circle and was headed at the boat again. This time, he knew, there was no time to evade it, so he gripped the iron bar of a torpedo skid and waited. The silence in his ears was deafening, until it was broken at last by the lookout's voice in the phones: *"Missed again."*

Bob loosened his grip on the torpedo skid. Slowly, they all shook off the scare. Then the order came down to prepare to fire torpedoes. The men readied themselves, and Bob listened through his phones. When the fire order came down, he repeated it, and the boat lurched slightly as compressed air launched the fish from their tubes. A few seconds later they heard a shattering boom. "Got him," the lookout cried.

Photo 15. The *Eisho Maru* sunk May 29, 1943, on the *Tambor's* eighth war patrol. Photograph taken through the *Tambor* periscope. (U.S. Navy)

After the engagement, when the torpedo room had been secured from battle station, Bob sat on his bunk and wrote in his war diary: "One of the fish ran erratic and came back at us. We gave her full rudder & it missed us—a little more & she would of blown us all to hell. It wasn't half an hour ago so am still a little shaken—first time really scared." Still, the peak and roll of his handwriting, rising and falling like the waves of the sea, showed no sign of perturbation. He concluded: "One hit on the ship & she went down fast—it makes quite a sight to watch as long as it's the other guy. Have had a lot of trouble with the fish. Hope we get at least another ship. We sure don't want any more tangles with our own fish."

The Japanese officer, nicknamed "Gus," became a crew favorite. He helped with chores around the boat, doing everything asked of him, and the only time they had any trouble with him was when they were in the middle of an attack and he yelled "Banzai!"

"Can't tell if he's for us or not," Bob wrote. "We watch him pretty closely."

On June 7, back in the Hainan Strait, they sighted a four-thousand-ton enemy ship in shallow, murky water, and fired three fish. One found its target, and it was enough to sink the ship. The action had been so heavy that they were down to only two torpedoes, both aft, plus one forward that had been flooded but might be repairable. "We have been afraid of mines in this area," Bob had written in his diary, and one day, with the boat submerged in shallow water, he heard an odd noise from outside—like a dull saw scraping across the hull. It traveled slowly, forward to aft, and Bob reported the noise over the phones to the control room. They had heard it, too, and said it was a mine cable scraping along the side of the boat as they slid forward. All they could do was hope that the cable didn't catch on a railing or on the propeller guards. The noise receded from the forward room as the boat moved ahead and the cable moved aft, and Bob listened through the phones as the control room reported its progress: "Moving across the engine room . . . now across the maneuvering room . . . now the after torpedo room. . . . " If the cable scraped past the after torpedo room and cleared the stern planes, Bob knew they'd be safe. He waited and listened. Finally, a voice said in his phones: "All clear."

With the boat running low on torpedoes, the pace of the action eased. They sighted seven ships on the tenth but lost them, then headed back to the South China Sea, running on the surface. On the fourteenth they spotted another small freighter but were too close to the beach to battle surface, so they had to let it go. "We are going to try and get just one more before we head in," Bob wrote. On the 16th, they found four more ships and fired the rest of their torpedoes, but scored no hits. The ships fired back, aiming at the *Tambor*'s periscopes, and Bob wrote: "We could hear the slugs going through the water." They had sunk three ships on the patrol, but it had taken twenty-two torpedoes to do it. "Not a very good percentage," Bob noted. Now, out of torpedoes and armed only with the deck gun, they had no choice but to head home.

On the way back, Bergner resumed his workouts, always leaving his dumbbells to be tied back down by the forward-room crew. Fred Richardson was commiserating with Bob about it when he suddenly snapped his fingers. "If you don't want to stash 'em," he said, grinning, "why not trash 'em?" Like all the other American subs, the *Tambor* packed its trash into burlap bags, one or two per compartment, weighed each bag down with a brick so it would sink to the bottom, and threw the bags over the side every night that they weren't at battle stations. Fred had just been assigned to the nightly garbage detail, and so the next night, when he and the rest of the detail came to the forward room, there was an extra item in each of the two bags of trash. Fred had recruited two extra men so there would be two on each bag to manage the extra weight. Even without the usual bricks inside, they were heavier than usual. When the detail reached the control-room ladder, Fred hollered up "Permission to dump trash and garbage" and received the reply "Permission granted." The men in the control room, who were also in on the plan, helped boost the extra-heavy bags up the ladder to the bridge. Once the bags were topside, Harry Behrens, who was in on the plan as well, helped them lift the bags up and over the side. Bob was stretched out on his bunk in the forward room when he heard first one thump, then a second, as the bags hit the side of the hull where it bulged out at the waterline. Then he rolled over and dozed contentedly.

~~~~~~~~~~~~~~~~~~~~~~~~~~~~~~~~

They pulled back into Fremantle on June 27. "The end of another patrol run," wrote Bob. "That makes eight—as many or more than any other sub in the Navy." By this time, Bob was one of the only men left who had made all eight runs; most of the rest of the *Tambor*'s original crew had been shipped out to other boats or opted to stay behind on the relief crew, like Ernie Costa. After a run as harrowing as the one they had just undergone, with the circular run and the mine-cable scare, there was liable to be even more attrition. Captain Kefauver's patrol report noted: "The medical officer reports 15 men who have made seven or eight war patrols show various degrees of fatigue or staleness, with some pallor, rapid soft pulse, and low blood pressure. On inspection there were other ailments of minor nature and one of valvular heart disease." Despite the celebratory air of the crew's return to port, this time the rigors of their patrol had left them too worn out to wish for much else than to shower, shave, and get rid of all their dirty laundry. (Bob, who liked a fresh change every couple of days while on patrol, had accumulated forty-five pairs of undershorts and almost as many T-shirts.) The crew was pale, their hair was long, and some of them wore beards as well. Many stared with glazed eyes, as if they were still looking for bumps on the horizon. They didn't really want to talk to anyone but each other. As an ex-submariner explained succinctly years after the war: "Brother, we were alone. . . . When we came back, hell, we didn't want to mix with guys from destroyers and cruisers. We was in submarines. We was different."[1]

What happened after they tied up at Fremantle only increased their feelings of alienation. Gus wished to say goodbye to the crew, and he made a point of shaking each man's hand, bowing as he did so. For his departure, he'd been given a pair of dungarees, a Brooklyn Dodgers sweatshirt, and a white navy cap, which he wore tilted at a jaunty angle like the American crewmen. Half a dozen Marines, having been informed that the *Tambor* was returning with a prisoner, waited on the deck. As soon as Gus poked his head through the hatch, two Marines hauled him up while the others covered him with their guns. Then he was handcuffed, blindfolded, and led away. The crew knew he was an enemy officer, but they'd grown genuinely fond of him, so the scene upset them. They never found out what happened to the man.

That wasn't the worst of it. As Bob walked across the deck, trying to suppress his anger, he came upon a group of his shipmates clustered around Sailor's cage. They looked even more desolate than Bob felt, and he asked what was wrong. The man nearest him merely took a step back, so Bob could see. The little finch, whose indifference to danger had boosted everyone's morale, lay dead in the bottom of the cage.

"What happened to him?" he asked.

"When we brought him topside," one of the men said, "we all gathered around to see how he'd like his new home, but he took one breath and fell over."

"Guess he got to be just like us," someone else said. "Couldn't stand the fresh air anymore."

Some homecoming, Bob thought and felt a need to be alone and apart, even from his shipmates. He climbed to the bridge and sat in a gap in the railing, but had been there only a moment when he noticed a civilian on the dock, aiming a camera at him. Bob started to move, but the man held up his hand. He wanted to get his picture, but Bob told him, in the plainest and most vivid language he could muster, what he could do with his camera.

~~~~~~~~~~~~~~~~

The *Tambor's* ninth war patrol lasted from July 20 to September 12, 1943. "This one will take us back to Pearl Harbor and then to the States, or so we hope," Bob wrote. The longer they stayed away from the States, the wilder everyone seemed to get, and they were rapidly wearing out their welcome in Western Australia. Bob himself, perhaps because of his frustrating leave, had gotten into not one but two scrapes the day before they left. The first time was in the bar at the Ocean Beach, where he and Louie were having a farewell beer or three. Louie said something that Bob interpreted as an insult, and Bob poured his beer over Louie's head, inadvertently setting off a chain reaction among the other sailors at the bar, who also poured their drinks over the heads of whoever sat next to them. Soon beer, chairs, fists, and other objects were flying through the air and across the bar, and the hotel manager called the shore patrol. Louie hustled Bob out to his cab and drove him back to the boat—a pretty sporting thing to do under the circumstances, but that was the kind of fellow Louie was. It was the last Bob ever saw of him.

That evening, the farewell party at the Ocean Beach spilled out onto the strand outside the hotel, despite the fact that the crew's departure the next morning was supposed to be a secret. The ethic of the silent service had seen better days. Earlier that day, when Bob was in downtown Perth, he had encountered his shipmate John Scaduto leaning out the window of a taxi and yelling, "*The Tambor's leaving tomorrow and those Japs are gonna catch hell!*" Now, as Bob sat in the sand outside the hotel and chatted with one of the many girls who were at the party, a sailor he didn't recognize walked up and started to cuss him out. Bob invited him around to a shadowy corner to settle the matter. The man wasn't much with his fists, and after taking a few punches to the face, he turned and ran toward the hotel. He was halfway up a wooden staircase leading to a service entrance in the back when Bob caught up to him and grabbed his ankle. The sailor fell and hit his head on one of the steps, knocking himself out. A group of his shipmates then ran up, apologized to Bob, and carted the man off; Bob thought that was the end of it. The next morning, however, as he was handling the number-one line, his hands aching and his knuckles skinned raw from the punches he had landed on the guy's face, the shore patrol came looking for a submariner who bore the marks of having been in a fight. The sailor, it seemed, had suffered a concussion when his head hit the step. They were also looking for the sub sailor who caused the ruckus at the Ocean Beach bar, not realizing that the two were one and the same. Bob managed to avoid them until the boat shoved off. Maybe it was a good thing he wouldn't be back in Western Australia for a while.

The ninth war patrol saw many opportunities, but meager results. They headed for the South China Sea again, by way of the Lombok and Makassar straits, the Java Sea, and around the northern tip of Borneo. For once, they enjoyed fine weather the whole time, but the only action they saw for the first two weeks was a dive after making radar contact with an enemy plane and firing a shot across the bow of a sampan that wandered too close. Then, on August 3, they sighted a convoy of five freighters escorted by a destroyer. They executed a perfect end-around maneuver, running ahead of the convoy, then laying in wait for a shot. When the freighter drew within eight hundred yards of them, they fired a spread of four fish, two of which hit the freighter and sank it. The destroyer then dropped eleven depth charges on them, and Bob wrote that "three of them came quite close." They tried to attack again via a surface approach after dark but were screened off by the destroyer.

The next twelve days were filled with frustration, as the enemy ships that were reported to be in the area eluded them. "There is a lot of water to cover," noted Bob, "so it's easy to miss them. It's been a good run so far—on the surface most of the time, and plenty of sun, but I sure wish we could get rid of some fish forward." On the sixteenth, however, a four-thousand-ton freighter was sighted, apparently unescorted. It was close to the beach but, at about five thousand yards away, out of torpedo range. The crew saw no large guns mounted on the ship, so Captain Kefauver decided on a daring maneuver: the *Tambor* would battle-surface and try to force the freighter onto the beach with fire from their new 5-inch gun. It had been installed on the boat's deck during its last refitting, replacing the old 3-inch gun. Bob was the rammer on the gun crew; his job was to force the big shell into the gun's chamber with a long ramrod. The powder and explosive device were then loaded, the breech was closed, and the gun was ready to fire. When the battle-surface order was given, Bob and the rest of the gun crew scrambled to the control room to go up the conning-tower ladder, out the hatch, and onto the deck. The 5-inch gun required a larger crew than the 3-inch—in addition to Bob there were the gunner's mate, a pointer, a trainer, and ammunition handlers—and getting the ramrod up the ladder and out the hatch proved to be quite awkward. When the gun crew finally made it onto the deck and were readying to fire the gun, a patrol boat came roaring up out of Cam-ranh Bay and fired on them. The shots fell short at first but kept getting closer, the bullets zinging through the water as the men struggled to load the gun. The order to commence firing came down the line, but at the crucial moment only a loud metallic click rang out from the deck gun.

It had not fired. Everyone looked at each other, not knowing what to do next, and the gunfire from the patrol boat drew closer. Somebody yelled to abandon the gun and somebody else yelled to man it. Half the gun crew obeyed the first order and the other half obeyed the second. Confusion reigned. Bob stood in the middle of the chaos with his ramrod, trying not to bean anyone with it as they ran past him. Finally, in pure exasperation, he heaved it as far over the side as he could. The ammunition handlers followed his lead and dumped their ammo, and since there was no longer any reason for them to be topside, they ran for the hatch and slid down the ladder to safety, with shots from the patrol boat ringing in their ears. Moments later, Kefauver gave the order to dive, and they remained submerged for almost seven hours, until they had reached the shipping lanes in the middle of the South China Sea.

The rest of the patrol was plagued by the same sort of bad luck, mostly with the torpedoes. On three separate occasions—August 21, 22, and 24—they worked the boat into perfect position to attack enemy ships and were betrayed by the fish each time. On the twenty-first, they fired seven torpedoes at an unescorted eight-ship convoy but scored only one hit, which did no damage. The next day they got three hits on a 17,000-ton *Nissin Maru*, one of the largest of all the Japanese tankers, but the fish merely bounced off the ship's hull. "It is damn disappointing to have things like this happen," Bob wrote in his diary. Kefauver, in his patrol report, was more laconic but no less dismayed: "Fired five torpedoes at *Nissin Maru*. Saw three perfect hits amidships. Torpedoes bounced off side and one exploded in wake. No damage." On the twenty-fourth, they got the stern tubes trained on the same *maru* again, but a short-circuit in the torpedoes' indicating-course motors caused a firing malfunction, and by the time it was corrected, the huge tanker had lumbered out of range. Bob was so frustrated that he threw his lucky Buddha into the forward-room bilges, but retrieved it soon after. Running out of torpedoes, and with their equipment going bad, they headed for home.

After the long homeward cruise, when they approached Midway on the night of September 7, they were suddenly challenged by a blinker. It was the *Finback*, another submarine in their squadron, and despite all the precautions taken to prevent subs from drawing friendly fire, no one on board either ship was aware of the other's presence. Had the *Tambor* not responded immediately with the proper recognition symbol, the *Finback* would have blown it out of the water. The two boats ran to Midway together, and after refueling there they both headed for Pearl Harbor, reaching it on the twelfth. From there it was on to San Francisco and a major overhaul at Bethlehem Steel that would last two months. It would be the longest Bob had spent on dry land since the start of the war.

Captain Kefauver's first two war patrols as the boat's skipper had shown that this man with the basset-hound eyes was quite a hunting dog. He was aggressive and imaginative without being reckless, and he got the best out of his crew by making it clear, in his own quiet way, that he trusted them. His air of calm confidence was infectious, inspiring the crew to stay cool in tight spots. His decision to battle-surface and run the Japanese freighter aground with 5-inch fire was the sort of bold maneuver that tacticians would have noted—if only the gun had worked. With any luck, in fact, the *Tambor*'s ninth war patrol would have been talked about for a long time; they had come tantalizingly close to a clean sweep and the sinking of a 17,000-ton tanker. But they had had only the worst kind of luck.

~~~~~~~~~~~~~~~~~~~~~~~~~~~~~~~~~~~~~

Each member of the *Tambor* crew was scheduled to spend one of his two months in San Francisco working on the docks at Bethlehem Steel and one on leave. Bob was one of the group that went on leave the first month, and he set off for Decorah for the first time in almost two years. The train to Cedar Rapids wasn't very crowded this time, and most of the passengers were wearing uniforms. With the war effort going full steam and travel restrictions in effect, it was hard for a civilian to get a train ticket. When Bob got to Decorah, R. C. called the local newspaper to tell them his son was back home, then got busy lining up speeches and appearances for him all over town, despite Bob's pleas for him to stop. All Bob wanted to do was get some rest, and there was very little he was allowed to tell anyone about his experiences anyway. But R. C. could not be dissuaded. He even made Bob go to church with him, the first time Bob had been in a house of worship since entering the service.

After the places he had been and the sights he had seen in the past two years, Decorah seemed smaller than ever, and when R. C. wasn't keeping him busy, Bob struggled to find ways to pass the time. One night he went to a local dance hall and met an attractive, dark-haired girl who took an immediate interest in him. She lived in Cresco, twenty miles away, so he suggested that she spend the night in Decorah and go home the next morning. She eagerly accepted, leaving only the problem of *where* they would spend the night. Bob was staying in the basement of R. C.'s apartment in back of the store, and although a bed was down there, it was not a good place for an overnight guest, since the apartment's only bathroom was also in the basement and R. C. might come down the stairs to use it in the middle of the night. After some discussion, they decided to check into the local hotel as husband and wife. They spent a very enjoyable evening together, but the next day word was all over town that Bob had spent the night with a girl in a hotel room—quite a scandalous bit of gossip in 1943. Nevertheless, Bob saw the girl a couple more times before he left town and even ended up taking another girl, whom he met at a country-club dance, to the bed in R. C.'s basement. The conditions weren't ideal, but if serving on a submarine had taught him anything, it was that an unfinished basement was no special hardship.

Those were the good times, such as they were in Decorah; there were also some bad experiences, such as the time Bob was invited to a dinner party at the home of one of his old high-school football teammates. Bob was expecting a small, informal dinner, and his heart sank when he walked into the dining room of his friend's house and saw the white lace tablecloth, fine china, and crystal wineglasses. Not only that, but his friend's entire family—Mom, Dad, and even his Aunt Hattie and Uncle Charley—were all there to get a look at the "war hero." When Bob sat at the head of the table he felt like a fish in a bowl, everyone staring at him curiously as if not quite convinced he was real. After he was seated, coffee was served, and Bob was confronted with the additional problem of trying to drink out of a dainty porcelain cup. On the *Tambor*, Bob, like most of his shipmates, drank coffee by the gallon, but always in a mug large enough for him to hold steady with both his trembling hands. He tried to bring the tiny cup up to his lips quickly and take fast sips between tremors, but it was hard work. Only by locking his other hand firmly onto the cup was he able to manage the trajectory from saucer to lips. When he looked up from his exertions, he saw that all eyes were still on him, staring more wonderingly than ever. Somehow Bob got through dinner, but when one of the other guests, a girl with whom he had gone to high school, said she needed a ride home, Bob volunteered immediately. He dropped her off in front of her house with barely a good-night and went straight back to R. C.'s apartment, his safe haven.

A few days later, R. C. came down to the basement to shake Bob awake and tell him he had an emergency phone call upstairs. Through the fog and throb of a pounding hangover, Bob recognized the voice on the line as that of a girl he had met a week or so ago, the fiancée of another high-school friend. They had invited him to their wedding breakfast, and he had forgotten all about it. Now she was calling, in tears, to say that there were thirteen people at the breakfast and they needed him to come at once so they wouldn't have an unlucky number of guests. Bob resisted, but finally relented, and staggered back downstairs to put on his wrinkled uniform. When he arrived, everyone immediately sat down to eat, and the bride stopped crying, so he felt he had done a good deed. The feeling, however, did nothing to help him through the next hour, which was filled with the sights and aromas of food and coffee, which set waves of nausea through his stomach. He tried to distract himself by talking to the priest, who was seated next to him, but he knew so little about Catholicism that he didn't even know how to address him. Since the priest was the head man, he decided to call him "sir," as he would a Navy officer. The priest didn't seem to mind, but talking to him did nothing to ease the pounding in his skull. As he had at the dinner party, he found a way to endure, but the unfamiliar situations taxed him.

By the time his leave was over, he was eager to get back to the boat and back to business. It was useless to try to rest. It felt as though he would never get as much sleep as he needed until the war was over, and he could do nothing in Decorah that would make that day come any sooner. And, strangely, the *Tambor* felt more like home to him now than anywhere else. Also, it felt different to be in Decorah now, not because the town had changed, but because he had.

~~~~~~~~~~~~~~~~~~~~~~~~~~~~~

When Bob got back to San Francisco, Captain Kefauver sent him to the engineering and design department at Bethlehem Steel to discuss a modification Bob had suggested in the design of the forward torpedo room. On a previous patrol, during a torpedo reload in high seas, a fish had gotten loose and a crewmate had ducked his head away just in time as two torpedoes rolled and clanked together. His hand had been caught, however, and was smashed. After the accident, Bob recognized that the small H-shaped beam across the front of the room was not heavy enough to support the torpedoes during reload and, further, that if the hinge that held the beam in place were replaced by pins, the cumbersome process would be easier to manage, especially during rough weather. A design draughtsman listened to Bob's ideas attentively, prepared a sketch, and soon every boat that came in for refit received the modifications. Bob felt gratified. The redesign probably prevented injuries, and it may have saved lives. Sometimes the Navy got things right.

Bob also developed an appreciation for the Navy way while working on the boat's overhaul with the civilian yard workmen at the Bethlehem Steel shipyard. The civilians were unionized and their ways of doing things involved elaborate procedures; when a lightbulb burned out, the yard workmen would report it, write a purchase order for the lightbulb, and fill out a work order for an electrician to screw it into the socket. A sub sailor, on the other hand, would either just get a lightbulb from spare parts and screw it in or steal one from somewhere else. There was a saying around the shipyard about sub sailors that Bob really liked, and that summed up nicely their way of doing things: If a submariner finds something that's in the wrong place, he picks it up; if he can't pick it up, he moves it out of the way; if he can't move it, he paints it.

While in San Francisco, Bob spent his free time either hanging around with Fred Richardson or drinking in a bar near the shipyard where the other sailors and workmen gathered. Fred had a lot of connections in the area, and it seemed that Bob always met someone interesting when he was with him. They were in the club room at the Bay Meadows racetrack, betting a few dollars and enjoying watching the horses run, when a man walked up to Fred, took him by the arm, and asked in an authoritative voice, "What are you doing here?" Bob thought they were in trouble until the man started laughing and pumping Fred's hand. It turned out that he was the president of one of the biggest banks in Los Angeles. Fred had been his regular caddie at the Los Angeles Country Club and used to drive him home and sneak him past his wife when the man had spent too much time at the clubhouse bar. Fred also introduced Bob to a fellow named Buster Wildes, a Hollywood stuntman and a good friend of Errol Flynn's. Fred also seemed to know all the jockeys at the racetrack and was glad to introduce Bob around.

The most interesting person Bob met while in San Francisco, though, was a very attractive young woman. One of Bob's friends lined her up as his date for a ship's party, and Bob recognized her charm right away. He might have been interested in seeing more of her, but he learned that she was married. She was, in fact, married to three men. She specialized, it seemed, in finding men about to go overseas or into battle and convincing them to marry her. That way, she got an allotment check from the government every month for each husband—if he survived—and a $10,000 insurance payoff if he didn't. Presumably she had a plan if more than one of her men survived the war, because she seemed to be in the market for yet more husbands. She had picked the wrong man in Bob, however, who had no intention of getting married. In any event, the war saved him from having to resist her charms, which were considerable. The *Tambor* was ordered back to Pearl Harbor on December 7, 1943, the second anniversary of the Japanese surprise attack, to prepare for its tenth war patrol.

Before the boat left for Pearl, they took on a very young-looking chief yeoman who needed a ride to Oahu. He was assigned to bunk in the forward torpedo room, and during the cruise Bob asked him how he made chief at such a tender age. "I just went to my exec and asked for it," he replied. The words had barely escaped his mouth when the *Tambor*'s own executive officer, Ed Spruance, appeared in the forward room, on his way to the head. Bob thought it must be some kind of sign, so he waited until Spruance came out and told him he wanted to be a chief.

"Okay, you got it," Spruance said as he ducked through the watertight door. "I'll do the paperwork when we get to Pearl."

So Bob had made chief. It was an old Navy tradition to throw a man over the side when he made that grade, so Bob knew what was coming. When the boat had tied up at Pearl on December 15 and his shipmates began to gather around him on the deck, Bob was wearing a chief's cap that Chesty DeBay had given him when he heard about the promotion. So Bob took the cap off and handed it to Tom Handley for safekeeping. The water in the harbor was still oily from the attack two years earlier, and Bob didn't want the cap to get ruined when they threw him in. True to tradition, Bob's crewmates picked him up and tossed him into the water. Then Tom Handley threw the chief's cap in after him. Then all the other sailors on deck started throwing each other in, until the slick, glistening water was filled with their bobbing, white-capped heads. Ed Spruance happened to walk by, and despite his rank he got thrown over too.

CHAPTER TEN

The Tenth Mission:
Peril and the Navy Cross

On January 5, 1944, soon after the *Tambor* departed Pearl Harbor on its tenth war patrol, there were difficulties controlling the boat during practice dives. Bob blamed the new armor plating that had been added to the conning tower and wrote in his journal: "Doesn't look too good for operating in enemy waters." After taking on fuel at Midway and cruising westward, Bob added on the fourteenth: "Weather isn't too good. It's hard on the new members of the crew. We are now in enemy waters so anything can happen." Bob usually wasn't so fretful in his diary; perhaps he had a premonition. The *Tambor*'s tenth patrol would bring its closest brush with destruction—and perhaps its finest performance of the war.

Its mission—to seek and attack Japanese supply convoys—would take it to the East China Sea, near the southern tip of the main Japanese islands, and to the northern entrance of the Formosa Strait. The boat would log roughly ten thousand miles and arrive back at Pearl after sixty-one days at sea—ten days overdue. Two weeks out, as the boat neared the Bonin Islands, 620 miles due south of Tokyo, the rough weather continued. Radar officer Robert Dye recalled standing topside watch "with one foot on the deck and the other on the bridge starboard bulkhead" to steady himself as the boat pitched. It was winter, and the men wore sheepskin coats that quickly became soaked through with seawater washing over the bridge. To sleep, Dye tucked himself between a pillow and a rolled blanket to keep from being thrown from his bunk.[1] In the forward room, the high seas complicated the delicate job of working over the torpedoes. Bob and his crew completed the task, however, and the fish would perform well.

Along for the rough ride was Lt. Cdr. G. N. Schiff, a Navy physician. His stated purpose for going out with the *Tambor* was to conduct tests of air and drinking water quality, and he did culture water samples in an incubator. But he also found occasions to talk with members of the crew, and it was widely believed that his true purpose was to observe them under the stresses of a long war patrol. "There were a lot of sub sailors cracking up," Bob said, "and I guess he was trying to understand why."

Schiff spent a lot of time in the forward room, near his bunk in the adjacent officers' quarters, and Bob liked him. "He was a big guy—he had kind of a Santa Claus way about him—and I tried to keep the guys from messing with him too much." They enjoyed toying with his experiments—dropping raw eggs or bits of food into his incubator—and saying strange things to him during their little "chats." "They thought he was a shrink," Bob said, "and they'd say things to him like, 'I love my dog but I hate my sister.' He seemed to take all this seriously, so I tried to tell them to stop."

The Navy physician could not have picked a better patrol on which to observe sub sailors under the stress of battle. Seventeen days out, on the morning of January 22, a lookout sighted the masts and stacks of a *Natori*-class cruiser escorted by two destroyers. As the ships moved in and out of rain squalls, the *Tambor* ran ahead and lay in wait, preparing for its shot. But the ships did not appear as expected. Captain Kefauver speculated that one of the destroyers had picked them up on radar and that the ships had changed course when hidden by the weather. "A cruiser would have been nice to start off with," Bob wrote. "Two destroyers would have made trouble, but I think most of the crew wanted a shot at them."

Two nights later the *Tambor* slid into the East China Sea, past Amami-Oshima, the northernmost island of the Ryukyu chain that includes, to the south, Okinawa. Now on station less than three hundred miles south of Nagasaki, periscope sightings included a patrol boat, a Zero fitted with float pontoons, and searchlights sweeping the sea out from Amami-Oshima. Then, three days later, on January 28, the boat spotted what it had come for. First, in the early light, a patrol boat appeared, and shortly afterward smoke rose above the horizon. Submerged, the *Tambor* investigated and discovered a convoy of nine ships steaming south, including at least one destroyer and three patrol boats for protection. Kefauver decided to conduct training drills and shadow the convoy as he waited for dark. Then, at 8:35 that night, a second convoy appeared, heading north. The Americans sat in the middle of a shipping lane and saw targets all around them. Visibility was poor, however, and it was difficult to fix position and course to plan an attack. But finally, at midnight, Kefauver fastened to the northbound convoy and approached it from astern of port.

There were seven ships—three large *maru* escorted by four patrol boats—and Kefauver diagrammed the formation in his patrol report. As the *Tambor* maneuvered to attack the near *maru*—a ten-thousand-ton freighter—crewman Tom Lampley stood a lookout post and gunner's mate "Nip" Howard was assigned to the 20-mm machine gun, in case a battle surface was called. Bob Hunt manned the

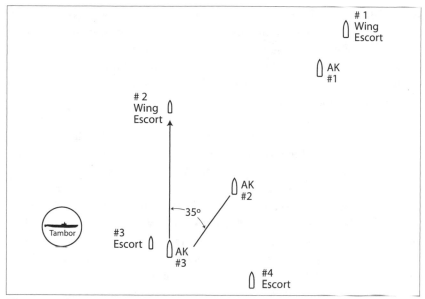

Figure 3. In his report on the *Tambor's* tenth war patrol, Lieutenant Commander Kefauver sketched the formation of ships the boat attacked in the East China Sea. The *Tambor* sank two ships before a Japanese destroyer drove it to the bottom and depth-charged it for seventeen hours.

phones in the forward room, prepared to fire a spread of three torpedoes on orders from the conning tower. In the conning tower, Captain Kefauver stood near Bob Dye as the radar officer monitored range from target. The captain asked XO Ed Spruance to man the bridge, explaining later, "I didn't want to scare myself by seeing the ships so close."

It would be a close shot—closer, even, than Kefauver intended. He had brought the sub to within 1,650 yards of its target when the freighter zigged 45 degrees to the left, unwittingly nearing the *Tambor*. When the captain gave his order to fire, the range was just 600 yards, near the minimum for the torpedoes to arm before they struck their target. No sooner was the first fish away than the escort turned on its red truck light, increased speed, and headed for the *Tambor*. Kefauver ordered the second torpedo away, then turned the boat hard to port to evade the onrushing escort. In the forward room, water flew as the tubes vented into the bilges, sucking air bubbles and seawater back into the boat to prevent detection and maintain the sub's trim. Then the reload process began, but Bob knew something was happening above when the boat went left full rudder and all ahead frantic.

Both torpedoes ran properly, and when they hit their target smoke and fire shot from the freighter. At such close range, the impact knocked the *Tambor's* lookouts back against the periscope shears. Tom Lampley, the starboard lookout, saw bodies and debris spinning in the flash. The patrol boat, however, continued to come on, its bow pointed straight at the *Tambor*, its searchlight probing for the sub. As it loomed, gunner's mate Howard saw Japanese sailors in white uniforms running to man their deck guns. Kefauver, who had stepped to the bridge to fire the torpedoes, reported: "All hands . . . were convinced that ramming amidships was inevitable."

On the 20-mm gun, Carlos Clifton "Nip" Howard was a recent addition to the crew. A former Golden Gloves boxing champion, he had enlisted with his brother Raymond, and the two had hoped to serve on the same ship. But after the five Sullivan brothers from Waterloo, Iowa, all died when the cruiser USS *Juneau* went down, siblings were not permitted to fight together. Raymond was posted to the submarine *Grayling*, and when it went missing in the Philippines, September 1943, he was lost with the rest of the crew. Nip then volunteered for sub duty. It was the best way, he said, to "even the score."

Tom Lampley, on his lookout perch, braced for impact. "I considered that [the patrol boat was] twelve to fifteen feet from hitting us," he recalled. "I know when their searchlights hit me I thought they were bullets and I thought, well, it really don't hurt to die, after all." The bullets, however, were flying in the other direction. Firing in a continuous burst, Nip Howard raked the deck of the patrol boat, knocking out the searchlight, sending a hail of fire into the bridge, and stopping the sailors racing for their guns. As the 20-mm blazed, the escort was so close that Kefauver read the numbers on its bow by the light of the tracers. Bullets may have struck the Japanese helmsman, because the patrol boat veered off course and passed a mere twenty yards to the *Tambor*'s stern. Lampley, who had a front-row balcony view, later said: "I believe that when Nip was shooting out the searchlights and raking the bridge with his fire that the helmsman was knocked down while holding onto the wheel, and as he went down he put right full rudder on his craft."[2]

By the time the escort recovered itself, the *Tambor* had escaped into the dark, having sunk a ten-thousand-ton freighter. In view of the near ramming, that might seem to have been enough, but once the *Tambor* lost the patrol boat, Kefauver ordered the sub to reverse course and pursue the other two freighters. Back charged the escort, however, this time dropping depth charges, so the *Tambor* changed course again, still hoping to regain contact with the convoy but without luck.

Bob had heard the gunfire from below in the forward room, and once he had secured his room from battle stations he learned the full story of the encounter. "We are very lucky to get by with this deal we just pulled," he wrote in his diary. "This guy on the machine gun will probably get a medal, as he really saved us from getting rammed."

When daylight arrived that morning, the *Tambor* submerged and patrolled southward along the Ryukyu Islands, then surfaced in the evening and head-ed west to intercept convoys at the mouth of the Formosa Strait. On the way, however, noise in a stern-plane drive revealed a burned-out bushing. The boat carried no spare, so the machinists had to fashion a replacement, making repairs submerged in enemy waters. By the evening of the next day, January 30, the boat was underway again. On February 1 the *Tambor* arrived at its assigned area to patrol near Japanese-held Formosa, and at dawn on the second its radar detected ships that proved to be a freighter and tanker escorted by what looked to be a brand-new destroyer. They were traveling southward, toward the entrance to the strait, moving in and out of rain squalls. Though they had not detected the *Tam-bor*, they made routine turns, zigging and zagging to make it more difficult for an enemy sub to set up for a shot. The tactic succeeded—and, to further complicate matters, the destroyer was shifting from one side of the merchantmen to the other—forcing the *Tambor* to stalk the convoy all day and night.

In the conning tower the tracking group included plotting officers William Wood and Elmer Atchison, radar officer Vito Vitucci, and Walter Post on the Torpedo Data Computer. Spruance and Kefauver manned the bridge. Tom Lam-pley stood the starboard lookout again, with Bill Reynolds on the port side and Clarence Erich to the stern.[3] Timing and plotting the ships' maneuvers, the tracking group planned an approach that would allow the *Tambor* to fire at both the freighter and tanker with the destroyer—the "can"—on the far side of them. "We sure have a lot of nerve cruising with this can all night," Bob wrote in his diary, "but he still doesn't know we're here."

At 4:00 AM on February 3, the boat finally made its attack approach. Bill Reynolds, the portside lookout, faced the Japanese ships. "As always, the queasy feeling in my stomach and the trembling of my legs and hands returned when I heard the target ranges shorten up and eventually when the targets were discern-able," he recalled. In the forward room, Bob and his crewmates had readied all six tubes. The plan was to fire at both of the big ships and dive before the destroyer could respond. At 4:16 AM Bob heard through his headset the order to commence firing a spread of three torpedoes. Everyone on the boat felt the familiar, gentle tug as a burst of compressed air sent each fish out of its tube. As soon as they were on their way toward the freighter, Kefauver turned the boat and fired a spread of three at the tanker.

On the bridge, as soon as the first torpedo left its tube, Kefauver saw the destroyer turn, and Red Mayo heard it change its sonar pinging to a short scale. What happened next the captain recorded tersely in his patrol report: "Saw and heard two hits amidships in freighter followed immediately by one hit just forward of tanker's stack. Swung right with full rudder and increased speed to flank. Passed 400 yards abeam of tanker. Saw men on fantail of tanker in light of huge fire which followed explosion on tanker. Intense light silhouetted *Tambor*, and destroyer began closing the range."

The lookouts remembered that the tanker's explosion was like nothing they'd seen before. First, Bill Reynolds had his binoculars trained on the freighter *Ariake Maru* when the torpedoes struck it. A plume of seawater flew up, followed by the boom of the explosion that would send it to the bottom. Next he shifted his glasses to the tanker:

> . . . the same geyser, the same report. A flicker of flame came from the stack and completely died down. Then a sight I'll never forget. Suddenly night turned into day. The tanker exploded and [it looked] as though the noon-day sun was shining in the East China Sea.
>
> The radar had given the relative position of the destroyer, but until then, I hadn't seen it. The angle of the bow was 90 degrees starboard and within seconds it was 0 degrees. In that hellish light I felt like a naked person on a crowded street with no place to hide. Dive! Dive! All hands below! The claxons [sounded and] I was the last man down and closed the hatch. Vents were open, all eyes were on the depth gauge, it just hung there, finally a down angle on the bow and [from] there on my memory is vague. I think I was on the stern planes until we hit bottom. I honestly can't remember.

As the *Tambor* dove, the destroyer passed directly overhead, and the crew heard splashes when the depth charges hit the water. Three exploded close by, shattering gauges and sending cork flying, then three more boomed just as close, then two more. Reynolds remembered a momentary panic in the control room—the explosions were closer than anything he'd experienced. But Kefauver gave orders calmly, and due to the captain's demeanor, Reynolds said, "discipline was returned and we were a crew again." Kefauver took the sub to the bottom at 268 feet and the boat went quiet.

By World War II everyone had the basic "ash can" that rolled from a stern-deck rack or was hurled by a small catapult as an antisubmarine weapon. The depth charge was a British invention, developed during World War I and copied by the Americans. The standard World War II charge carried three hundred to six hundred pounds of Torpex or cordite, materials with twice the explosive power of TNT. Most sank at a rate of eight to twelve feet per second, but by 1943 Americans were using newer tear-shaped depth bombs equipped with fins that sank faster and straighter. Detonation was triggered by a water pressure–sensitive fuse preset to a chosen depth. A standard depth charge would sink to three hundred feet in roughly thirty seconds, and a single charge could destroy a sub only if it exploded within ten yards of the hull. Within thirty feet, however, a depth charge's "water-hammer" effect would damage a hull, and several such hits could kill a sub. Depth charges were also good for flushing a submarine gone deep and quiet, allowing the surface ship to regain contact. The effect of the weapon was psychological as well as physical. As Lt. Sheldon Kinney, skipper of the destroyer escort USS *Bronstein*, remarked, "A depth charge has a magnificently laxative effect on a submariner."[4]

Early in the Pacific war the Japanese depth-charging tactics were unsuccessful, but were corrected thanks to U.S. Representative Andrew J. May, a member of the House Military Affairs Committee. At a press conference after a fact-finding trip to the Pacific theater, he blithely remarked that our subs were safe because the Japanese were setting their devices to explode at shallow depths. Several papers, including one published in Honolulu, saw fit to publish the remark, making it available to enemy intelligence. Vice Adm. Charles Lockwood, Commander of Pacific subs beginning in February of '43, wrote to his counterpart in the Atlantic, Rear Adm. Richard Edwards: "I hear . . . Congressman May . . . said the Jap depth charges . . . are not set deep enough. . . . He would be pleased to know the Japs set 'em deeper now." Later, he estimated that the "indiscretion" cost ten subs and the lives of eight hundred submariners.

The Japanese commander pummeling the *Tambor* knew his business. Methodically, the destroyer made pass after pass, dropping two charges at a time, all of which exploded extremely close by. Each time the entire crew heard its approach, a rumble that grew louder until it roared like a steam locomotive crossing a trestle directly overhead. Then, through the hull, the crew heard the splash of the charges, waited as they sank, then heard and felt each explosion. The shock was like a hammer striking the hull. It shattered glass, sent cork insulation and paint fragments flying, and loosened pipe fittings, causing leaks throughout the boat. A bad leak in the conning tower flooded its bilges and ran down to fill the bilges in the pump room below.

Enginemen Ray Bouffard and Warren Link, standing in the engine room's throttle area, felt a blast and saw a wall of water. Their first thought was that the hull had been breached and the *Tambor* was finished. Jack Semmelrath and John Scaduto were there, too, and threw out their arms, but the wall of water, instead of flooding over them, persisted eerily in the room. Their arms had passed through a veil of water backlit by a lantern. A cooling water gasket flange on one of the engines had been jarred loose, sending the thin stream across the entire room. As soon as the men realized what had happened, Ray Bouffard tightened the connection and stopped the leak—but there was a more serious problem. The men heard the unmistakable sound of air escaping the boat and quickly concluded that a ruptured line in a nearby ballast tank was leaking. Rising bubbles, they knew, would give away their position to the relentless destroyer.

Back in the control room, Nip Howard and Bill Reynolds were sitting on the deck with broken cork lying all around them. "Hey Bill," Nip said, "Are you scared?"

Photo 16. *Tambor* crew members, including (from left) torpedomen Ernie Costa and Ole Clausen, and, peering through rails, Max Muller. (Courtesy Robert Hunt)

"No," Bill lied.[5]

"Me, neither," Nip said. Perhaps saying it would make it so.

After an hour of listening to the destroyer churn over them and absorbing the blows of its depth charges, the crew heard a new sound through the hull. It was a loud crackling noise that the long-timers recognized as the sound of a ship's hull breaking up. One of their targets was imploding as it sank. Then the destroyer passed again and two more close charges banged the *Tambor*. When one of them struck, Bob was standing on a crossbeam used as a support during reloading, and the vibration burned his feet as if he stood on hot coals.

After two hours there was a lull in the attack, and no sound of the destroyer's screws came through the hull or sound gear. Kefauver decided to make a move. But this involved starting the loud drain pump to clear the flooded pump-room bilges so the boat could be properly balanced. Kefauver later wrote in his report, with heat: "This pump is a *menace*." Within minutes the destroyer was upon them again—it had stopped to conceal its presence and listen. Red Mayo, on the sound gear in the forward room, yelled: "The guy is right on the track and coming like hell." When the sound of the screws came through the hull, Bob felt like they were drilling right into his head. "A very bad moment for all hands and about that time we got what we knew was coming," he wrote. In 268 feet of water the depth charges sank for thirty agonizing seconds while the crew waited for the inevitable explosions. Two charges went off close to the *Tambor*, and minutes later another pair exploded even closer to starboard, causing the sub to hog and sag. Bob's diary says, "This old boat just about broke in half and didn't seem like she would ever stop shaking." Kefauver quickly ordered the *Tambor* back to the bottom.

During this action Claude Brown, who had celebrated his sixteenth birthday earlier in the patrol, met Johnny Scaduto in the engine room. Brown remembered: "We stopped, facing each other, and he had his right hand on the cover of the Kleinschmidt salt water evaporator while I clutched the railings beside the engines. [The destroyer] roared over and dropped two. . . . I saw a streak of blue fire start from the forward bulkhead, travel the length of the electric cable, and shatter the light bulb over Scudato's head raining pieces of glass down into his hair—then he took off running aft as the deck plates shifted under our feet, and I took off running forward to the aft battery compartment." In that room, after he closed the watertight door and dogged it tight, he turned to find crewmates clutching the sides of their bunks, "their faces whiter than usual." At the same time portly "Guts" Martin snored softly, his hands folded across his belly.

When Brown got to the forward torpedo room he found Bob Hunt "still fleecing Richardson and a few others in their nonstop poker game." And when the can "laid two off the bow, upsetting the bucket and board they were using for a table," poker chips and cards went flying. "Bob jumped up," Brown remembered, "shook his fist at the overhead, and yelled at the enemy: 'You bastard! Do that again and I'll swim out a tube . . .and punch a fuckin' hole in your hull!'"

It was now 6:55 AM, and the *Tambor* had been under attack for nearly three hours. As the depth charges continued to explode around them, one crewman shook his head, saying: "Some boat—she sure can take it." But they had to wonder how much more she could take. The *Tambor* was the first of its class, an older "thin-skinned 250," which meant that its steel pressure hull was rated to a maximum depth of 250 feet, compared with the 400-foot rating of the later, thicker-skinned subs. Sitting on the bottom at 268 feet, absorbing blow after blow, the *Tambor* had taken damage in every compartment.

In the maneuvering room, near the back of the sub, water leaked through the packing glands around both screw shafts. When close charges exploded near the aft of the boat, Rex Harvey and Robert Galloway swore they could see flashes around the shafts, followed by the scent of cordite. In an attempt to stem the leaking, Roy "Foo" Rausher fastened a wrench to the tightening nuts and cranked hard. Foo was the strongest man on the boat, and the crew had a saying: "When Foo tightens something it takes two men and a boy to loosen it." But he couldn't stop the leaks around the shafts. If water overflowed the shallow maneuvering-room bilges and rose above the deck plates in the motor room below, the main motors would get wet. So, between depth chargings, Harvey, Foo,

Galloway, Robert Koostra, and Chesty DeBay, chief of the maneuvering room, formed a bucket brigade, frantically transferring water from the maneuvering-room bilges to the deeper ones in the aft torpedo room. When they heard the destroyer approach again, they stopped, closed the watertight doors between compartments, and sat out the attack.

The attacks kept coming, sometimes thirty minutes apart, but for one terrifying hour they arrived every ten minutes. The destroyer crossed them from port to starboard, then back again, then down the port side, then down the starboard side. It had a fix on the *Tambor*. With air leaking from the boat, and given good depth and current charts, the Japanese captain could pinpoint the sub's location. At 8:40 AM Kefauver recorded: "Destroyer ran down the port side, close aboard and dropped two duds. These were labeled *Tambor* and were close enough to be heard falling through the water." Some crew members recalled hearing these charges land on the deck, roll off, and bounce against the side of the boat.

At this point in Kefauver's report, a page is missing. What followed was the worst of the depth charging, and one wonders whether the page was lost or deliberately removed, and if removed, by whom and for what reason.

As the attack continued, the aft torpedo room was taking considerable damage. The escape and torpedo-loading hatches had been sprung by a nearby explosion, and the latch dogs wouldn't tighten them. Carl Johnson, Ole Clausen, George Venditelli, and others in the compartment had to secure both hatches with chain falls. Also, air lines were leaking, fresh water leaked from a ruptured emergency tank, the torpedo tube spindles had been bent by the concussions, and a spirits tank fastened to the bulkhead with ¾-inch bolts had been blown free.[6] Meanwhile the forward torpedo room was crowded. With the sub sitting on the sea floor, the main sound heads on the bottom of the boat were useless, so radiomen Bill Shoop and Red Mayo were using the auxiliary sound gear in Bob's room. And since this was the only way to track the destroyer—except when its screws were audible through the hull—the captain was there, too. This, in addition to the regular torpedomen and the reload crew, made for a full house. Bob, in charge of the room, tried to keep everyone occupied between attacks, instructing them to shut down leaks, mop up water, and sweep up debris. It was better than having everyone just standing around waiting for the next big jolt.

Then a big blast came. It sheared a pair of bolts from the overhead and sent them ricocheting through the compartment like rifle bullets. One bolt with its nut still attached struck Bob Dye, but most of its energy was spent and he was not badly hurt. Bob Hunt knew that the bolts held motors to the overhead, and if more of them were blown off the heavy machines would crash down. He told the men in bunks under them to move so they wouldn't get hurt when the motors fell. "This did scare the hell out of them," he wrote in his diary, "but it [got] them moving rather than laying [sic] in a bunk and getting smashed by [a] motor."

As the attack wore on Kefauver made his way from room to room, assessing the *Tambor*'s condition. As he went, he made a point of speaking with every man. And as he departed each compartment he said the same thing, over and over: "I am honored to have served with you."[7]

If it sounded like the captain was preparing for the end, it only made plain what everyone was thinking. Nevertheless, the crew kept working, and gradually the air leaks were brought under control. One daring effort was made by machinists Gus Builder and William Wood, who crawled across the top of the sub's powerful batteries on a rubber blanket to get into the pressure hull and tighten fittings inside the #1 air bank.[8]

During the long ordeal, there were periods of quiet when the men tried to get some sleep. One lull persisted for three hours, raising hopes that the destroyer had finally departed. Bob wrote in his diary: "Most of us had turned in for some rest as best we could at depth charge stations with water and cork all over everything. About noon we came out of our bunks like divers as the can had eased in and laid one right on top of us. It looks like the end as we thought he was gone and can't figure out how he found us there on the bottom. It could only be one thing—oil leaks. . . . After that, he turned around and headed back—so close we could hear those screws right through the hull. Right over us again, up one side and down the other letting us have a pasting that we were sure the boat wouldn't stand. We just stood around and waited."

It was now past noon, and the *Tambor* had been under depth-charge attack for eight hours. And still the destroyer dropped charge after charge, all of them on target. Captain Kefauver was in the forward room where Red Mayo continued to listen to the destroyer's movements. Bob, in dungarees and a T-shirt, stood next to Kefauver, who wore khaki pants and shirt. The two men had served on the *Tambor* since the beginning, when Bob was a new submariner and Kefauver was diving officer. They had been through a lot together, beginning with the first peacetime depth-charge tests conducted live on the *Tambor*. Now, in a pause between blasts, Captain Kefauver turned to his longtime crewmate, looked him in the eyes, and asked, "Bob, did you ever hear depth charges this close before?"

"Not that close, Captain," Bob replied.

Then Kefauver said, "We've got to get out of here."

Bob would later speak of this moment often. He felt consulted by a captain he respected, and it meant a lot to him. Immediately, Kefauver turned and headed to the control room, making his way as quickly as possible through the closed watertight doors of each compartment. Once there, he ordered Chief Bill Blakenbaker to start pumping so the *Tambor* could get under way. He warned the men, "We may have to surface and fight it out." A destroyer, bristling with guns, would make short work of a sub, but the alternative was waiting for the charge that would breach the *Tambor*'s hull.

Checking the depth gauge, diving officer Blakenbaker saw that the boat had settled twelve feet into the sea bottom. The explosions had churned up sand and muck, and the boat's vibrations had settled it downward. As he gave instructions, the control room became a hive of activity to break the sub free. The trim manifold men pumped bilges into the sea to lighten the boat, the man on the hydraulic manifold opened and closed valves to shift weight from tank to tank, the men on the blow and vent manifolds did the same, and the crew in the maneuvering room applied power to the screws, running them forward and reversed, one at a time or both at once. The idea was to shift the boat from side to side, forward and back, like rocking a car stuck in mud.

Jack Semmelrath, in the forward engine room, watched anxiously as the lights dimmed with every attempt to break free. He was concerned about the waning battery power. "That was the real danger at this point," he thought, ". . . NO BATTERY, NO PUMPS."[9] The *Tambor* was stuck fast with dwindling air and power, and it was making a lot of noise for the destroyer above.

The crew on a submerged sub, after fourteen hours, began to experience shortness of breath as the oxygen content of the air dwindled. Bob remembered several occasions when the sensation came on quickly. "Suddenly [the crew is] gasping for air, making a sound with each breath, taking in air deeply and slowly, especially while working or moving around. Also, almost everyone smoked, and as soon as the oxygen was that low even matches wouldn't stay lit. So the guys with lighters used those. But even a lighted cigarette only lasted a few puffs before it would extinguish due to lack of oxygen." At this point the smoking lamp would be turned off, the diving officer would be notified of "bad air," and he would inform the pharmacist's mate, who would test the air in each compartment. To "doctor" the air, he would spread a white CO_2-absorbing powder on the bunks and other flat surfaces and bleed oxygen from bottles in each room. It was a short-term, emergency solution in a dire situation. During the nearly fatal East China Sea depth charging, the *Tambor* remained submerged for seventeen hours.

Methodically, Blakenbaker searched for just the right combination of weight distribution and thrust to free the boat. Every source of buoyancy was sought out; even the small tanks in the sub's heads were blown. Bob remembered the ordeal of freeing the sub from the bottom lasting for about two hours. Clarence Erich thought it was five.

When, at last the *Tambor* broke loose, the crew was in for a white-knuckle ride. With flooded rooms, the boat—badly out of balance—tipped side to side and nosed upward, out of control. The control-room gauges no longer worked or flying debris had knocked their hands crazy, so Blakenbaker worked by feel, continuing to pump water and air among various tanks. The trick was to keep the *Tambor* more or less upright and to keep it from breaching the surface where the destroyer would finish it off with its guns. Blakenbaker asked for full power on both screws to steady the boat, but trim was hard to establish. With great expertise and with quick responses in the control and maneuvering rooms, he gradually brought the sub under control and kept it beneath the surface. Given a stabilized boat, Kefauver maneuvered it submerged, running for deeper water. The destroyer dropped another charge, and Red Mayo, still in the forward room, listened intently to its movements.

For another two hours the *Tambor* took evasive action submerged, listening for the destroyer and waiting for full darkness. Finally, at 9:00 PM, Kefauver dared to surface the boat. As he did, he improvised a tactic to conceal his position. On the way up, the helmsman at the wheel had a hard time maintaining his given heading, indicating a strong underwater current. Observing this, Kefauver ordered him to steer directly into the flow, causing any leaks of air or fuel oil to be carried far behind.[10]

When the *Tambor* reached the surface, Kefauver couldn't be sure he'd lost the enemy, and even opening the conning-tower hatch would be a risky venture. Without functioning gauges, equalizing the pressure in the boat with the pressure outside was a matter of guesswork, and when the hatch popped it nearly carried its man up the ladder. With the sudden change of pressure, the air in the conning tower turned smoky and blue. When the lookouts ran topside and scanned the area, however, they were relieved to see that a battle surface was not necessary. The East China Sea was dark around them, and after more than sixteen hours under attack, the *Tambor* had escaped.

It had been one of the worst depth chargings survived by an American sub during the war. Years later, when the crew wrote letters to compile a room-by-room report of the action, they made possible an account unique for two reasons: No other crew wrote coordinated letters about a severe depth charging, and most who had undergone a similar experience died in their subs.

That night, the crew members who went topside were hit by the smell of fuel oil. Immediately they understood that the boat had a serious leak that could lead enemy ships to its location. As quickly as possible, the main engines were brought online and the sub got out of the area. As it did, relief passed through the boat with fresh air from the open hatch. Bill Shoop, one of three men on the *Tambor* from Philadelphia, sought out his buddies, Bill Raymond and Jack O'Brien, and when they met in the control room they embraced. "I was completely overwhelmed by the feeling that overtook me," Shoop remembered. "It was as if we were in some other world and returned."

Bob Dye, as officer in charge of the ship's safe that contained codes, cipher keys, and the liquor supply, had the happy task now of dispensing shots of brandy to the repair parties. For Bob, however, relief was mixed with continued anxiety. They were near Japan, five thousand miles from home in a shattered boat. That night he wrote in his diary:

> We surfaced about nine . . . and we don't know whether we'll get back or not. The engines run all right, but just about everything else is out. Both air compressor bases are smashed which means we can't jam any air, which means we can't make many dives. Maybe we can rig something to hold them down, but we don't know. The after tubes are out of commission along with a lot of motors. Our ice machine went off to spoil our meat. Rich says, "When you hear the rumble of the depth charge, you know the *Tambor* has made another attack." We took thirty-four depth charges in all and most of them right on. . . . A couple more and we could never have gotten underway.

Rex Harvey felt a more immediate anxiety. Now that the *Tambor* was cruising the surface on its main diesel engines, it was time to recharge the batteries. But virtually every electrical box on the boat was grounded out, and it would be the first time they'd attempted a charging with a full voltage ground. "What a way to go," he thought, "survive the depth charges, then have a battery explosion wipe us out." But Chesty DeBay and his electrical crew managed the recharge successfully and began an effort to repair circuits that would consume the rest of the patrol.

That night Kefauver received a grim damage report. In addition to the items Bob listed, the turbo blower, which circulated air, had been torn loose and damaged; the heavy deck hatch to the dry stores locker near the galley was knocked off its hinges; the number-one periscope and the SD radar mast were flooded; the radio antenna had been blown off the sail; seawater had leaked into the radio transmitter; charts, cork, and glass littered the conning-tower deck; the Torpedo Data Computer hung from its fastenings and two of its dials lay at the bottom of the periscope well.

By daylight the next morning, repair parties examined the scene topside and were shocked by what they found. Jack Semmelrath marveled at the white blotches on the superstructure that smelled like TNT. Jagged pieces of depth-charge shrapnel were embedded in the wooden decking. On the aft deck, the heavy 5-inch gun had been knocked off its trunnions, despite the bracket that held its barrel in place. The conning tower had been driven back three inches against the pressure hull and was misaligned. And, most disturbing, a 21-inch crack was visible in the outer hull. From the split, thousands of gallons of fuel oil leaked from the port side fuel ballast tank.

The *Tambor* continued to trail oil, its ability to dive was compromised, it could not radio its location or condition, it was nearly blinded by the damage to its periscopes and radar, and its only remaining weapons were the machine gun, small arms, and the forward tubes. But without a working Torpedo Data Computer, it would be hard to hit anything with the remaining fish. Again, the crew went to work.

To reattach the turbo blower to its base, Gus Builder and Warren Link used the boat's lathe to fashion new bolts from raw stock. Builder hand-filled the bolt's hex heads and retapped the old holes, and the blower was soon back in place. Chesty DeBay then rebuilt the blower motor, restoring it to use. Then Builder and Art Strickle cannibalized the two ruined compressors to make one good one, and the *Tambor* could once again jam air for future dives.

Bill Shoop, Harvey Refensterf, and Red Mayo worked to reestablish radio communication, drying the transmitter and running a lead up through the control room and the conning-tower hatch to serve as antenna. In case of a crash dive, a man was stationed at the hatch with an axe to chop through the lead. In this radio work Red Mayo was hampered only slightly by the deafness in one ear caused by the explosions that had boomed in his headset. The radiomen managed to achieve a short-range signal, but it was not strong enough to reach an American outpost. So they did not hear that Tokyo Rose reported the *Tambor*'s destruction, a report that did reach gunnery officer Vito Vitucci's wife, who worked at the Naval Communications Station in Washington, D.C.

As the repair parties worked, Bob realized that he hadn't seen the Navy "shrink" for quite a while. When Bob saw the captain in the forward room, he asked him about the man who was monitoring their responses to stress. "Do you really want to see him?" Kefauver asked.

"Yes, I do," Bob said, and the captain led Bob to a bunk in the officers' quarters and pulled back a curtain. Bob saw a lump in the bunk, and Kefauver flipped its blanket back, revealing Schiff, face down, silent.

"He's been like that for a couple of days," the captain said, then reached to prod the figure. Bob stopped him.

"No, that's enough," he said. At the end of the patrol, the man was removed from the boat, and the captain's report noted briefly: "Lieut-Comdr., G. N. Schiff, (MC), USNR, conducted extensive tests of air conditioning condensate water throughout the patrol. The findings of his experiments are being made the subject of separate report by him."

~~~~~~~~~~~~~~~~~~~~~~~~~~~~~~~~~

As repairs continued, Bob Dye sat on the control-room deck, examining the burned out leads on the tube that drove the SD radar coils. Without radar, there would be no advance warning of nearing planes. And without the Torpedo Data Computer, their most potent weapon was compromised, so a plan was devised to retrieve its dials from the bottom of the periscope well. Warren Link was the skinniest man on board, and he agreed to be lowered into the narrow well. Walter Post and Elmer Atchison fashioned a yoke out of heaving lines and a pillow, and Link went down head first, with ropes tied to his ankles and a flashlight hanging from his neck. It was a tight fit, and only the grease smeared on his skin allowed Link to slide thirty-five feet down the dark well. When they pulled him out after several tense minutes, he was holding the crucial dials. Then, after fourteen hours of continuous work, Post had the TDC working again.

The boat would have no aft protection, however. Neither the deck gun nor the aft torpedo tubes could be repaired, and no matter what Carl Johnson and his men tried, both of their hatches continued to leak. More serious than the leaking hatches was the cracked fuel ballast tank. After three days of repair work, on February 7 Bob wrote in his diary: "Still have an oil leak and we're spreading oil all over the ocean—tried again to send the message but can't get it through . . . . [H]ave all repairs made in the forward room and are now looking for the Jap again—we're in very bad shape to be operating out here, but if we can get the oil leak stopped we won't be in so much danger."

The next day the search for the oil leak continued. "Have been emptying one tank at a time trying to find it," Bob wrote. Thanks to the improvisations of the radiomen, the *Tambor* could now pick up radio transmissions. "Got a message late yesterday of a convoy heading this way, but still haven't run into it. . . . As usual about this time the crew isn't in very good spirits—a few arguments here and there. Still can't send a message."

Later that day the leaking tank was finally located and a repair plan devised. First the remaining fuel was shifted to other tanks, but the only way to stop the oil trail fully was to flush the damaged tank. To do this its pumps had to be converted, allowing the tank to draw and expel seawater like a regular ballast tank. The task would require two men to go under the main deck, crawl through a jumble of lines, and remove a set of banking plates. And this task would need to be done with the boat on the surface in broad daylight. Warren Link and John Scudato, nicknamed "the Oil King" for his work with the fuel supply, volunteered for the job. Kefauver warned them: He would not jeopardize the boat and the entire crew if the *Tambor* was spotted. He would have to dive, even if the two men could not crawl out and reach the hatch in time.

Working in close quarters by the light of a lantern shone down through the slats of the topside deck, Scudato and Link worked quickly but carefully, tucking nuts and bolts into their breast pockets as they went. Deep in enemy waters, just miles from Japanese territory, a plane could appear at any moment, especially with the early-warning SD radar out. If the *Tambor* had to make an emergency dive, not only would Link and Scudato be left on the surface, but they would probably be trapped below the decking and drowned. There would be little chance of freeing themselves, treading water, and waiting for the boat to resurface. The men understood the situation, and they finished their work with dispatch. When, at last, they tightened the final bolts, an order was given to test

Photo 17. Lt. Cdr. Russell Kefauver (center), in the officers' mess, was captain of the *Tambor* for its eighth through eleventh war patrols. (Courtesy Robert Hunt)

the converted valves, and when the air pressure hit them, the valves roared. It was the same sound the boat made when it dove, and Scudato got out and ran for the hatch, shouting as he went: "Don't get in my way!"

The job was completed just in time. "Sighted a periscope quite close and really got out of there in a hurry," Bob wrote in his diary. "We figured he was ready to fire when we sighted him." That day—February 8—Kefauver wrote in his patrol report: "All vital repairs completed. All tubes will fire by hand; continued electrical work. Considered boat to be in fighting trim again. Commenced patrolling an easterly course."

The *Tambor* and its crew had been at sea for thirty-six days, nearly all of that time in enemy waters. After the boat's near destruction, first by ramming and then during the long depth-charging—and operating now with extensive damage that included foggy vision through its single remaining periscope—the *Tambor* resumed its mission.

Four days later it claimed another sinking. Still patrolling in the East China Sea, ten miles west of Okino Erabu, the small middle island of the Ryukyu chain, lookouts spotted smoke on the horizon, then the masts of three ships. Kefauver addressed the crew on the boat's PA system. Clarence Erich remembered the captain saying "Boys, I've just made a thorough inspection of our boat, and, as you all know, we're in one helluva shape. But I think she's good for one more shot at old Tojo. So if you'll all back me up, I'd like to get just one more ship out of that convoy out there, and I promise we'll head for the barn immediately." There was no dissent from the crew.

At 8:52 that evening, after two hours of pursuit, only eight minutes remained before moonrise would make the sea too bright for a surface attack. The foggy periscope made a submerged attack impossible, so Kefauver decided on a long shot. Bob's forward room fired three torpedoes at the largest target from a distance of 3,500 yards. Immediately an escort turned toward the sub, and the *Tambor* submerged and rigged for another depth-charge attack. A minute later they heard one of their long shots hit its target. Then the depth charges came—seventeen of them in the next hour—but between the explosions the crew heard through the hull that loud crackling sound of a ship breaking up. The *Ronsan Maru*, a 2,700-ton passenger-cargo ship, was going down. Minutes later the crew heard a different explosion, as the boilers of the *Ronsan Maru* blew up. At midnight, having evaded the escort, the *Tambor* surfaced and looked for new targets.

Contrary to Kefauver's promise, the boat stayed on station for another five days, dodging patrol boats and planes, then departed for Midway, as assigned, on February 19. It still could not reach a friendly operator by radio, and Vito Vitucci's wife remained in her dreadful suspense.

The *Tambor* was leaving a very dangerous area, and before she reached home two other American subs patrolling there would be lost. The *Scorpion*, operating in the East China Sea, is thought to have struck a mine, February 24. All hands were lost. On the day that the *Tambor* left for home, the *Grayback* reported sinking two ships in the Formosa Strait. Five days later, operating east of Formosa, it sank a tanker, then damaged two more ships before leaving the area. On February 26 it was caught on the surface by a carrier plane and suffered a direct bomb hit that sank the boat and killed all aboard. Before the year was out, the *Tang* would go down in the Formosa Strait, sunk by a circular run of its own torpedo. Its captain, Richard O'Kane, and eight of his crew survived and were taken prisoner.

As the *Tambor* made its way home there was one scare when a destroyer appeared suddenly out of a rain squall, and another when a flying boat headed for the *Tambor*, but both times the boat dove and escaped. Finally, on February 29—leap day—they moored at the Midway base. They were ten days late, and because they were presumed lost, the crew's mail had not been forwarded from Pearl Harbor. The next day, however, they were sent on to Pearl and its Navy yard, since the Midway base could not repair a boat as badly damaged as the *Tambor*.

But the sub had seen its crew through their harrowing ordeal. "She always brings us home," the men repeated, and Clarence Erich attributed her toughness to the fact that she was a "peacetime boat," built with extra care before the pressures of wartime production schedules. In their recollections, the *Tambor*

Photo 18. Crewmates on leave in Hawaii: *(top, from left)* Bob Hunt, Red Mayo, Harry Behrens, and Donald Hodges; *(bottom, from left)* Bill Shoop, Harvey Refensterf, and Jack O'Brien. (Courtesy Robert Hunt)

sailors spoke of their sub with affection; it was a weapon of war, but also their home and haven. It had almost become their tomb in the East China Sea, but now, when they emerged after the two-month patrol, it was more like a womb that birthed them, white and drawn, into the light of a familiar place.

After the patrol Kefauver recommended fourteen crew members for awards ranging from the Legion of Merit to the Bronze Star. The list included officers and enlisted men Ed Spruance, Charles DeBay, Bill Blakenbaker, Carlos Nip Howard, William Wood, Gus Builder, Vito Vitucci, Elmer Atchison, Walter Post, Carl Johnson, Art Strickle, Warren Link, Gordon Red Mayo, and Bob Hunt. Nip Howard, as Bob predicted, did receive the Silver Star for his performance on the 20-mm machine gun, and Warren Link received the Bronze Star for his heroic repair work. Radioman Gordon Red Mayo also received the Bronze Star, and remembered:

The captain and I were at the sonar and when every depth charge hit the water I would say there's another one . . . and would take the phones off and count for a minute and it would explode [and] then I would put the phones on again. Well I heard another hit the water and waited and nothing happened so I put the phones on again and then it exploded. When I put the phones on again I discovered that I couldn't hear out of one ear, and told the Captain he should get someone else to man the sound gear. He replied saying that I would stay where I was and that he and I were going to save the ship, so I was there until it was over.

After we were back safely on the surface and after I had finished securing the sound gear, I started aft and the Captain called me into the officers' mess hall and said we had saved the ship and we needed some libation. He broke out a quart of Old Grandad and we half finished it in about 20 minutes.

I went back to the crew's quarters and fell soundly asleep for 13 hours (he had told them not to wake me . . . I couldn't hear out of one ear for ten days).[11]

Captain Kefauver, for his part, received the Navy Cross. He recommended Bob Hunt for the Bronze Star and proposed a citation for "heroic and outstanding duty. . . . During a severe and prolonged depth charge attack you directed repairs in the forward torpedo room. Your fearless and skillful performance of duty on this and eight previous war patrols aboard the USS *Tambor* has been an inspiration to all with whom you served."[12] As a result of Kefauver's recommendation, Bob received a commendation ribbon and the following citation from Admiral Chester Nimitz, Commander in Chief, United States Pacific Fleet:

For meritorious conduct in action in the performance of his duties in a United States Submarine during a war patrol of that vessel. As a Member of the Crew, his exceptional skill and proficiency at his battle station materially assisted his Commanding Officer in conducting successful attacks which resulted in sinking one enemy tanker and three freighters for a total of approximately 30,000 tons. His calm manner and devotion to duty contributed directly to the success of his vessel. His conduct throughout was an inspiration to all with whom he served and in keeping with the highest traditions of the United States Naval Service.

CHAPTER ELEVEN

Wave the Flag on Market Street

E ven at the height of Japanese military success in late 1941 and early 1942, their definition of victory was never to force an Allied surrender but merely to achieve a draw, in the form of a peace settlement that would allow them to retain the riches they had snatched up in Asia and the Pacific islands. After Midway, that dream had grown increasingly remote; by the end of 1943, although neither side was saying so out loud, the dream was dead. Instead of attaining a stalemate, the Japanese found themselves on the losing side of a forced mate: all that remained was for the final, inevitable moves to be played out, and the only questions left were how long Japan would drag out the contest and how many lives would be lost on both sides. The supply of fuel for both the Japanese war machine and the domestic economy was rapidly evaporating, and the greatest share of blame or credit went to the American submarine fleet. Once they had shaken off their early material and tactical shortcomings, the once-ragtag fleet had become the most destructive force of the war on either side, so efficient that a Japanese captain remarked, whenever a tanker was sent to Japan, "there wasn't much doubt in our minds that [it] would not get [there]."

At the beginning of the war, Japanese military planners estimated that the country possessed only a two-year supply of oil; the Pearl Harbor attack was meant to buy them the time needed to take control of the vast supplies of oil in the East Indies. That the Japanese passed up a chance to hit the American submarine fleet during the attack indicated how fatally they underestimated the U.S. subs' capacity to disrupt the shipping of East Indian oil to the Home Islands. American strategists, too, underrated the abilities of their own subs in their war planning, but in the summer of 1943 they finally shifted the focus of their submarine fleet from enemy warships to oil tankers and other Japanese merchant ships—a change for which "Uncle Charlie" Lockwood was largely responsible. American subs, which had sunk only nine tankers in the first year-and-a-half of the war, promptly downed fourteen in the last four months of 1943 and added eight more in January 1944. In November 1943, the Japanese Imperial Navy responded to the mounting losses by organizing a convoy system to escort their merchant vessels. Ironically, however, the new escort system only increased the U.S. subs' hunting efficiency, since American cryptographers had broken the Japanese merchant code earlier in the year, and the increased radio communication between the members of the convoys and their escorts allowed U.S. forces to pinpoint their locations. By the end of the year, U.S. submarines had gone on over 300 patrols, fired nearly 4,000 torpedoes, and sunk 335 ships with a total tonnage of 1.5 million—far more than the flagging Japanese shipyards could replace. And that was only the beginning.

By January 1944, in sharp contrast to the early months of the war, it was the Japanese who could do nothing right and the Americans who appeared invincible. The same newsreel footage that Americans had seen in their movie theaters in late 1941 and early 1942 now seemed to be running in reverse, as the Japanese acquisitions of those early months slipped out of their grasp. MacArthur was on the move, into New Britain and New Guinea; the Gilbert Islands were retaken and the Marshalls were within the Allies' reach. The ruthless efficiency of American submarines in sinking tankers had reduced oil imports to Japan by more than 50 percent from the year before, and the Japanese Imperial Navy was reduced to the humiliating contingency of sending its convoys skulking along coastlines by day and hiding in harbors at night, a practice which only reduced the flow of oil even further. Desperate to get any oil at all through, they tried to ship it on freighters, in huge rubber bags towed by tugboats, and even in submarines, but nothing worked. In the Home Islands, any available substance—pine roots, castor beans, and sake—was requisitioned for use as fuel. By the beginning of 1945, oil imports had stopped completely. The submarine-enforced blockade was watertight.

The fuel shortages had also begun to cripple Japanese military strategy. In June 1944, their battle fleet lacked the fuel to get to the Marianas, enabling the Allies to achieve a walkover victory. The imperial fleet was forced to separate into two groups, one stationed in Japan and the other near Singapore, to stay close to oil supplies, further hindering its strength and readiness to attack. New Japanese replacement pilots went into battle inadequately trained, in sputtering planes fueled by wood turpentine and alcohol. Japanese ships were powered by highly inflammable Borneo crude, and some were even rebuilt to burn coal.

When the Allies recaptured Guam in August 1944, the Japanese mainland came within the range of the B-29 bombers, and in September MacArthur moved to within three hundred miles of the Philippines. American submarines so dominated Pacific waters that cowed Japanese sailors nicknamed the area around Luzon "the sea of the devil" and told each other the dark joke that they could walk back home to Japan atop all the American periscopes. American sailors called the target-rich area "convoy college." In response to the interdiction of their shipping, the imperial navy pinned their waning hopes on the Battle of Leyte Gulf in October, thus fulfilling the forty-year-old prophecy of War Plan Orange that the climactic battle of the Pacific war would be fought in the Philippines. Again, the lack of fuel hampered the Japanese. Forced to remain close to their fuel supplies and to travel at less than full speed to conserve oil, many of their ships arrived at the scene of the battle late. Even the introduction of the kamikaze pilots (whose tactics conserved oil, since their planes did not require the fuel necessary for a return trip to their carriers) was not enough to save the Japanese from a crushing defeat.

Around the same time, the Japanese also introduced the lesser-known submarine counterparts to the kamikazes, the *kaiten*—manned torpedoes equipped with pilots' compartments, canvas seats, and crude periscopes. The men in their metal tubes were launched on their suicide missions from the torpedo tubes of Japanese subs. Ninety-six *kaiten* pilots sacrificed themselves during the last months of the war, but only two hit their targets, destroying a U.S. fleet oiler and blowing the bow off the U.S. destroyer escort *Underhill*. The *kaiten* pilots who missed their targets faced the choice of self-detonating or suffering a lingering death in the vastness of the Pacific.[1]

As Japanese and American fortunes continued to reverse, 1944 was an even more effective year for the American submarines than 1943. In addition to sinking over 500 merchant ships totaling almost 2.3 million tons, they also downed 7 Japanese aircraft carriers, a battleship, 9 cruisers, 30 destroyers, and 7 submarines. Not only did they throttle the supply of oil almost completely, they also severely curtailed the importation of food and raw materials to the Home Islands. They were so successful, in fact, that they began to run out of targets and were diverted to other tasks. Foremost among these was lifeguard duty, picking up American pilots who had been shot down over the Pacific. American submarines rescued 504 fliers during the war, and on September 2, 1944, the *Finback*, which a year earlier had almost fired mistakenly on the *Tambor*, changed the course of American presidential history when it picked up Ens. George Herbert Walker Bush off Chichi Jima in the Bonin Islands.

By the time the *Tambor* cast off on its eleventh war patrol, on April 9, 1944, Bob was one of only two crew members left who had been on every mission. He had always intended to see things through until the war was over, but after the near disaster of the tenth patrol he had begun to wonder if he was tempting fate. With his old comrades opting off the boat, he was going out with a less experienced crew every time, and he wondered if all the trouble they had encountered on the last patrol was a forewarning that their lack of experience might soon catch up with them. The new men sent to Bob in the forward torpedo room for a bunk and a locker were getting younger and greener all the time. They were so lost that they were effusive in their gratitude for his help, and so naïve that they were astounded by the way he ignored most of what the officers said. Captain Kefauver was also concerned about his increasingly inexperienced crew, noting in his report on the *Tambor*'s eleventh war patrol that out of the sixty-seven men on board, forty-four had less than three years of service. "At present over fifty percent of the crew have two or less war patrols," he wrote. "Daily school and drills have made it possible to keep up the operating standard of the past. The vanishing of men with extensive submarine experience is, however, being felt more and more. The loss of these experienced men is proving a decided handicap in effecting repairs while underway. The willingness to work and learn displayed by the new men cannot be effectively substituted for the detailed knowledge of machinery and trade skills of our pre-war submarine men."

Bob was beginning to weary of the whole routine. True, there was important work left to be done, but he had spent so much time at sea the past couple of years that he felt as if barnacles were growing on his hide. Also, sheer numbers suggested that he was, indeed, pushing his luck. Four of the twelve subs in the *Tambor*'s squadron had been sunk in 1943. By the end of the war three more would be lost—more than half of the squadron. During the entire Pacific conflict the Navy would lose roughly one in six subs. Of the 16,000 submariners who made war patrols, 22 percent were lost, the highest casualty rate among all U.S. armed services. In the latter stages of the war, the men knew the odds, and it was commonly said that after your fourth patrol you were tempting fate.

In addition to his sense of mounting risk, Bob was also wearying of this business of meeting a girl he really liked, then getting shipped off and never seeing her again. An old chief he knew from magnetic-exploder school invited him to a Pearl Harbor beach party, where Bob was introduced to a Kanaka woman—a native Hawaiian who had lived in the islands all her life. The old chief was her older sister's boyfriend, and the three of them, plus the sister's teenaged daughter, all lived in the sister's house. It was crowded, but no one seemed to mind Bob sleeping on the living-room couch. He was glad to have a place to stay other than the Royal Hawaiian, which had become wilder than ever. When Bob threw a party for the crew after they returned from the tenth war patrol, one of his shipmates had so much pink lady and Coca-Cola he decided he could fly, and jumped out of the window flapping his arms. Luckily, he was only on the third floor and in a very relaxed state when he landed, so he only broke his arm. The pilots based at Pearl, jealous of the sub sailors' posh residence, also thought it funny to buzz the hotel early in the morning with full props, shaking the hungover sailors out of bed with the vibrations and noise.

Photo 19. Bob's Hawaiian friend. When a woman gave you her picture, "it was so you could remember her for the rest of your life," however long or short that might be. "This was heavy stuff and represented a deep emotion," Bob remembered. (Courtesy Robert Hunt)

As soon as the older sister and her boyfriend went to work in the morning and the niece went to school, Bob was free to crawl into bed with his girlfriend. One morning, after he had dozed off in her bed, he was awakened by something cold against his cheek, and when he opened his eyes she was sitting beside him, pressing a cold bottle of beer against his face and laughing. They spent the mornings in bed and the afternoons on the beach, a routine pleasant enough in its domesticity to encourage his growing feeling that he should leave the rest of the fighting to someone else. But when the call to duty came, Bob set off on the *Tambor* once again. Was it patriotism, a sense of responsibility to the other men, the ingrained habit of moving between land and sea—between cutting loose and concentrating on important work? He didn't know. But on April 9, 1944, there he was again, reclaiming his familiar bunk and locker in the *Tambor*'s forward torpedo room.

The boat was accompanied on its eleventh war patrol by the *Drum*, a submarine from another squadron. The *Tambor* had been overhauled so poorly, however, that it wasn't seaworthy, and it had to stop at Johnston Island for ad-

ditional repairs. While at Johnston, the crew received word of the sinking of the
Grayback. "That makes five out of our original twelve," Bob noted in his diary.
He had been promoted to junior officer of the watch, and his regular station
was now in the control room, where he served as diving officer, although his
battle stations post was still in the forward torpedo room. Kefauver, who was
himself the *Tambor*'s former diving officer, used his most experienced chiefs as
diving officers during regular watches. He would not allow his young officers to
dive the boat until they had stood behind the chiefs and learned enough to do
it properly—a procedure which did not sit well with some of them, but suited
the rest of the crew just fine. Bob was serving as diving officer when a plane was
sighted early in the patrol and the diving alarm was sounded from the bridge.
When Kefauver came down the ladder from the bridge, Bob thought the captain
would take over the controls, but he merely told Bob to take her to 150 feet and
level off, then invited Chesty DeBay to play a game of acey-deucey on the board
that had been painted on the gyro table. Kefauver never looked at him, but
Bob felt his presence right behind him all the while. It was Bob's first time as
diving officer under the pressure of an impending attack, but he executed the
dive flawlessly.

On April 18 they sighted a small vessel loaded with fresh vegetables and other
food for the starving Japanese soldiers isolated on Wake Island. Though the vessel was an armed naval boat, there was no need to waste a torpedo on the small
target, so they made a surface attack. At battle stations in the forward room, Bob
took his diary out of his locker and wrote: "Sighted ship early this morning. We
are now making a surface run on him—what will happen? I won't see this show
as I have a station in the F.T.R. I'll check off the five-inch as we fire." From the
torpedo room Bob listened to voices in his headset and to the gunfire echoing
through the boat. One voice was that of Vito Vitucci, who stood on the cigarette
deck and directed fire by the 5-inch gun and machine guns. As Bob continued
to write, his quick scribbles captured, perhaps more vividly than any of his other
diary entries, the fitfulness, uncertainty, anxiety, and sudden violence of battle,
the notations tumbling down the ruled lines of the diary page as the action occurred. In the entry he indicated each shot with a pencil slash:

> First shot out / / / / / 8500 yards / / / / / / no hits yet / / / / / / / /
> good thing we got plenty of shells / his shots / / looks like a couple hits
> / we move in closer / / / range 5500 / hit / / just sighted a periscope
> / / / / / / / / / / fired a burst of 20 MM—probably at periscope—we
> can still see the periscope—we're coming around to make another run
> on him / / / / / / he took a shot at us this time / / 20 MM / / / /
> shooting at periscope with 20mm / / / / / 4850 range / / / better rub
> Buddha's belly—only two more high-explosive shells left in the control

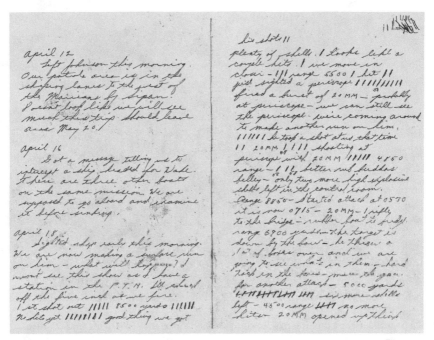

Photo 20. Bob, while at battle stations in the forward torpedo room, listened to the surface battle with the supply boat and recorded its progress in his diary, marking shots with pencil strokes. (Taken by David Cavagnaro)

room. Range 8850—started attack at 0530, it is now 0715—20 mm—1 rifle to the bridge—rubber boat to bridge—range 6900 yards—the target is down by the bow—he threw a lot of boxes over the side and we are going to see what's in them—hardtack in the boxes—man the gun for another attack—5000 yards . . . six more shells left—4500 range . . . no more hits—20 MM opened up think we're closing the range. Short bursts 20 mm firing at 0830—range 3600 yards—2500 range—firing 6″ again . . . firing 20 MM again—2300 range—can't figure out why planes from Wake haven't gotten here yet. We got a couple of hits out of the last few shots—we are going in to use the 20 mm—2000 yards—stand by—if he's got anything we'll get it now. 1500 yards—1400—1200—1000 yards coming in for the kill—900—20 MM's open up—800 yards very close—30-caliber—tommy guns & rifles on the way to topside—750 yards—600 yards—wonder where that enemy sub is now—still shooting—rubber boat to the roof—three men going over—we shot all their crew—shot them right under the guns.

Three men went aboard and loaded their lifeboats with rifles, papers, and the captain of the boat, who is still alive. Then the boat sank when they jumped in—all we have left is the skipper and lots of money he had.

Photo 21. This photo, which appeared in newspapers across the country, shows the *Tambor* sinking an armed Japanese supply boat headed for Wake Island and taking a Japanese officer prisoner. (U.S. Navy)

We have him in the forward room. The boat was about 200 tons and was of course sunk. They didn't get any of us but came close with two high-powered machine guns. Our prisoner has a flesh wound on his neck, but he is okay other than that.

We think the periscope we saw was the *Drum*.

Captain Kefauver's report of the incident was much terser: "0530: Sighted small 250-ton wooden trawler acting as cargo ship loaded with food and fresh vegetables. Commenced maneuvering to attack with deck gun. 0855: Boarded trawler and searched ship. Killed seven members of crew and took second officer prisoner."

One of the men who boarded the trawler was Ole John Clausen, Bob's friend who always fell asleep when he drank too much. Later he told Bob that he wished the whole thing had never happened. The Japanese had guns so they had to shoot them. It was closer combat than a submariner usually experienced. Ole John said he saw blood jump from the bodies with each bullet that struck them.

Three days later, they transferred their prisoner to the *Grouper*, which was on its way back to Pearl Harbor, and headed west of the Marianas. Three days after that, they got word that the *Trout*, with Bob's old friend Joe Magner aboard, had been sunk on February 29. "Six down and six to go," Bob wrote in his diary. The *Gudgeon*, the first U.S. submarine to sink a Japanese warship, went down in April, the seventh and final sub in the squadron to be destroyed, with the loss of seventy-eight men.

A fire in the *Tambor*'s engine room on May 6 caused no major damage; on the tenth they scored hits on two six-thousand-ton freighters, then got pinned down by seventy depth charges, a new record for the *Tambor*, but none exploded close enough to inflict damage other than the usual broken glass and showers of paint and cork. On the afternoon of the twenty-sixth they spotted a freighter and its escort, tracked it all day, and attacked successfully that night, sinking it with two torpedoes and making a clean escape from the escort. On the twenty-ninth they sighted an enemy sub but were forced down by a plane overhead before they could take a shot at it. Japanese planes were a constant nuisance on this patrol; they were now working in concert with the convoys and forced the boat to dive a number of times after it had maneuvered itself into good position for an attack.

The *Tambor* finally made it back to Midway on June 2, ten days late, and to the crew's extreme displeasure another fire in the engine room kept them there for three extra weeks. Lloyd Schuermann, a quiet, likeable fellow who had been a motor mechanic on the *Tambor*, was in Midway with a new sub called the *Shark* and paid the crew a visit. Bob had a unique connection to Lloyd: when Bob was on liberty in Western Australia the year before, he had met and kept company with Lloyd's old girlfriend. The girl had been knitting a sweater for Lloyd and had planned to present it to him the next time he came back to port—only Lloyd had gone back to the States, without informing her, to put the *Shark* in commission. Bob and Lloyd were about the same size, so the girl had planned to give Bob the sweater when *he* came back to port—but he never returned either, as the *Tambor* was reassigned to Pearl Harbor after its next war patrol. When Bob told Lloyd about it, they both wondered which sailor wound up wearing that sweater.

As usual there was very little to do at Midway. They drank, played softball, went deep-sea fishing in Navy power boats, ate the fresh tuna they had caught, swapped war stories, and drank some more. The news of the invasion of Normandy had broken soon after they arrived, and everyone but Bob seemed confident that the war would be over in a couple of months. One night he was sitting around a table in the chiefs' recreation area, drinking beer and discussing the war with a group of his shipmates, when their repeated insistence that he was a dumb son of a bitch to think that the war wouldn't be over by autumn made him so angry he leapt to his feet and shouted, "I'll lay one thousand dollars that the war in Europe will *not* be over in the next six months, and you smart-asses can take any part of the bet you want." Lewis Payne, Bob's old crewmate in the forward room who was now stationed on the *Trigger*, took a hundred, a sailor

Photo 22. *Tambor* crewmates Ole John Clausen (left) and Harry Behrens. Clausen was a torpedoman, and Behrens a quartermaster. (Courtesy Robert Hunt)

Bob didn't know took another hundred, and the rest of them kept their mouths shut. Bob had no firsthand experience with the Nazis, but he knew that if they were nearly as tenacious as the Japanese, the war would drag out into 1945 and perhaps beyond.

Another night, Fred Richardson organized a beach party with the help of an ex-*Tambor* sailor who was in charge of the island's beer hall and helped them sneak two cases past the armed marine guards. Fred made everyone in attendance stand up and provide some kind of entertainment. One crewmate sang a song, one did a little magic show, and Fred recited some of his poetry. When it was Bob's turn he'd had five or six bottles of beer. Sitting on a beach in the middle of the Pacific with crewmates after a war patrol, he stood and delivered a speech—he was feeling sentimental—in which he envisioned them all back home after the war, staying in touch with each other, and gathering each year in reunion. Then the Marines showed up, chased them back to their barracks, and confiscated what was left of the beer.

When he'd arrived at Midway, Bob had been pleasantly surprised to find his old friend and former shipmate Harry Behrens waiting to receive the *Tambor*'s number-one line. Harry was now in charge of the night lookout school at Midway, and he and Bob got together one evening for a few drinks, along with Ole John Clausen. After three full nights of drinking, interrupted only by naps during the day, they decided to go to the base hospital and persuade the doctors to write Bob a ticket out. It was a volunteer service, after all, and you were only supposed to make four war patrols before transferring to the relief crew anyway. After an orderly took a urine sample from Bob, the doctor came in and asked him what the trouble was. Bob showed the doctor his trembling hands and told him that he couldn't even hold a cup of coffee anymore without spilling it all over himself, even with both hands. Just then, the pharmacist's mate came in and announced the results of the urine samples. "Ninety proof, sir," he said with a smile. Then the doctor instructed Bob to face the near wall, reach out his hands and arms, and lean against it.

"See," he told Bob coolly, "your hands aren't shaking anymore."

Bob discovered later that some of his shipmates had seen Harry and Ole John escort Bob toward the infirmary and hurried over to Kefauver's quarters to tell him what was going on. Kefauver had called the doctor and told him to pay no attention to Bob's complaints, that he was needed on the next war patrol "for purposes of morale." When Bob heard this, he wondered if the captain considered him to be some kind of good luck charm.

Captain Kefauver had already been relieved of command of the *Tambor* and was being sent to New Construction. The *Tambor* was getting a new captain, but before Kefauver left he asked Bob who he thought should be put in charge of the forward torpedo room, Ole John or Link Handley. Bob told him to put Ole John in the forward room because he had more experience and to put Link in charge of the after torpedo room. It didn't dawn on Bob until later that this left him without a job, except for standing his watches as diving officer. So on July 16, 1944, under the command of the new captain, Lt. Cdr. William J. Germershausen, they set off on what would be Bob's final run. "An Empire run for a change," he wrote in his diary. It was the farthest north the *Tambor* had ever ventured, to the Kuril Islands off the northeast coast of Japan, then all the way into the Sea of Okhotsk, off the eastern coast of Russia. The assignment was another indication of how slow business had gotten in the South Pacific. "This should be a short run and maybe a good one if we are lucky," Bob wrote, as if he were eager to get it all over with. A couple of sentences later, though, he added, "Sure hope to get back off this one, as it's my last for a while."

As if to echo his ambivalence, the entire patrol was shrouded in fog. Submerged, feeling their way along the coast of Japan north of Tokyo, they almost blundered into a trap when they surfaced to attack a small vessel called a spitkit that had appeared in the mist. Just as they were about to break the surface, the fog lifted and revealed that the enemy boat was laying in wait for them, with a 3-inch gun and several machine guns aimed at them. The surface was aborted, and they sneaked away safely.

Not long after, a member of the crew came down with appendicitis and kept passing out. "Hope they don't have to operate," Bob wrote, remembering Lipes and Rector. On July 26, still submerged, they passed within forty miles of Honshu. On the twenty-eighth still operating in fog, they made a radar attack on an image that appeared on the screen, fired three fish, and heard three explosions, at which point the image disappeared from the radar screen.

On August 1 they entered the Sea of Okhotsk. "It's colder than hell up here," Bob wrote, adding bleakly, "We don't leave here until the 23rd of the month." A week later the fog cleared long enough for them to sight a convoy of four ships and two destroyers. They had made the tubes ready and were about to fire when one of the destroyers turned and headed right at them, so they dove and rigged the boat for depth charges, but none came. They surfaced to chase the convoy, running all the way to Paramushiro, at the northern tip of the Kurils, but couldn't find it. Then they had trouble with a deep dive. At one point, the boat was tilted at a 20-degree angle. "What a lash-up," Bob commented. "Sent all hands forward on the up angle." The next day, periscopes were sighted. "Don't like the idea of enemy subs," Bob wrote. "Sure will relax when the run is over." Every encounter raised the specter of being killed on what he planned to make his final war patrol. After eleven previous missions, it was a special kind of pressure.

On the thirteenth they made another radar approach, breaking through the fog to face a six-thousand-ton freighter. They waited for it to come within range, fired a quick spread of four fish, and scored one hit, which was enough to sink it and send its crew scrambling over the side in lifeboats. They circled back around to try to take an officer prisoner for interrogation, but a patrol boat and two ships came into sight and the *Tambor* raced to safety. "The first time we've attacked for a long time without getting rapped," Bob noted.

Traveling submerged on August 15, they saw smoke on the horizon, chased it, and found a single unescorted tanker—an inviting target, but they couldn't get into firing position and so had to surface and chase it. When they caught up with it, they fired another spread of four torpedoes. "Watched one torpedo broach near target," Captain Germershausen wrote in his report. "Torpedo made a large splash in line with target's screws. Thought this was a sure hit but heard no explosion. Then saw torpedo pass about one hundred yards astern of target." The tanker dropped four depth charges on them and escaped. They were so far north that they began to wonder if they had mistakenly fired on a Russian tanker, since, as Germershausen wrote, "we could find no similar tanker in Jap identification manuals." They later received a message that the Russians had complained that an American sub had fired on one of their ships, and figured it was a good thing they had missed it.

Finally on the twentieth they came back through the pass and out of the Sea of Okhotsk, on their way home. Seven days later they hit Midway for an overnight stop, and on September 1 they arrived in Pearl Harbor. "Most of the old gang are back in the States," Bob wrote. "There are only two of us left who have made all the runs and we both leave this time. This was my last run for a long time." Again he sounded ambivalent about leaving the boat, but added, as if to reassure himself that he had done the right thing, "Sure will be glad to get a change."

Back at Pearl, he moved into the chiefs' quarters at the sub base, and no one seemed to care, or even notice, that he was there. He spent most of his time with his Hawaiian girlfriend, not even bothering to check in at the base or wear his uniform most of the time. The guys in charge of mustering the troops assured him they would count him as present and contact him if he was needed. He never was. It almost felt as though the war was over, but Bob knew that battles were still being fought and soldiers and sailors were still getting killed, and he believed that the outcome was still in doubt.

One of the few times Bob made sure to be at the base was October 3, when the *Tambor* took off on its thirteenth war patrol, the first one without him aboard. Bob entrusted his lucky Buddha to Link Handley, who had been put in charge of the forward room when Ole John had also opted off the boat. Bob claimed the privilege of throwing off the number-one line when the boat set off. He wished them good luck and good hunting, and then he heard the refrain he'd called out from the bow so many times himself. "If we don't come back, wave the flag for us on Market Street," the line crew said to him.

~~~~~~~~~~~~~~~~~~~~~~~~~~~~~~~~~~~~~

Two days later Bob was lounging in bed at his off-base hideaway when he got a call that he was to report right away to the offices of the big brass. He showered, shaved, put on his uniform, and rushed to the base, where he was ushered into one of the offices. The ensign behind the desk handed him a sheaf of papers without even looking at him.

"You're being transferred back to the States," he said.

Bob backed away from the papers as if the ensign were a process server. "Wait a minute," he said. "I bet nearly every serviceman on this island wants to go back to the States, right?"

"So?"

"So send one of them. I'm not going."

The ensign looked up at him with an uncomprehending stare, as if Bob were speaking a foreign language. When the young man's stare turned plaintive Bob sensed that he had the advantage on the junior officer, so he asked to speak to his superior. The ensign's stare instantly brightened into a relieved smile, and he led Bob into a bigger office with a larger desk, behind which was ensconced a much older and more composed officer with lieutenant's bars on his collar tabs. The ensign murmured something into the man's ear and hurried out of the office; the lieutenant invited Bob to sit down with a cordial wave of his arm and listened patiently as Bob told him that he had no desire to leave the island. As soon as he paused to take a breath, the lieutenant took another sheaf of papers off his desk and handed it to Bob. "According to information I have been given," he said, suddenly no longer sounding or looking so friendly, "Chief torpedoman Robert R. Hunt is spending most of his time on the beach with his girlfriend instead of on the base, which is where he is supposed to be. It doesn't seem to me as if you're much use to the United States Navy while you're playing volleyball on Waikiki Beach. Don't you agree?"

Bob thought the United States Navy had put him to enough use already, but it was easy to see that saying so would only make matters worse, so he merely nodded.

"Well, then," the lieutenant said, pushing the papers squarely beneath Bob's nose, "don't you think it would be a much better thing for all concerned if you were to accept your transfer to Hunters Point, San Francisco, and put your considerable expertise and experience to work as a member of the Advanced Training and Relief Crew?"

Bob nodded again and took the papers. He would have been better off sticking with the ensign.

He was sent back to the mainland on a Navy transport ship loaded with men from all branches of the military—uncomfortably crowded for most of them, but for Bob, who had never been to sea on any other vessel but a submarine, luxuriously spacious—so much so in fact that he kept getting lost in the ship's labyrinthine corridors. Finally a fellow CPO took pity on him, found him a bunk in the chiefs' quarters, and helped him find his way around. Since his promotion Bob had spent all his time as a chief either on the *Tambor* or avoiding duty in Hawaii, so this was his first taste of the respect and privileges afforded one of his rank. After all the years of sleeping on a skimpy mattress perched above a torpedo, and showering, shaving, and evacuating in a head the size of a broom closet, the chiefs' quarters seemed so much like a luxury hotel that he was sorry to see his trip come to an end. The accommodations at Hunters Point weren't bad either. He was assigned a bunk in a large, open dormitory-like area lined with beds and lockers and then largely forgotten, to the degree that he felt as if he were a parcel being stored in a warehouse until some use for him was found. His one and only duty was to be sure that a voice answered "here" when his name was announced at roll call every morning, and the voice didn't even have to be his, which suited Bob fine.

With little else to do, Bob explored San Francisco. Most nights he took the cable car to the corner of California and Hyde streets, where there were bars on three of the four corners. The ones Bob liked best were the one on the ground floor of a hotel that was frequented by local gangsters and one on another corner, which had the best-looking girls and the best music in town. As long as you avoided guys like "Big Bad Charlie," a permanent fixture at a corner table where he brokered his deals for bootleg liquor and gasoline, you didn't have a problem with the gangsters. Bob met a girl there who he started running with, one of a pair of sisters, both of whom had good jobs and good connections in San Francisco. Bob's girl made all the travel arrangements for a large clothing store on Market Street, and her sister was running with a Navy captain, one of the big brass at Bethlehem Steel in the submarine division. Bob's girl had the run of the town and introduced him to some of the city's finest restaurants and nightclubs. She was quite beautiful and always wore a fur piece draped around her neck, even in bed. She would let him do anything he wanted, but, she said, she didn't know him well enough to take her clothes off for him.

As one of the most experienced torpedomen in the Navy, Bob was called upon by submarine captains who were assembling crews for new boats. Like suitors, they flattered him and asked him to join their crews, but he turned them all down. When one put the pressure on him to serve, Bob told him he had already been on enough war patrols to last him for a while. "I know plenty of sailors who have been on more than four patrols," the captain barked back at him, pointing to Bob's service record, which was open to the first page on his desk. Bob told him to turn the page, and the captain counted: "Five, six, seven, eight, nine, ten, eleven, twelve." His face reddened, then he said, covering his embarrassment, "Get the hell out of here."

Captain Kefauver, who was now skipper of the *Springer* and was at Hunters Point between war patrols, was also looking for him, but Bob was able to duck him until the morning when two shore patrolmen jabbed him awake with their nightsticks and escorted him to Kefauver's office. He knew his former captain was going to ask him to volunteer for the *Springer*, and Bob already had the "no" half-formed in his throat. But Kefauver surprised him by asking him to serve as chief of the boat. It was the most important post next to that of the captain himself, and it was a great honor to be asked, especially by someone Bob respected so much. But before he could wither under Kefauver's level stare and accept the offer, then spend the next couple of years regretting it, he remembered something he had learned from Kefauver himself: When under attack, take the offensive.

"Mr. Kefauver," he said, "remember when you got transferred off the *Tambor* back at Midway? You left me to make the next war patrol with a boat full of inexperienced men. You bailed out on me then, so I'm bailing out on you now." It wasn't exactly true, and they both knew it. Kefauver had no choice but to obey his orders, and Bob could have gotten off the boat any time he wanted. But a lesson Bob had learned from the war was that you fought with whatever weapons were available and worried later about whether or not you had fought fair.

Kefauver leaned back in his chair and gave Bob a long look. "I was afraid that would be your answer, but I just wanted you to know that you were my choice."

With that matter settled, they lingered for a while to reminisce about past battles. On Kefauver's desk sat a jagged piece of depth-charge shrapnel he had pried from the *Tambor*'s deck; it was bronzed and inscribed with the coordinates of the seventeen-hour assault they'd survived at the bottom of the East China Sea. Finally they wished each other good luck. Bob wanted to ask Kefauver if he had really considered him a good luck charm, but he couldn't work up the nerve, and he didn't want to give him another opening.

Not long after that, Bob was again awakened by a shore patrolman's truncheon. At first he thought that Kefauver was after him again, but the SP told him he was to put on his full dress uniform and get over to the public relations office immediately. He'd been ordered to do so the day before, the man informed him gruffly, but Bob had been off the base and missed the order. While he was donning his uniform, he asked the SP if he had any idea what they wanted with him at the public relations office.

"To give you a medal and take your picture," the SP replied scornfully.

The reply caused Bob to remember a long-forgotten encounter, the only other time he'd heard the words "you" and "medal" uttered in the same sentence. On the way home from the nearly disastrous tenth war patrol, exhausted after a full day of cleaning the forward room and trying to repair all the depth-charge damage, Bob had crawled into the "bridal suite," the bunk that was hung from the overhead high in the middle of the room. From deck level, no one could see whether or not it was occupied, so when the yeoman came into the forward room looking for Bob, his crewmates told him he wasn't around. After he couldn't find Bob anywhere else on the boat, he came back, figuring he had been lied to, and said that he had orders from the captain. Bob poked his head over the side of the bunk and asked him what he wanted, and the yeoman started asking him questions and writing his responses in a notebook. *How long have you been in the Navy? How long have you been on the boat? How long have you been in charge of the forward room?* Bob eventually got tired of answering the questions and asked what was going on, and the yeoman said, "You're being recommended for a medal."

"I'm not interested in any goddamn medal," Bob had shouted down to him, and the yeoman had simply turned and left.

Three other chiefs and a lieutenant commander stood in the public relations office, all looking a little sheepish. He joined them and waited, feeling every bit as self-conscious as they looked. Finally an officer strode into the office, bringing a timid-looking Navy photographer in his wake. The officer lined them up against the wall as if he were about to bring in a firing squad, but instead had each man step forward to have a ribbon pinned on his chest while the photographer snapped picture after picture. As soon as the officer stopped pinning and the photographer stopped snapping, Bob was dismissed without a word of explanation. Bob ducked into the bathroom, and one of the other chiefs came in, holding his ribbon out in front of him as if it were something unclean. He went into the stall next to Bob, a loud flush immediately sounded, and the chief

Photo 23. Bob's father, R. C., received this photo in the mail, without explanation, then read in the Decorah newspaper that his son had received a commendation ribbon for his "exceptional skill and proficiency at his battle station" during a war patrol. (U.S. Navy)

came out of the stall empty-handed, a contemptuous smirk on his face. About a month later R. C. sent Bob a clipping from the Decorah newspaper with a grainy photo of Bob receiving his ribbon from the officer.

~~~~~~~~~~~~~~~~~~~~~~~~~

By Christmastime it had become obvious that the war would extend well into 1945. Though the Japanese cause was hopeless, they fought on, and it appeared that nothing less than a full-scale invasion of the Home Islands would force them to surrender. In Europe the war was prolonged by the Battle of the Bulge. Bob had won the bet he made at Midway, though his victory caused him no pleasure—and he saw little chance of ever collecting it. To his astonishment, however, one of the sailors who had taken a hundred dollars of it tracked him down at Hunters Point and paid up, and only a few days later, Lewis Payne, on liberty from the *Trigger*, materialized on the barstool next to his and paid his hundred bucks. He also told Bob that the *Shark*, with Bob's old buddy and sweater-mate Lloyd Schuermann aboard, had been sunk on October 24, on its third war patrol.

On December 10 the *Tambor* came to San Francisco, and Bob was at Hunters Point to handle the number-one line. He learned from his old crewmates that their thirteenth war patrol had been in many respects an unlucky one. While patrolling south and east of Honshu, they got caught in a typhoon and the port lookout had been washed overboard. After searching for an hour in the heavy seas, they found him and picked him up. Five weeks into the patrol, having scored two sinkings, they were ordered to Saipan to participate in a top secret mission with six other submarines. Writing after the war, Captain Germershausen described the venture:

> The fleet commanded by Admiral William F. Halsey, Task Force 38, was planning a strike against the Japanese mainland. No such operation had been carried out since the Doolittle raid in 1942. Halsey hoped to use his carrier forces to destroy Japanese warships in their home waters and to wreak havoc on their aviation industry. The raid was code-named "Operation Hotfoot."
>
> Our mission, as envisioned by Vice Admiral Lockwood, COMSUBPAC, was to sweep ahead of Halsey's forces and destroy pickets known to be guarding the approaches to Japan, thereby preventing them from alerting the Japanese regarding the approach of Halsey's fleet.

Early on the morning of November 17, the *Tambor* sank an enemy patrol boat with machine-gun fire, but during the attack Bob Baggett, a member of the 5-inch gun crew, was seriously wounded in the knee by an enemy shell. Baggett and a Japanese sailor who had also been wounded were evacuated to the USS *Grayson* two days later.

The rest of the mission, Germershausen wrote, was "a masterpiece of confusion." A lone Japanese patrol vessel managed to hold off three attacking submarines; the *Tambor* was ordered to join this attack but never received the message. Germershausen noted, "300 rounds of deck gun ammunition were expended without destroying the target." During a subsequent attack on two armed trawlers, the *Ronquil* blew two holes in its own pressure hull. Finally, Germershausen wrote succinctly, "COMSUBPAC called the whole thing off at 1630 on November 17."[2]

The submarine sweep had been designated "Burt's Brooms," named after Cdr. T. B. "Burt" Klakring, who captained its lead sub, the *Ronquil*. Wolf pack operations had never been a strength of the U.S. sub fleet, and this one was hampered by high seas which made accurate shooting from the slick, pitching decks of the subs impossible.

When Bob told Link Handley that at least the lucky Buddha he had given him had gotten them all home, Link replied that the Buddha had been stolen.

Bob had grown tired of being warehoused in the chiefs' quarters, so he tried working in a local defense plant, but soon quit, in part because the neighborhood was almost as dangerous as enemy-controlled waters. He also ran the officers' quarters and the base motor pool for a short time, although he had no experience with either. The *Tambor* had been assigned to training exercises in Port Angeles, Washington, in March 1945 and served as spotting target for anti-sub pilots training there. As a result, none of his old buddies came to San Francisco anymore. One benefit he gained from the *Tambor*'s reassignment was that he had taken over the downtown apartment of Link Handley's girlfriend Bonnie, who had moved north to be with him.

The wheels of the Navy's bureaucracy ground slowly, but finally the captain of the sub base gave Bob an assignment for which he was eminently qualified—designing and running the Navy's first torpedo-tube school. Until then, the sailors who worked on the tubes had to learn by trial and error, on the boats and with relief crews. Now, however, with so many new boats being commissioned during the last big Pacific push, too many sailors were going into battle with neither the necessary experience nor the chance to get it. With twelve war patrols in the forward room of the *Tambor* on his resume, Bob was judged the ideal man to run the school, and he had to admit that he couldn't think of anyone better. His only condition was that he be allowed to do things his way, with no interference from above, and the officers over him were only too happy to shift all responsibilities from their shoulders to his.

Bob soon discovered that he enjoyed teaching and was good at it. His combat experience gave him instant credibility with his students, and being only a few years older than them helped him communicate effectively. When he was giving his introductory talk to his first class, one of the men in the back pulled out a six-pack of beer and opened one. Bob walked to the back, grabbed a can, opened it for himself, and, sipping from it as he walked to the front of the room, instructed the trainee to share the remainder equally with his classmates. Whenever he had a class that wouldn't pay attention, he set up a problem with their practice tube and water tank that sent water spraying out of the tank and all over the room. "Your room is flooding," he announced. "Fix the problem or sink."

Never was his students' perception of him more evident than in a sketch one of them turned in on an exam sheet. It pictured Bob in full uniform with a submarine combat pin and a chest full of medals, leaning against a signpost. A long chain with a miniature submarine attached to it looped from the waist of his pants, zoot-suit style. The picture required a caption, "CPO Hunt," not because of any defect in the drawing, which was excellent, but because Bob was rendered in it as a long-jawed wolf. And at the top of the signpost an arrow-shaped sign read "Waves BRKS." Bob gave the young sailor an "F" on the test, but he kept the drawing.

~~~~~~~~~~~~~~~~~~~~~~~~~~~~~~~~~~~~~

On January 8, 1945, MacArthur landed at Lingayen Gulf and drove quickly through to Manila, forcing the Japanese army to retreat into the mountains of Luzon. Now, ironically, it was they who were the guerrillas, fleeing the occupying force. The more ground the Japanese lost, however, the harder they fought. At Iwo Jima it took three marine divisions a full month to capture a rocky island less than five miles long and three miles wide. Marine losses totaled 6,800, and 19,000 were wounded in the effort, and only 216 of the more than 20,000 Japanese soldiers survived. The blood flowed almost as freely in the invasion of Okinawa, where American forces suffered a 35 percent casualty rate.

Despite the fierce Japanese resistance, the war effort begun with the Pearl Harbor attack was running dry. The oil ports in the East Indies had been abandoned, the Home Islands refineries were out of fuel, and when one last tanker convoy tried to make it past the American submarines in March 1945, it was promptly sunk. On April 13, the U.S. submarine *Bashaw* had just surfaced to outrace a pursuing destroyer when its crew was astonished to see the destroyer stop dead in the water, out of fuel.

On the other side of the world it was still April 12, and the stunning news of President Roosevelt's death in Warm Springs, Georgia, had begun to circulate. The greatest war machine the world had ever known was now under the command of a former senator from Missouri named Harry S. Truman, who was known to the American public—to the extent that he was known at all—for his crusade to combat waste and fraud in the military-industrial complex.

The litany of American military successes in the first half of 1945 seemed to bring the Japanese no closer to surrendering. Their cause had long since been lost, but soldiers, sailors, and civilians continued to die by the thousands, and ships and submarines continued to be sunk. Among the eight U.S. subs lost in 1945 was the *Trigger* in late March, with Bob's old crewmate Lewis Payne aboard. An Allied invasion of the Japanese mainland seemed inevitable, with millions of casualties expected on each side.

On August 6, however, the world was startled by the news, delivered over the radio by President Truman in his calm, clipped Missouri twang, that the United States had dropped an unfathomably destructive new weapon on the Japanese city of Hiroshima. Three days later, a second atomic bomb was dropped on Nagasaki. On August 14, despite protests and even a coup attempt by members of the Japanese military, Emperor Hirohito recorded a surrender message that was

Figure 4. A student in Bob's Hunters Point torpedo tube school turned in this drawing in lieu of exam answers. Bob complimented him on his artistic abilities, kept the drawing, and gave him an F on the exam.

broadcast on Japanese radio the next day. It was the first time Japanese citizens had heard the emperor speak, and most were stunned and moved that he had spoken to them in a human voice.

Bob heard the news on a car radio. At the end of the workday, August 15, 1945, he and five of his friends took a pool car into downtown San Francisco. There had been lively talk in the car about the bombs that had been dropped on Hiroshima and Nagasaki, but as soon as the radio announcer began to report the surrender news, they all fell quiet. Each had made war patrols in the Pacific, and each felt keenly the import of the moment. "I was the first to get out," Bob remembered. "They let me off at the cable car on Market Street so I could get up the hill to California and Hyde. My apartment—the one I was keeping for Bonnie—was only a block or so from there. I had one thing on my mind: to get cleaned up, put on my dress uniform, and head back to Market Street to wave the flag for all my shipmates and all the sub sailors who had gone down on the boats."

Around him, people were streaming out of the buildings and onto the street with wide, almost dazed smiles on their faces. Those still in their offices threw shredded paper out of the windows that floated down, shimmering in the afternoon sunlight. Quickly the streets filled with smiling people literally jumping for joy, shouting and embracing. Some climbed light poles and whooped while others below them danced in the streets. One woman took off all her clothes and climbed a statue to pose.

Eagerly Bob made his way to the apartment, showered, put on his uniform, and headed for the cable car to go back down the hill. "We'll all be dead, so wave the flag on Market Street." Now it was time. He thought of Lewis Payne, Lloyd Schuermann, Joe Manger, and so many others. It was time to remember them all. But he needed a flag. Bob recalled: "I no sooner got on the street when I noticed a little boy playing at a storm sewer grate and he was holding a small American flag. I told the boy I wanted to buy his flag, and he said 'No way!' But then I said, 'I'll give you twenty bucks for it,' and I had my flag."

When he reached Market Street and got off the cable car, however, he was shocked by what he saw. "Instead of happy people I saw a mob of hoodlums with the look of kill on their faces. Every criminal in the city must have come downtown and everybody else, it seemed, just went along." The crowd rushed and seethed, some of them running in and out of the shattered windows of stores, filling their arms with whatever they could carry. Desks and display tables and wooden manikins had been dragged out, piled in the street, and set ablaze. Dark smoke rose from bonfires while fire trucks stood at intersections, blocked by the crowd. The police were helpless, and several of their cars were overturned. Underage recruits staggered drunk, bottles in their hands from looted liquor stores. The young trainees, cheated of their chance to go to war, fought each other or whoever came along. Others fought over looted goods or just because all hell had broken loose. Sirens wailed above screams and shouting, punctuated by the pop and crash of storefront windows. Shattered glass crunched under Bob's feet the way it had in the *Tambor* after a depth charging.

In the chaos Bob looked for an open space where he could stand and wave his flag, but someone knocked him down and then there were hands clutching at his uniform, trying to tear it off him. When someone tried to snatch his chief's hat he grabbed it and held on with both hands, then struggled to his feet. "I was mad now, too, and I wanted to fight, but there were too many of them, so I ran for the cable car. When I got there I saw that it had to be rotated to head back up the hill, but vandals had pushed the conductor out of the way and were trying to spin the car. In a scuffle several of us were able to drive off the vandals and get the conductor back to his car. Then we got the thing pointed the right way and all jumbled on and headed up the hill with a very large sigh of relief. In just a couple of blocks we were out of it and everything was quiet."

City officials and the national media were not eager to dwell on what came to be called the "peace riots," but the *San Francisco Chronicle* tried to tell the story. Initially "doctors weren't sure [of the precise number of casualties] because they were still too busy taking care of the injured to bother with bookkeeping." One of the hundreds injured was a friend of Bob's, a mild-mannered old chief who showed up at Hunters Point the next morning with a big shiner. He had taken one step out of his Market Street apartment, he explained, when he was punched in the eye by a complete stranger. He scrambled back inside and stayed there until morning, listening to the havoc in the street. He was luckier than the eighty-year-old retired bank clerk whom the *Chronicle* reported had been hit by a wastepaper basket filled with water and thrown from a high window. It struck him in the head and killed him instantly. In the final accounting he was one of eleven who died. There were several rapes, and no one knew how many had gone unreported. According to the *Chronicle*, 107 plate-glass windows and 300 street-car windows were broken, at least 135 parking signs were destroyed, barber poles were broken off their bases, and policemen were disarmed and beaten. The utter senselessness of the violence was typified by an assault on city hall, also reported by the *Chronicle*. A "crowd of civilian hoodlums" smashed in a door of the municipal building, tore a phone off a wall when a night watchman tried to call for help, and made off with a time clock. "I'm lucky that I'm alive," the watchman was reported as saying.

"That was a very sad day for me," Bob recalled. "When I got off the cable car I went to my neighborhood bar and had enough drinks so when I got back to the apartment I just fell into bed and didn't wake up until the next morning. To this day I don't know what happened to my flag. I sure wish I still had it."

CHAPTER TWELVE

"Echoes of the Past"

On the same day that the atomic bomb fell on Hiroshima, the USS *Bull-head* was sunk by depth charges from a Japanese plane while patrolling off the coast of Bali. It was the fifty-second and final American sub-marine to be sunk in the war. On the day of the Japanese surrender, the USS *Torsk* sank two eight-hundred-ton Japanese frigates in the Sea of Japan, the last submarine victims of the war. At 11:04 that night, Admiral Nimitz ordered all naval units to cease fire.

The final record of the U.S. submarines during World War II showed a total of 1,392 Japanese naval and merchant sinkings, or nearly one ship sunk for each of the 1,347 days of U.S. involvement in the war. The 5.5 million tons of Japanese shipping downed by the subs represented just over half the total sunk during the war. During Bob's service on the *Tambor*, the crew recorded twenty-one ships sunk and eight more disabled or damaged, plus seventeen merchant ships under five hundred tons that they destroyed. After the war, however, the Joint Army–Navy Assessment Committee was able to confirm only eleven of the *Tambor*'s sinkings.

After the war millions of soldiers and sailors would rejoin the new world they had helped to create; millions more civilians who had been engaged in war work would find their jobs—and the factories and offices where they performed them—either transformed or eliminated. Even the instruments of war that these men and women had labored so devotedly to create and so diligently to use were no longer needed in such overwhelming numbers. Among these instruments was the *Tambor*. After its last war patrol in December 1944, on which it earned its eleventh battle star, it was overhauled at Mare Island Navy Yard and sent to Port Angeles, Washington, to commence training operations with Navy patrol aircraft. The boat also picked up a new captain in Mare Island, as Lt. Cdr. A. M. Ferrara relieved Commander Germershausen. In September 1945, it began the long trip back to its birthplace in Portsmouth, New Hampshire, for decommissioning. Larry Vincent, who joined the *Tambor* crew in October, described the last leg of the boat's final journey in a 1986 letter to Bob Hunt:

> I caught her in Mare Island during 10/45 and shortly after Navy Day (10/27) we sailed with four other subs (*Tuna*, *Thresher*, *Tautog*, and *Gar*) for the East Coast and eventual decommissioning. We were decommissioned at the Portsmouth Navy Yard on 5 December 1945 [the Navy's official records list the decommissioning date as December 10] and the crew at that time had been reduced down to about 12 or 15 persons. At the topside ceremony the commissioning pennant, the jack and the standard flag were awarded to 3 plank owners whose names I have long since forgotten.

In 1947, the *Tambor* was sent to the Naval Reserve Training Center in Detroit to serve as a training boat. One of the reservists assigned to the boat as an instructor was none other than Detroit native Larry Vincent. The boat was finally found unfit for further duty in 1959 and sold for scrap, along with the other two surviving subs in its squadron, the *Tautog* and the *Gar*. The *Thresher* had been scrapped in 1948. The other boat in the squadron that had survived the war, the *Tuna*, had served as a target during the atomic-bomb tests at Bikini in 1946 and was sunk as a target off San Francisco Bay two years later.[1]

Bob Hunt's transition to civilian life began in November of 1945, when he was transferred to Mare Island for the last few weeks of his enlistment. Bob had six years of service and a rating of chief, which would have assured him of prime duty and good pay for as long as he chose to stay in the Navy, but he had no thoughts of doing so. With no duties and nothing else to do but wait for his discharge papers, Bob spent most of his time in the nearby town of Vallejo. It had been a Navy town for many years and was still a pretty tough place—you didn't want to go there alone in case you got into a fight and needed backup—but it also housed all the familiar recreational requisites. Sub sailors passed through all the time, so Bob ran into many of his old shipmates and celebrated with them each time he did. Sometimes the celebrations went on for several days, as they did when he got together with Harry Behrens and Ole John Clausen. "This was a good way to end my time in the service," Bob remembered. Bob's friends had a couple of young women with them, and of course Bob had found a woman in town, as well. The ladies, however, were forced to spend most of their time listening as Bob, Harry, and Ole John sorted memories and pieced together the stories they shared in common. It was an opportunity for them to sum up their experiences, to tag an exclamation point on the end of their adventures and ordeals, and to celebrate the unlikely fact that they had survived.

Four months earlier, before the war had ended and when he'd still been teaching torpedo-tube school at Hunters Point, Bob had looked ahead in a letter to his dad:

Barb said she stopped in to see you. Bet you had quite a talk about the farming situation. . . .

I plan to go in business after the war & Dick & I will no doubt be together. It's a cinch we'll need plenty of help. The regular navy will have a much harder time getting out, but we plan to fight for equal rights with the reserves. I think we at least rate that. The people that get out first will certainly have the best chance. Even though the big money will be on the coast I plan to start back your way. It would be hard to say anything definite right now as we don't know how long this deal will last. . . . People will be a lot different after this war than before.

On Christmas Day, 1945, Bob received his discharge. And, true to his planning, he returned to Iowa.

~~~~~~~~~~~~~~~~~~~~~~~~~~~~~~

In October of 2006 I traveled back to Decorah to visit Bob Hunt. I had moved to Virginia two years before, and I was accompanied by my co-writer, James Shell. The three of us were going to drive together to Manitowoc, Wisconsin, to tour the USS *Cobia*, the *Tambor*-like sub moored at the Maritime Museum there. James and I flew into Minneapolis, rented a van, and drove south past dark fields, woodlots, and scattered farmhouses, passing through small towns—Chatfield, Preston, Harmony, Canton—and descended finally the long, gradual hill of state highway 52 as it enters the Oneota Valley, a dark bowl dotted with the lights of Luther College and the town of Decorah, population 8,172.

The next morning we drove down Water Street, past the bank façade that covered the site of the old Hunt Variety Store and past the Vesterheim Museum, a handsome brick building with Renaissance-style windows and a small balcony where the king of Norway had stood and waved to the crowd below during his visit in 1995. We steered toward the earthen dike that holds back the Upper Iowa River when it floods in springtime, and turned onto Goose Island Drive. At Heritage Haven Apartments, a long, blue one-story building, we parked next to the camouflage-painted dumpsters of the Army Reserve post next door. Bob immediately came out to greet us, still trim and wiry at 87.

It is the first time he has met James, after much correspondence—including an exchange in which Bob and the smart, attractive women who helped him with our book—Mary and Julie—sent him an official-looking document certifying him for submarine duty. Bob figured James had earned his rating, having mastered in prose the intricate workings of ballast tanks, bilges, and poppet valves. It's a damp, cool morning in Decorah, but Bob is in high spirits and he takes us inside. As he unlocks a side door, he explains, "This is a very secure place. It has to be. Sometimes, after the bowling alley closes, drunks come through this way."

From a narrow central hallway we step into a small apartment—bathroom to the left, bedroom straight ahead, a kitchen to the right that opens to a sitting room with couch, chair, coffee table, and bookshelves. At its far end, outside the picture window, chickadees hop and flutter at a bird feeder mounted on a metal pole. In the kitchen Bob's bike leans against the small Formica-topped table. The table is spread with things he wants us to see—his war diary with its spine taped where the rat gnawed it, photo albums, newspaper clippings. Today his wife Barb is much on his mind, and many of the clippings and photos he has laid out to show us are about her. He speaks with pride of her long career in journalism. For sixty-two years she wrote for and helped to edit the two weekly Decorah papers. Bob repeatedly says, "She's the smart one." Their Christmas card from the year before is printed with a photo of Bob and Barb in red Norwegian vests as he helps her into a convertible for the Nordic Fest parade the year she was chosen to be its Grand Marshal. Every morning now he goes to the Aase Haugen Home to have breakfast with her and returns to eat lunch there, as well. "She needs some help, and it's nicer if I can do it," he explains. When the weather is okay he rides his bike across town for the visits. After we have gone through the materials on the table, we will go to see Barb.

"Between us, she was always the brains of the outfit," Bob says. "And she was beautiful. Not like a cover girl. I mean, during the war I went out with girls that were beautiful. And Barb was good-looking. But she was—she still is—a beautiful person."

On the wall I see a blue commemorative plate painted with the words, "Bob and Barb, July 14, 1946." In the summer they had marked their sixtieth wedding anniversary.

When Bob and Dick had gotten out of the service they had gone to Waterloo, Iowa, about seventy miles southwest of Decorah, to work for a cousin at the Iowa Paint and Glass Company he ran there. While in Waterloo, Bob cashed out of the eighty-acre farm he had bought with his dad when Bob was operating out of Australia. At the time, R. C. still lived behind his downtown store, rented out the farmland, and sometimes helped the tenants with the crops as recreation from his work at the store. After Bob sold his share in the farm, he had his poker winnings back—plus a little profit—as a stake for civilian life.

Barb lived in nearby Grundy Center where she ran the Farm Bureau *Spokesman* newspaper. She had written Bob a couple of letters during the war, but, holding to his strict policy, he had not answered. Now they started dating, and within a year Bob said to her: "Why don't we get married and give it a try and see how it goes." Ignoring the tentativeness of the proposal, Barb accepted. The ceremony at the Little Brown Church in the Vale north of town included only the couple, Dick as Bob's best man, a relative of Barb's as her maid of honor, and the pastor.

Dick met his wife, Peggy, in Waterloo, and the couple moved to Madison,

Photo 24. Barb Hunt in the 1940s—Bob's favorite photo of her. (Courtesy Robert Hunt)

Photo 25. Bob and Dick Hunt, ca. 1943. Both men enlisted before the war and rose to the grade of chief. (Courtesy Robert Hunt)

Wisconsin, where Dick opened his own glass and paint company. They prospered, had two children, and bought an A-frame on a lake in northern Wisconsin, where Bob and Barb visited twice a year, catching muskies, walleye, perch, and crappies in the lake. Bob saw his sister Marge less frequently. She and her husband Bill worked as educators all their lives, raising their two children in Atlantic, Iowa.

In 1950 Bob bought his dad out of the Hunt Variety Store and ran it for twenty years. Once the couple returned to Decorah they lived an outdoor life, ranging the streams and fields together in the summertime. Bob hunted deer and pheasants in the countryside around town and ducks along the Mississippi. He bought a brand-new shotgun for Barb, which she fired once; then it found a permanent home in a rack on the wall. "There's no way she would ever shoot a bird," Bob said. She did go bow hunting for deer with Bob, and had her own bow. "She never hit anything with it," Bob said. "She probably didn't want to."

Their son David, who had been born in Waterloo, went to Luther College, earned a master's degree in Political Science and History at Iowa State University in Ames, and taught high school in Tipton, Iowa. An annual highlight of his history course was a visit from his father to talk about World War II with his students. In mid-career David was voted Iowa Teacher of the Year, received a $20,000 award, and was funded to spend nine months visiting schools around the state to describe his teaching methods.

Younger son Craig was born in Decorah—February 29, 1952—the eighth anniversary of the *Tambor*'s arrival at Midway after its near-fatal tenth war patrol. After graduating from the University of Iowa, his work for the short-lived 1976 presidential candidacy of Fred Harris took Craig to the East Coast. When he returned to Decorah his dad had sold Hunt Variety Store to the bank and had become head of the Decorah Parks and Recreation department, a position Bob held through the 1970s. Craig joined his dad in this work and, since Bob's retirement in 1980, has continued to operate the Decorah Municipal Campground.

Bob and Barb sold their house on Pine Street in 2003 when Barb, after a fall, was confined to a wheelchair. They moved together into an assisted-living apartment, but that arrangement proved expensive, and when Barb's health declined further, she went to the Aüse Haugen Home and Bob moved into his Heritage Haven apartment behind the bowling alley and next to the Army Reserve post.

Even after Barb had retired from full-time editing, she had continued to assemble a weekly feature, "Echoes of the Past," a selection of local news items that had appeared in the paper ten, twenty, or fifty years before. The feature still runs in the paper, produced now by a successor. One of the items Bob had cut out for us to see had appeared just a few weeks earlier. It was the obituary for

Bob's mother, Bessie, reprinted from 1936: "The entire community has received the sad news that Mrs. R. C. Hunt has passed away. The 40-year-old well-known resident will be sadly missed. She and her husband operated the Ben Franklin Store here."

"That really hit me hard when I saw it," Bob offered. "I wasn't expecting to see it. I was just reading the paper and there it was. It really hit me hard." He paused. "It made me realize how little I've thought about all that—my mother dying so young when I was in high school." At the time the family had lived in a two-story, wood-frame house with a porch on Oak Street. An aunt who was a nurse had moved in with them to help take care of Bessie, who stayed at home through her illness and death. "Sometimes I just had to get out of the house," Bob remembered. He'd walk out the front door, into the pasture across the street, and straight on into the woods beyond. "There were no trails there. I just went out into the woods and walked."

～～～～～～～～～～～～～～～～～～～～

Driving to the Aüse Haugen Home to see Barb, we cross the Upper Iowa where it curves beneath high limestone palisades. Bob and Barb used to fish it from their canoe, catching smallmouth bass and, where spring-fed streams chilled the river, wild trout. The Home, like Bob's apartment, is situated next to the dike, but on the other side of the river. Inside, it is brightly lit and clean. All the staff and residents know Bob, and he greets them and introduces us as we make our way past the dining hall and through a common area. A dark-haired resident, a woman with dramatic eyebrows and a piercing gaze, stares fixedly at Bob, waiting for him to notice her. When she catches his eye she smiles broadly and nods at him.

Barb has a private room, where she sits in her wheelchair, facing the window. Bob sits beside her on the narrow bed, and James and I stand. Bob introduces us, and Barb lifts her head to smile at me. "See, she remembers you," Bob says, beaming. "You got a good smile out of her."

He tells her he will be gone until the next evening, reminding her that we're traveling to the maritime museum. He tells her that the nurses know he'll be gone, and that they'll watch out for her. Barb understands and nods. James and I step into the hall and Bob takes a few minutes alone with his wife. On the way out of the building he tells us: "She always loved reading. She was always reading some kind of book. She can't do that anymore, and that's a shame." We walk on to the van in silence.

Driving to the museum, the three of us have five hours together on the road. We ask questions and Bob replies, usually with a story. He goes back to the war years and takes us with him. In the forward room of the *Cobia* he stands at his old post between the torpedo tubes and explains each valve and lever. Standing next to the H-beam that bisects the room to support torpedoes during reload, he explains how it was strengthened, according to his specifications, after an accident on the *Tambor*. In the crew's mess I ask where he played poker, and he takes his habitual seat at the end of a bench and leans into the galley bulkhead. "This was my spot," he says. "But there was always a pinup here." He pats the bulkhead next to his shoulder.

With the museum director, Michelle Hill, we are able to tour the boat from end to end, and Bob explains everything—engine room, maneuvering room, battery room, the complex of valves and levers in the head. In the control room he shows us his watch station at the bow planes and explains the Christmas tree. From the control room, James and I are permitted to climb the ladder into the conning tower. It is about the size of an overturned hot tub, a stark, claustrophobic space beneath the bridge where three or more officers conducted attacks, steering the boat from an iron wheel at the front, peering through the 'scope in the middle of the room, and using the Torpedo Data Computer in the back. Even with only two of us in it, we feel cramped, and knowing what occurred in this space, my muscles tense.

Back topside, James takes a picture of Bob and Michelle. He throws his arm over her shoulder and she smiles into the camera. Bob, even now, continues to surround himself with attractive women—his assistants, Mary and Julie; his longtime Decorah friend, Judy; the women who teach ski lessons with him. (On the way home Bob points out the Wisconsin ski resort where he still gives instruction in the winter!) They sense how much he likes women, how he genuinely enjoys their company, and his charm continues. One understands why he was never alone between patrols. Yet, equally evident has been his devotion to Barb, his admiration for her, and the pain he feels at the loss of the easy companionship they shared for so long. "She doesn't talk so good anymore," he tells us on the drive home, "and I don't hear so good. So that makes it tough."

We talk for another five hours in the van—the questions and the stories continue—and when we arrive back at Decorah Bob's voice is hoarse.

In the summer of 2005 I'd made another trip from Virginia to Decorah, this one for my son's wedding. On a Saturday morning I sat with Bob in his small bedroom-study with photos of the *Tambor*, crewmates, friends, and his Great Lakes training class hanging on the walls. There was a single bed in a nook against the wall, a desk with computer, and two chairs. The room was smaller than most compartments on Bob's sub, and we sat almost knee to knee. I'd asked Bob whether his twelve consecutive patrols on the same boat might be a record and he was resisting such talk. "We didn't think like that," he said. "Anybody who came out and served on a war patrol was one of us. We were all volunteers and we were doing a tough job, so we had a lot of respect for everybody on the boat." I knew that Harry Behrens had done twelve patrols on three different subs. I hadn't discovered anyone who had gone on more patrols than that, and no other sailor on the *Tambor* served on the boat as long as Bob had. Finally, he did allow: "I've never met the guy who did more."

Bob had told me that he didn't expect to survive the war, and I wanted to understand what motivated him to keep going out. At first he made jokes.

"After a mission we'd come in and had two weeks off. We might get hammered for two or three days, but we always knew when we were going to leave. We were partying so much the night before we went, the first thing I know is I'm on the boat and I feel a swell. We're going out on war patrol, and I said, 'Shoot, I've done it again!'" He laughed and I laughed with him. I asked again.

"Well, you got pay-and-a-half and nobody bothered you. It wasn't regular Navy. We didn't pay a lot of attention to the officers. Besides the captain and the navigator, they were mostly a box of rocks." We laughed again.

He paused, and we let the quiet settle in the tiny room. "They were killing my buddies like crazy," Bob said. "I wanted to get out there and fight back."

"So it was very personal," I said.

"Yes," Bob agreed. Then he thought some more. Finally, he arrived at what I took to be the bottom line.

"When it came time to go," he said, "I wasn't not going to do it.'"

~~~~~~~~~~~~~~~~~~~~~~~~~~~~~~~~

When I met Bob in 1985 he was retired, but still did some work under the banner of Hunt Enterprises as factory rep for companies that sold playground equipment or built tennis courts and swimming pools. He and Barb still lived in the tidy, ranch-style house with the white siding and red brick front. In the summer I would see him in his yard, wearing a sweat suit in the 90-degree weather, something I only understood after hearing about the 130-degree temperatures inside the *Tambor* when it operated in tropical waters without air conditioning. Then it seemed to me that his body's thermostat had been permanently readjusted during the war.

When we spoke of making a book together, Bob took me to his basement study, an unfinished room with concrete floor, exposed pipes and wires, bookshelves, and a desk lit from above by bare lightbulbs. Outside the sunken window wells and the tiny basement windows, the upper Midwest stretched all around, a vast inland sea. Perfectly at home, he pulled binders from the shelves and opened them on the desk. They were filled with photographs ranging from his enlistment to the present; with clippings from *Polaris*, the sub vets' newsletter; with drawings and documents; and with letters from former crewmates or their wives, sons, or daughters. One letter noted that the only remaining part of the *Tambor*—its periscope—survives at the Dossin Great Lakes Museum, where visitors can press their faces to the rubber eyepieces and peer through its magnifying optics at the Detroit River and the city's skyline. Several binders contained snapshots of shipmates at conventions and reunions, middle-aged men in SS-198 ball caps and vests sewn with patches. As I flipped the pages the men aged.

Bob's *Tambor* archive included a complete set of captains' logs covering each of the boat's war patrols. The dark photocopies were sometimes hard to read but the pages were firmly bound between hard covers. Out of a cardboard box, Bob produced what looked like a rolled pillowcase and unfurled the *Tambor's* handmade battle flag. "We flew it from the number-one periscope shear the last time we sailed under the Golden Gate Bridge," he told me. "That was the only time, I think."

A small, pocket-sized booklet wrapped in blue-green cardboard and sewn with a red thread was a memento from a crew's party in San Francisco, February 16, 1945, after the boat's final war patrol. The cover featured a drawing of a submarine labeled USS *Tambor*. Inside, after a full listing of the crew members, the night's entertainment was previewed, including "For your pleasure: 'The Kilgore Dancers, Princesses of Precision'; 'Zenith Sisters, Boogie Babes'; 'Edyth Dennis, Pin-up Girl'; 'Francis Dainty & Co., Feats on Wheels'; and 'Music for Dancing' styled by Ray Hackett's CBS Band." The back pages were to serve, apparently, as a "little black book." Nine ruled lines appeared below column headings labeled "Name," "Height," "Bust," and "Phone."

We paged together through the *Life* magazine that came to Bob and Barb's house in 1946, bringing an article on the Battle of Midway that included images mocked up to represent its key moments. One of them depicted the *Tambor* surfacing near the Japanese heavy cruisers. "That's when I learned that the two ships had collided because of us," Bob said. "That's the first I knew about it."

Over the years Bob had been the organizer of *Tambor* reunions at sub conventions in places such as Reno, Albuquerque, Vegas, and Norfolk, making good on his drunken prediction on the beach at Midway that they'd all get together after the war. In the process he had collected current information sheets on his former crewmates that included contact information and photos from then and now. And he'd also made contact with a wider circle of veterans. When he saw an article in the Cedar Rapids *Gazette* about a local man who had been stationed on Wake Island when the *Tambor* cruised offshore in the war's first days, he sent the man a letter. The man, Marvin Balhorn, replied promptly, giving Bob a full account of his experience on Wake and as a prisoner of war after the island fell. Bob even corresponded with the son of Chick Parsons, the man who had led the shore party to resupply the guerrillas on the Philippines. Bob admitted that he and the others in the forward room hadn't liked their passengers much "because they were officers and certainly let us know that," but he and the son conducted a genial correspondence, with Peter filling in details of his family's life in the Philippines before the war and his father's support of the guerrillas during the Japanese occupation. He also put Bob in touch with the radioman

Photo 26. Robert Hunt in 2008. (Taken by David Cavagnaro)

who had given Bob the typed 50-centavos note. Bob learned that the radioman, Bill Johnson, originally had served on one of the three PT boats that removed MacArthur from Corregidor. After he'd declined Bob's invitation to take him back to Australia on the *Tambor*, Johnson spent two years spying on Japanese shipping from the hills overlooking Davao Gulf, providing information that led to many U.S. sub kills. His service ended when a Moro man shot him in the back to steal his weapons. After the shooting a fellow radioman kept him alive, and now Johnson corresponded with Bob from his home in Florida.

Even as Bob had lived his postwar life as businessman, husband, and father, he'd reached back in a sustained act of memory, eager to fill gaps in his knowledge of what he'd lived through. These acts of reconstruction informed the yearly visits Bob made to area schools to talk with students about the war in the Pacific and his role in it. Some of the binders on the shelves around us contained materials for these visits, and he always took along a big map charting the *Tambor*'s missions, noting with color-coded dots the sites of depth chargings,

aerial bombardments, sinkings, and surface battles. If repetition eventually out-
weighed analysis, it was because the magnitude of remembered events eclipsed
the view of more distant causes. And Bob's wartime experiences could hardly
have been more mind-filling—living in a metal pipe in the middle of the ocean,
a small boat alone thousands of miles from home, men confined together in
cramped compartments for two months at a time, hunting and killing, literally
under pressure ("Pressure in the boat," the diving officer would call). And then
two weeks of utter freedom in a strange place, cut loose from normal time, awash
in gratitude for sunlight and touch, for another survival, at first exhausted, but
then effervescent with bottled-up sex and fear and anger. For two weeks they'd
purge and rebuild themselves, seeking what they felt they needed. Then out
again and back to the fight, because this was the work of their time, the time of
their youth.

~~~~~~~~~~~~~~~~~~~~~~~~~~~~~~~~

When I still lived in Decorah and when Bob and Barb still lived in their
house two doors up, I would go for walks, climbing the Pine Street hill,
descending the other side to the edge of town, passing the small pasture where
two horses grazed—if I'd stuck a carrot in my back pocket they would come to
the fence to eat it from my hand—then I'd climb again to hilly Phelps Cemetery
and circle among the headstones before returning home. Coming and going, I
passed Bob's house, and often in the year when he was writing down his memories I saw through the tiny basement window a single bare lightbulb burning in
what I knew to be Bob's room. I always pictured him there, in that unfinished
space—its exposed pipes, wires, and insulation—surrounded by his maps, note-
books, and photos, submerged again in that past time.

I did not stop to go in and see him, but as I walked on, part of me stayed
there, wondering at the submariner at home, underground in Iowa, remembering. And I wondered myself at a life so marked by early experience. When the
war ended Bob was twenty-six, and everything that followed—even love, mar-
riage, children, career—would be aftermath. He might disagree, arguing for the
primacy of his postwar life—and he would not use the word "aftermath"—but
when I spoke to him and he told me one of the stories that stood so clear in his
mind, his eyes widened and his voice took on a wondering tone, as if neither
one of us should credit such a tale. *But there it is*, that tone said again—*I can hardly
believe what I did and witnessed.* "I didn't figure I was going to make it," he told me
once. "I just knew I wasn't going to make it." *Yet, now, after everything, here I am.*

His past had become the great romance—they set ships on fire in the middle
of the sea; they had parties all over the world—and he responded to the enor-
mity of the war that had caught him up with a capacity for wonder that spilled
into the afterlife. "After the war it was liberty with no going back. Just driving

a car with the windows down was a great thing. Sometimes I even sang when I drove, or Barb and I sang together. It was something I'd never done before." I wondered that he had emerged from those years on the boat so apparently unscathed. When he wrote his memories the blunt sentences seemed unshadowed, one story leading to the next in an associative flow in which cascading events left no room for reflection. Once, when he used the word "flashback," I asked him what flashed back, expecting a patch of darkness. But he said, "The things that come back are the things I like to remember—the parties, the sex." The darkest aspect he ever showed me was the set jaw and straight gaze when he spoke of his friends who'd been killed. Then I glimpsed the resolve and simmering anger that saw him through, that kept him going out, and that provided the big story his generation shared: America had been attacked, they'd set all aside to avenge the wound and defeat the aggressor, and then they'd gone back to live normal lives. The war was an interruption, and they'd put it behind them with a resolve like that with which they'd fought.

But Bob kept going back. Eleven times during the war he returned to that forward room, to the bunk that pulled out from under a torpedo, where he heard water rushing past and the bow plane motors, and felt secure. At home in Iowa he went downstairs to the archive room and back in time. And lately, in his snug apartment, in the blue bedroom where we'd huddled together, he has reviewed these pages and remembered again, descending once more into the past.

Notes

CHAPTER 2. REAL WAR

1. Duane Schultz, *Wake Island* (New York: St. Martin's Press, 1978), 80, 150.
2. *Ibid.*, 150.

CHAPTER 3. TAMBOR CLASS

1. FDR had taken a keen interest in subs for many years. In 1915, as assistant secretary of the Navy, he had written:

   The submarine has come to stay. It has taken its place, not as the whole weapon in naval offense and defense, but as an adjunct to other weapons. That it is useful for coast defense, for commerce destroying, especially in narrow waters, for scouting purposes, and as a part of the protection and attacking power of a battleship fleet is established. . . . It would of course be most unreasonable to suppose that while the weapons for the destruction of underwater craft are being perfected, the improvement of the submarine itself will not continue. Without doubt its size will increase, its engine both surface and subsurface gain in horsepower and resulting speed, its radius of action grow and its seaworthiness improve.

2. Letter from Chet Smith, a *Tambor* shipmate and eventual Electric Boat executive, to Bob Hunt, February 5, 1986. "Most people do not know," Smith wrote, "that those tests were ordered by President Roosevelt personally, after Winston Churchill told him that the British did not think our submarine hulls, welded, could survive depth charging. You are a personal witness that they could and did, Bob."

CHAPTER 4. WAR FERVOR

1. Clay Blair Jr., *Silent Victory* (Annapolis: Naval Institute Press, 1975), 291–92.
2. James F. DeRose, *Unrestricted Warfare* (New York: John Wiley & Sons, 2000), 46.

CHAPTER 5. "POINT LUCK": THE BATTLE OF MIDWAY

1. Gordon W. Prange, *Miracle at Midway* (New York: McGraw-Hill, 1982), 19.
2. Stephen Budiansky, *Battle of Wits: The Complete Story of Codebreaking in World War II* (New York: The Free Press, 2000), 13. This book is a source for much of the information on U.S. code breakers in the current chapter.
3. Prange, *Miracle at Midway*, 15.
4. Budiansky, *Battle of Wits*, 16–17.

5. Prange, *Miracle at Midway*, 358.

6. Mitsuo Fuchida and Masatake Okumiya, *Midway: The Battle that Doomed Japan, the Japanese Navy's Story*. Foreword by Adm. Raymond A. Spruance (Annapolis: United States Naval Institute Press, 1955), v.

7. *Ibid.*, 245–48.

8. Prange, *Miracle at Midway*, 190.

9. From a statement made by Genda in response to a questionnaire from Prange, *Miracle at Midway*, 252.

10. *Ibid.*, 260.

11. *Ibid.*, 262.

12. *Ibid.*, 264.

13. *Ibid.*, 274–75.

14. Fuchida and Okumiya, *Midway: The Battle that Doomed Japan*, 185.

15. Blair, *Silent Victory*, 250.

16. Prange, *Miracle at Midway*, 81. In a 1965 interview with Robert E. Barde, Nimitz remarked, "It was a great day for the Navy when Bill Halsey had to enter the hospital." Knowing Nimitz's high regard for Halsey, one hears a note of jocularity in the remark. However, in the context of Nimitz's praise of Spruance's performance—notably for the discriminating application of aggression and restraint he displayed at Midway—Nimitz's remark about the ever-aggressive Halsey has force.

17. Fuchida and Okumiya, *Midway: The Battle that Doomed Japan*, vii–viii.

CHAPTER 6. "HOT, STRAIGHT, AND NORMAL": AT LIBERTY IN PEARL HARBOR

1. Blair, *Silent Victory*, 249 passim.

2. *Ibid.*, 250.

3. Thomas Parrish, *The Submarine: A History* (New York: Viking, 2004), 307.

CHAPTER 9. CLOSE CALLS IN THE SOUTH CHINA SEA

1. Drew Middleton, *Submarine: The Ultimate Naval Weapon—Its Past, Present & Future*. (Chicago: Playboy Press, 1976), 90.

CHAPTER 10. THE TENTH MISSION: PERIL AND THE NAVY CROSS

1. This information is drawn from a 1987 letter from Bob Dye to Warren Link.

2. Tom Lampley's remarks are from a Winter 2002 letter to Ann Adams, daughter of Carlos Clifton "Nip" Howard. Also in the letter Lampley recounted an incident in which Howard saved him from being washed overboard:

   A few months later we were in rough weather. I was on Starboard forward lookout. Binoculars were absolutely worthless with salt water pouring over us every few seconds. The officer of the deck brought me down from the post on the shears to the deck just above the conning tower hatch. Before long a huge wave came over and completely enveloped me and the next I knew was "Nip" had a wrist and [was] pounding on my fingers to turn loose and I tried but my fingers would not obey for a few seconds. "Nip" and someone else pried my finger[s] off the stanchion and dragged me back aboard. Since this was [the] middle of the night and in enemy water you come close to not having to read this blather.

Lampley went on to recount another instance of Howard's marksmanship:

The next day (after Nip had saved me the second time) a little guy name of H. Canaday was washed overboard. Call to Nip to get up on deck with heaving line. Trouble was experienced in staying close enough to Canaday to reach him with heaving line so Nip broke out his special gun that fired a steel pin attached to a small line. Nip layed the line right across Canaday's shoulder but he was so weak he couldn't hold it for being dragged in. So Chief Geo. DeLoria who had been a Marathon swimmer in his early manhood went after him and brought him in. Canaday passed out a few seconds after he said, Thank you, Cap'n. After a couple of days in the bunk Canaday was restored to duty.

In view of these incidents, Lampley wondered in the letter whether it might be possible to initiate a process whereby his crewmate would receive a posthumous Medal of Honor. Howard died at the age of fifty-nine of a brain tumor.

3. In my account of this action, I have drawn heavily from an article "We Remember the *Tambor*," authored by "The Crew" and published in *Polaris* magazine, October 1987. Crew member Warren Link circulated a draft account of the February 3 depth charging and solicited eyewitness additions from others serving at various stations. The original letters of response ended up in Bob Hunt's archive, and I also have drawn directly from this correspondence.

4. USS *Cavalla* Newsletter, www.aztechsoft.com/cavallanews/newsletter2.htm (accessed February 21, 2008).

5. This exchange is recounted by Bill Reynolds in an April 27, 1987, letter to Warren Link.

6. This account from the aft torpedo room is drawn from a 1987 letter from George Venditelli to Warren Link.

7. When Captain Kefauver was making his round of the compartments, he had the following exchange with eighteen-year-old diesel mechanic Thomas Levens: "I told Captain Kefauver in front of the crew, I said 'Captain, if my mother knew where I was right now, she would be worried to death.' The captain looked up at me and said, 'What are you, Levens, an atheist?' Well, that drew laughter from the crew and sort of lifted our spirits." Mobile *Press Messenger*, November 12–13, 1987.

8. This information is drawn from Rex Harvey's 1987 letter to Warren Link and from the article "We Remember the *Tambor*."

9. From Jack Semmelrath's letter to Warren Link, April 26, 1987.

10. Kefauver's tactic was recalled by Rex Harvey in his 1987 letter. Harvey was in the maneuvering room, receiving orders from the control room through headphones. He also remembered reports coming over the headset from the bridge that, when the *Tambor* had surfaced and lookouts checked for the destroyer, they saw searchlights scanning the sea hundreds of yards astern. This latter account varies from Thomas Lampley's information that radioman Mayo heard the destroyer retire in the direction of Nagasaki after dropping its final depth charge, either, Lampley conjectured, because the destroyer crew believed they had destroyed the *Tambor* or because they had used all depth charges.

11. Letter to Robert Schultz from Gordon "Red" Mayo, March 23, 2007.

12. In the official numbering of the *Tambor*'s war patrols, the Navy neglected to count the boat's participation in the Battle of Midway. By Bob Hunt's reckoning, therefore, the patrol narrated here was the *Tambor*'s—and Bob's—tenth. Bob's numbering of the patrols, and not the Navy's, is used throughout this book.

CHAPTER 11. WAVE THE FLAG ON MARKET STREET

1. www.combinedfleet.com (accessed January 2, 2007) is an invaluable source of information about the *kaiten*.

2. All quotations and information on the secret mission are from "Burt's Brooms," an unpublished and undated reminiscence by *Tambor* captain Germershausen.

CHAPTER 12. "ECHOES OF THE PAST"

1. www.globalsecurity.org (accessed February 20, 2008).

BIBLIOGRAPHY

BOOKS

Blair, Clay, Jr. *Silent Victory*. Annapolis: Naval Institute Press, 1975.

Budiansky, Stephen. *Battle of Wits: The Complete Story of Codebreaking in World War II*. New York: The Free Press, 2000.

Davidson, Edward, and Dale Manning. *Chronology of World War Two*. London: Cassell & Co., 2000.

DeRose, James F. *Unrestricted Warfare*. New York: John Wiley & Sons, 2000.

Fuchida, Mitsuo, and Masatake Okumiya. *Midway: The Battle that Doomed Japan, the Japanese Navy's Story*. Foreword by Adm. Raymond A. Spruance. Annapolis: United States Naval Institute Press, 1955.

Kimmett, Larry, and Margaret Regis. *The Attack on Pearl Harbor: An Illustrated History*. Seattle: Navigator Publishing, 1992.

——. *U.S. Submarines in World War II: An Illustrated History*. Seattle: Navigator Publishing, 1996.

LaFeber, Walter. *The Clash: U.S.-Japanese Relations throughout History*. New York: W. W. Norton & Co., 1997.

Middleton, Drew. *Submarine: The Ultimate Naval Weapon—Its Past, Present & Future*. Chicago: Playboy Press, 1976.

Padfield, Peter. *War beneath the Sea: Submarine Conflict during World War II*. New York: John Wiley & Sons, 1995.

Parrish, Thomas. *The Submarine: A History*. New York: Viking, 2004.

Parshall, Jonathan, and Anthony Tully. *Shattered Sword: The Untold Story of the Battle of Midway*. Washington, D.C.: Potomac Books, 2005.

Prange, Gordon W. *Miracle at Midway*. New York: McGraw-Hill, 1982.

Schultz, Duane. *Wake Island*. New York: St. Martin's Press, 1978.

Tuohy, William. *The Bravest Man: The Story of Richard O'Kane & U.S. Submariners in the Pacific War*. Gloucestershire, U.K.: Sutton Publishing Limited, 2001.

Wheeler, Keith. *War under the Pacific*. Alexandria, VA: Time-Life Books, 1980.

Yergin, Daniel. *The Prize: The Epic Quest for Oil, Money, and Power*. New York: The Free Press, 1993.

MAGAZINE AND NEWSPAPER ARTICLES

"Midway: Models Reconstruct War's Decisive Naval Battle," *Life*, February 18, 1946, pp. 93–101.

"My Favorite War Stories." Mobile *Press Messenger*, November 12–13, 1987, n.p.

"We Remember the *Tambor*," *Polaris*. October 1987, n.p.

WEB SITES

Battleship Yamato provides information and photos of the Japanese super battleship. www.battleshipyamato.info (accessed February 21, 2008).

Chance-Vaught SB2U Vindicator provides information on the torpedo bombers that fought in the Battle of Midway. www.microworks.net/PACIFIC/aviation/sb2u_vindicator.htm (accessed February 21, 2008).

Combat Aircraft of World War II includes information on the Douglas SBD Dauntless that fought at Midway. www.angelfire.com/fm/compass/SBD.htm (accessed February 21, 2008)

Deck Log provides lists of submarine crews and biographical information on crew members. www.decklog.com (accessed May 1, 2007).

Dictionary of American Naval Fighting Ships includes *Tambor* patrol summaries and a photo. www.history.navy.mil/danfs/t2/tambor.htm (accessed February 21, 2008).

Global Security includes information on the sinking, decommissioning, or scrapping of World War II subs. www.globalsecurity.org (accessed February 20, 2008).

Home of Heroes includes information and photos on the Japanese attack on Pearl Harbor. www.combinedfleet.com/map.htm (accessed January 2, 2007).

The Internet Movie Database contains information on the movie about the Sullivans and a biography of Buster Wildes, the stuntman Robert Hunt met in California. www.imdb.com (accessed October 5, 2006).

Japanese Imperial Navy History includes information about the Japanese suicide torpedoes, the *kaiten*. www.combinedfleet.com (accessed January 2, 2007).

Japanese Submarines at Pearl Harbor. www.combinedfleet.com/map.htm (accessed January 2, 2007).

Katanning Western Australia includes information about, and pictures of, the town of Katanning. www.katanningwa.com (accessed February 20, 2008).

Myron's Submarine Pages provides general submarine information. myweb.cebridge.net/myron/submarines/index.html (accessed October 5, 2006).

Naval Historical Center, an official U.S. Navy site, includes extensive World War II information, including extensive data and photos on individual ships and submarines and types of aircraft. www.history.navy.mil/index.html (accessed February 21, 2008).

Pacific Island and Australia Information. www.factmonster.com/atlas/pacificislandsand australia.html (accessed February 21, 2008).

Pacific Naval Battles includes maps and extensive information on all major World War II Naval battles. www.combinedfleet.com/map.htm (accessed January 2, 2007).

Submarine Photo Index includes specifications and photos of U.S. submarines, including the *Tambor*. www.navsource.org/archives/08/08198.htm (accessed February 21, 2008).

They Served Their Country at the Battle of Midway, part of an extensive site on the battle, includes links to eyewitness accounts. www.users.bigpond.com/pacificwar/Midway/TheyservedatMidway.html (accessed February 21, 2008).

Torpedo Junction offers books and films on submarines and U-boats. www.sonic.net/~books/sub.html (accessed February 21, 2008).

Valor at Sea provides extensive information on U.S. submarines in World War II and links to other major sites. www.valoratsea.com/links.htm (accessed February 21, 2008).

Wisconsin Maritime Museum is the Web site of the museum where the USS *Cobia* can be toured. www.wisconsinmaritime.org (accessed February 21, 2008).

World War II in the San Francisco Bay Area includes information on and photos of the Mare Island Naval Shipyard. www.cr.nps.gov/nr/travel/wwIIbayarea/mar.htm (accessed February 21, 2008).

INDEX

ABOUT THE AUTHORS

Robert Schultz's books include a novel, *The Madhouse Nudes*, and two collections of poetry. He has received a National Endowment for the Arts Literature Award in fiction, Cornell University's Corson Bishop Poetry Prize, and, from the *Virginia Quarterly Review*, the Emily Clark Balch Prize for poetry. He has taught at Cornell University, the University of Virginia, and Luther College; he is currently the John P. Fishwick Professor of English at Roanoke College.

James Shell has had fiction, nonfiction, and poetry published in the *Roanoke Times, Jazz, College Poetry Review, Single Living, Ideas at Work, Artemis, Raconteur, GlennGould,* and the *University of Toronto Quarterly.* He lives in Salem, Virginia.

The **Naval Institute Press** is the book-publishing arm of the U.S. Naval Institute, a private, nonprofit, membership society for sea service professionals and others who share an interest in naval and maritime affairs. Established in 1873 at the U.S. Naval Academy in Annapolis, Maryland, where its offices remain today, the Naval Institute has members worldwide.

Members of the Naval Institute support the education programs of the society and receive the influential monthly magazine *Proceedings* or the colorful bimonthly magazine *Naval History* and discounts on fine nautical prints and on ship and aircraft photos. They also have access to the transcripts of the Institute's Oral History Program and get discounted admission to any of the Institute-sponsored seminars offered around the country.

The Naval Institute's book-publishing program, begun in 1898 with basic guides to naval practices, has broadened its scope to include books of more general interest. Now the Naval Institute Press publishes about seventy titles each year, ranging from how-to books on boating and navigation to battle histories, biographies, ship and aircraft guides, and novels. Institute members receive significant discounts on the Press's more than eight hundred books in print.

Full-time students are eligible for special half-price membership rates. Life memberships are also available.

For a free catalog describing Naval Institute Press books currently available, and for further information about joining the U.S. Naval Institute, please write to:

Member Services
U.S. Naval Institute
291 Wood Road
Annapolis, MD 21402-5034
Telephone: (800) 233-8764
Fax: (410) 571-1703
Web address: www.usni.org